I0901013

IMAGES
of America

Around Neversink
From the Rondout Reservoir to the Neversink Reservoir

ON THE COVER: Teacher Evelyn Huntsberger is driving this Packard car around the mid-1930s. Bruce Denman Sr. lent the car so the students at the Unionville School could go for a last-day-of-school picnic and swim. (Denman Family Collection TVM.)

IMAGES of America

AROUND NEVERSINK

FROM THE RONDOUT RESERVOIR TO THE NEVERSINK RESERVOIR

Carol Gridley Smythe

ARCADIA PUBLISHING

ISBN 978-0-7385-9849-9

Published by Arcadia Publishing
Charleston, South Carolina

Printed in the United States of America

Library of Congress Control Number: 2012950612

For all general information, please contact Arcadia Publishing:
Telephone 843-853-2070
Fax 843-853-0044
E-mail sales@arcadiapublishing.com
For customer service and orders:
Toll-Free 1-888-313-2665

Visit us on the Internet at www.arcadiapublishing.com

To the families who lost their properties through eminent domain so that New York City residents could have drinking water and to the workers who lost their lives while building the Neversink and Rondout Reservoirs.

CONTENTS

Acknowledgments

I want to thank the Neversink Town Board for their continuing support of the role of town historian. (The role of town historian offers a wonderful opportunity to gather, share, and conserve local history for future generations.) Thanks also go to all the staff at town hall who have been very supportive of this project, including Lisa Garigliano, Janis Offringa, Brenda DeVore, and Teri Lockhart. My editors, Abby Henry and Rebecca Collingsworth, at Arcadia Publishing have stayed with me as I floundered with the loss of my husband and my involvement in beginning the new Time and the Valleys Museum. To some of those who have worked diligently with me—Joe and Mary Inghrim, George and Helen Elias, Lynn Priebe, and Lee Shader—I say thank you. Also thank you to Pat Giannotti, Wanda Terwilliger, Shirley Smith, and Bob Dorn. There are others who researched on their own and shared generously, including, but not limited to, Frank Carlsen, Joe Weise, Jack Denman, and Gloria Thompson. It is important to note that past Town of Neversink historians laid the groundwork for myself and other historians to follow. Present-day researchers help keep the flame burning both for today and for the tomorrows that follow.

To my sister Linda Gridley Lane, who gave me great sisterly support. And to Robert Curry, the Denman family, the Margaret Smith Dolan family, and all the others who either loaned photographs or gave them to the museum or the town. Thank you to Computer Doctor in Liberty who helped keep my old computer going through the project.

Images with no courtesy lines are from the Time and the Valleys Museum collection (TVM). Images courtesy of the Town of Neversink are marked TN, and images from special collections are marked accordingly.

Introduction

The town of Neversink in Sullivan County and the town of Denning in Ulster County are forever linked by geography and a series of circumstances. The Neversink Reservoir and the Rondout Reservoir cover two of the three valleys of the so-called Tri-Valley area. The third valley, where Grahamsville is located, was sometimes known as the Chestnut Valley because of the plentiful chestnut trees that could be found there. The Neversink Reservoir is completely located in Neversink, and almost half of the Rondout Reservoir is situated there also. The primary sources of water for both reservoirs are located in Denning.

The Ulster County Legislature created the town of Neversink in Ulster County in the year 1798. Prior to that time, the area had simply been known as Neversink country and was part of Ulster County. The details of the boundary changes often due to politics and geography are enough to confuse researchers. Meanwhile, present-day Denning was first part of the town of Woodstock, Ulster County, and then became part of the town of Shandaken, Ulster County. In 1849, the Ulster County Legislature created Denning, whose boundaries would change too.

Neversink became part of Sullivan County in 1809 when Sullivan was created by the New York State Legislature. Neversink's boundaries changed again. Denning remained part of Ulster County.

Determined early settlers came up the valleys, first to the Upper Rondout, then to the Chestnut Valley and the Upper Neversink. These hardscrabble adventurers looked for land they could afford and water to sustain them. Some went into Denning to settle and faced great challenges in this untouched Catskill Mountain area—Indians, wild animals, and large forests of virgin trees and stones. By 1824, the Post Office Department had approved post offices for both Neversink and Grahamsville. The first school in Neversink was taught by Christopher Darrow, who had fought in the Revolutionary War. Joseph W. Smith and Albert VanDover walked over the mountain to Shandaken to get permission to open the first school in Denning. The year was 1844.

The written words of Eli Bennett give clues as to what the area was like in the 1800s. Bennett lived near Willowemoc, as it is known today, and did business from Willowemoc to Grahamsville to Wawarsing and back. An October 4, 1834, entry in *The Eli Bennett Chronicles* reads, "One chair bought fifteen minutes after we settled agreed price—twelve shillings." On July 4, 1835, Bennett wrote, "Day and half's work to piling bark 30 trees 1.22." Further research shows it was not unusual for shillings to sometimes be used instead of dollars to record finances.

Juliana Hanford George was born in a log cabin on October 6, 1875. In later years, she wrote about her memories of the early days. She said in one entry, "People who talk about the good old days have short memories. Roads were all dusty—most of us walked. Just very rich or very lucky people had horses."

By 1899, local resident Emma Carney wrote an epic poem that described Grahamsville in a way that bears little resemblance to the area today. Three typed pages tell in detail what life was like. There were three daily stages, four dry goods stores, two blacksmith shops, three physicians, a sawmill, a gristmill, a creamery, two hotels, country homes for city guests, a meat market, an undertaker, a furniture maker, a print shop, three ministers, a village school, a public library, and of course the Grahamsville Fair, which was then in its infancy. One can only assume that the other nearby communities were booming as well.

In the years to follow, Neversink and Denning residents, along with the rest of the country, endured the Great Depression and World Wars I and II. But their endurance was tested when New York City took through eminent domain the beautiful Neversink and Rondout Valleys. The valleys marked the town of Neversink almost like bookends. One can see the beauty of the lost valleys in old images. Photographs and memories were all that was left once the taking of the land was finalized.

This development displaced 1,600 residents of the two valleys. Their homes, barns, and stores were mostly burned, and their churches and schools were demolished as well. A few barns and outbuildings were moved. In the Neversink Valley, a few of the smaller homes were moved. Deceased loved ones were taken from their "permanent" resting places and shuffled off to other cemeteries. The anguish of the former residents over the two valleys can only be imagined. Payment for properties was often too small, and there was no suitable payment for the lost family history of the generations who had come before.

Neversink and Denning residents have always shown a great resilience in the face of many changes. Perhaps this resilience has fostered the strong spirit of independence and cooperation that characterizes their lives today. This was evident in the years following the "taking" of the valleys. There was the small group of parents who banded together and fought the New York State Education Department so that the area could have its own school instead of high school students going to Ellenville or Liberty. Thus, Tri-Valley Central School district was born.

Among the area's distinct characteristics is a prohibition of alcohol on the Neversink books that up until now has faced down a number of challenges by voters. Also notable are a small community newspaper, the *Townsman*—over 50 years old and still run by volunteers—and the Grahamsville Fair, which has survived and flourished for more than 100 years without state support. The many achievements in the area are as enduring as the community's Quaker Meeting House, built in 1832 and standing strong today.

The story of Neversink and Denning is still being written. Future historians will find much of interest in this fiercely independent area, where neighbors still help neighbors and residents value the beauty of the region even as they strive to make Neversink and Denning an even better place to live and call home.

One

The Early Days

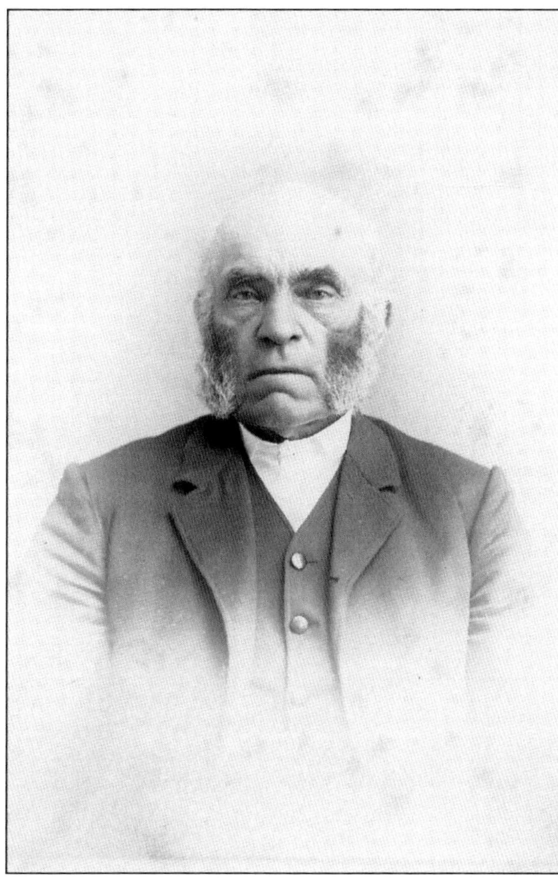

John W. Smith walked with Albert VanDover to Shandaken to get permission to build the first schoolhouse in what became the town of Denning. The schoolhouse was a log cabin on Red Hill. Smith owned a sawmill up the East Branch of the Neversink in the 1840s. This photograph of him was taken by J.E. Le Roy, a photographer from Newburgh, New York. (Helen Erts DuBois Collection.)

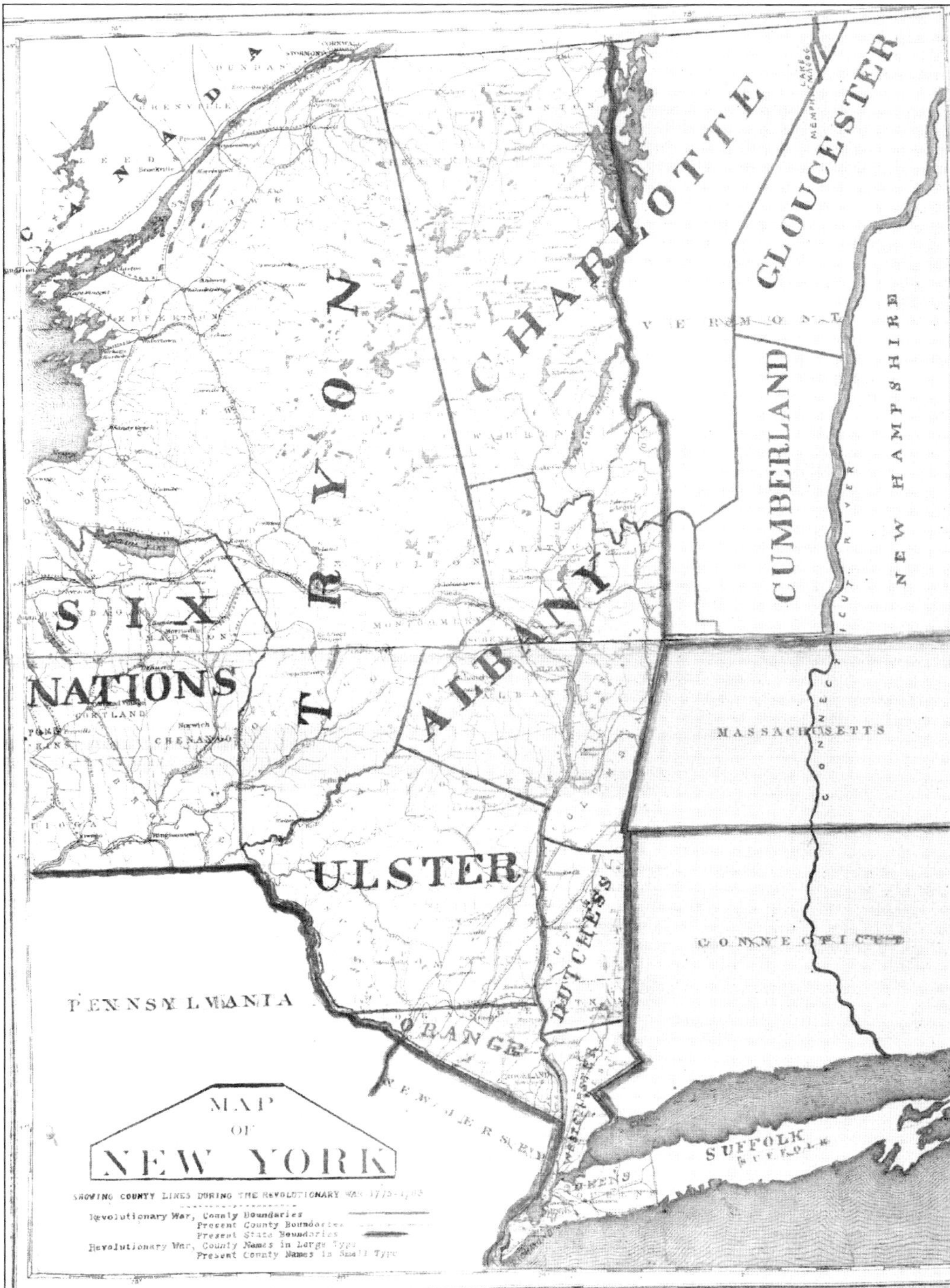

Ulster County as it is shown on this state map at the time of the Revolutionary War includes all of present-day Sullivan and Ulster Counties. (*NY in the Revolution*, 1904, published by New York State Education Department.)

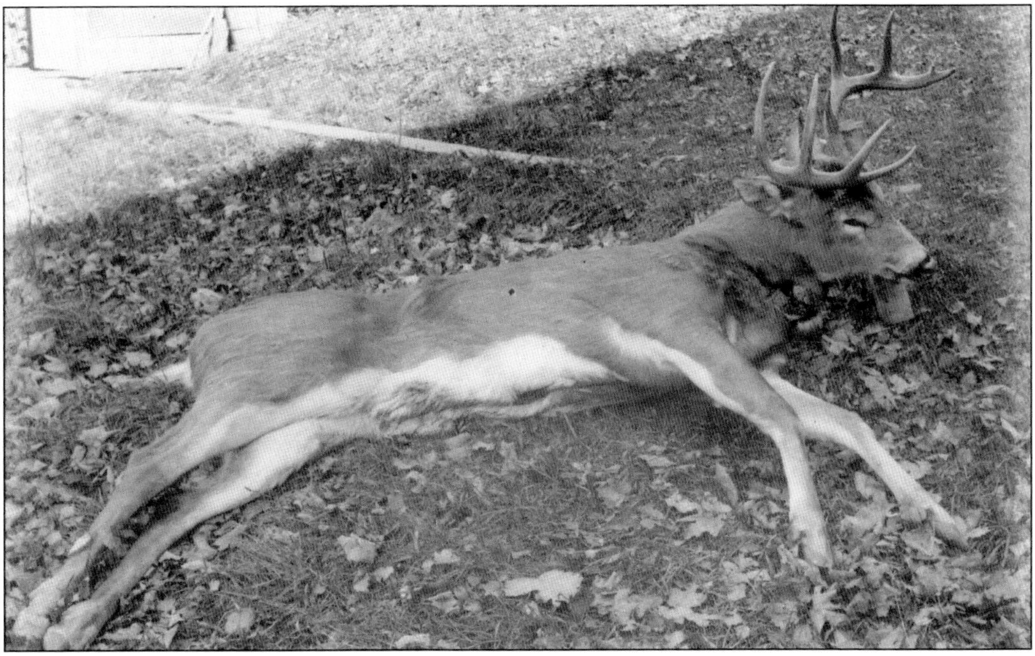

Pictured in a c. 1910 Raymond Erath glass plate negative, this buck with his handsome rack brought joy to the hunter and meat to the table. Today, hunters in the mountains of the Catskill Park and Forest Preserve focus on the sport and not the food, although a good venison stew can still be found in some area kitchens during hunting season.

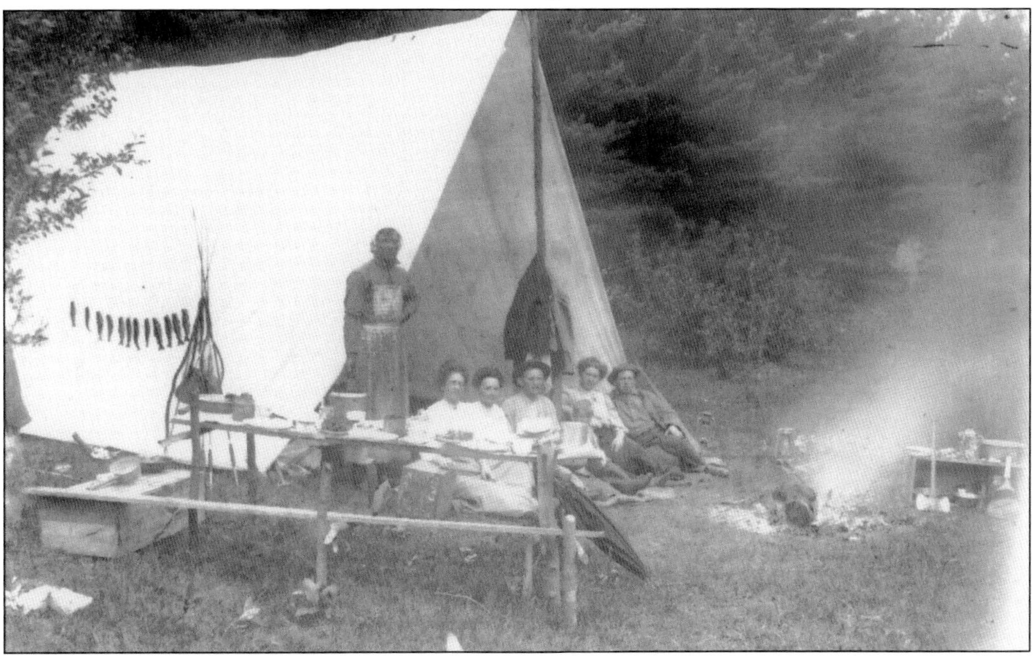

Fishing and camping were very popular in the early 1900s. This glass plate negative gives excellent details of an outing on the Rondout Creek. Note the string of trout to the left of the canvas shelter. The smoke from the campfire and the coffee pot give one a sense of what camping was like in those days. (Raymond Erath Collection.)

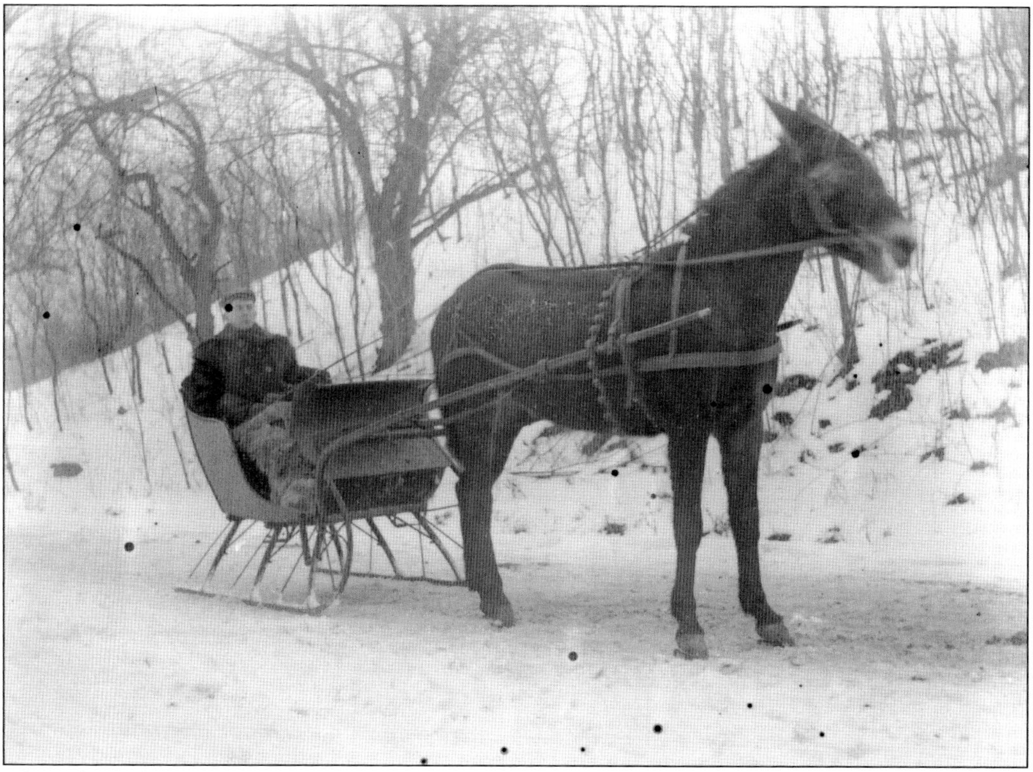

This glass plate negative print shows a driver and one-horse sleigh. Note the full string of sleigh bells encircling the animal's girth. The snapshot is from the early 1900s. (Raymond Erath Collection.)

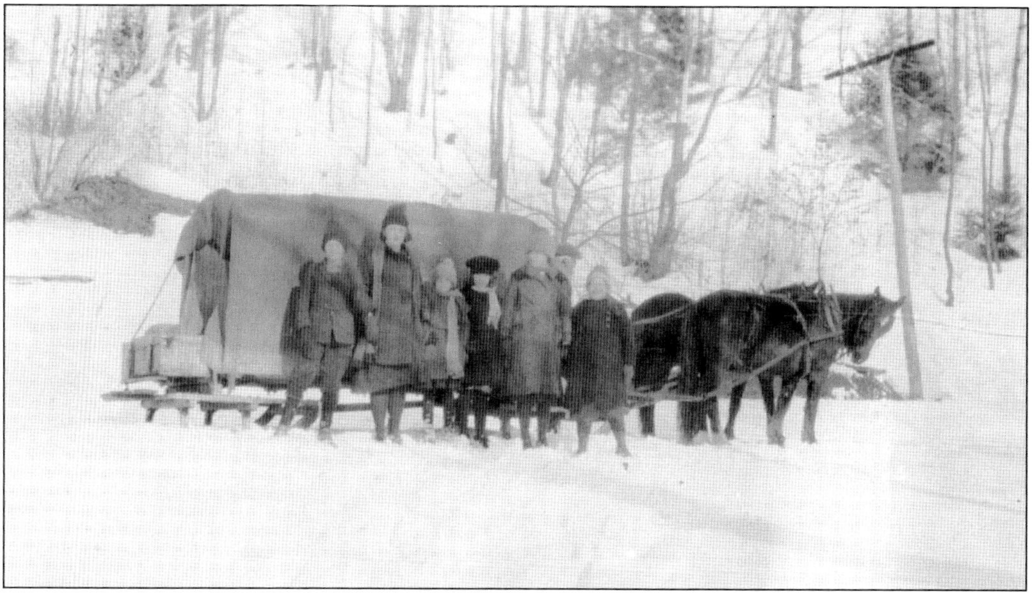

This stage functioned as a school bus; note the runners on the sledge and just imagine the hard wooden seats under the canvas frame. One would have to dress for a very cold ride. The group is bound for nearby Ellenville around 1922.

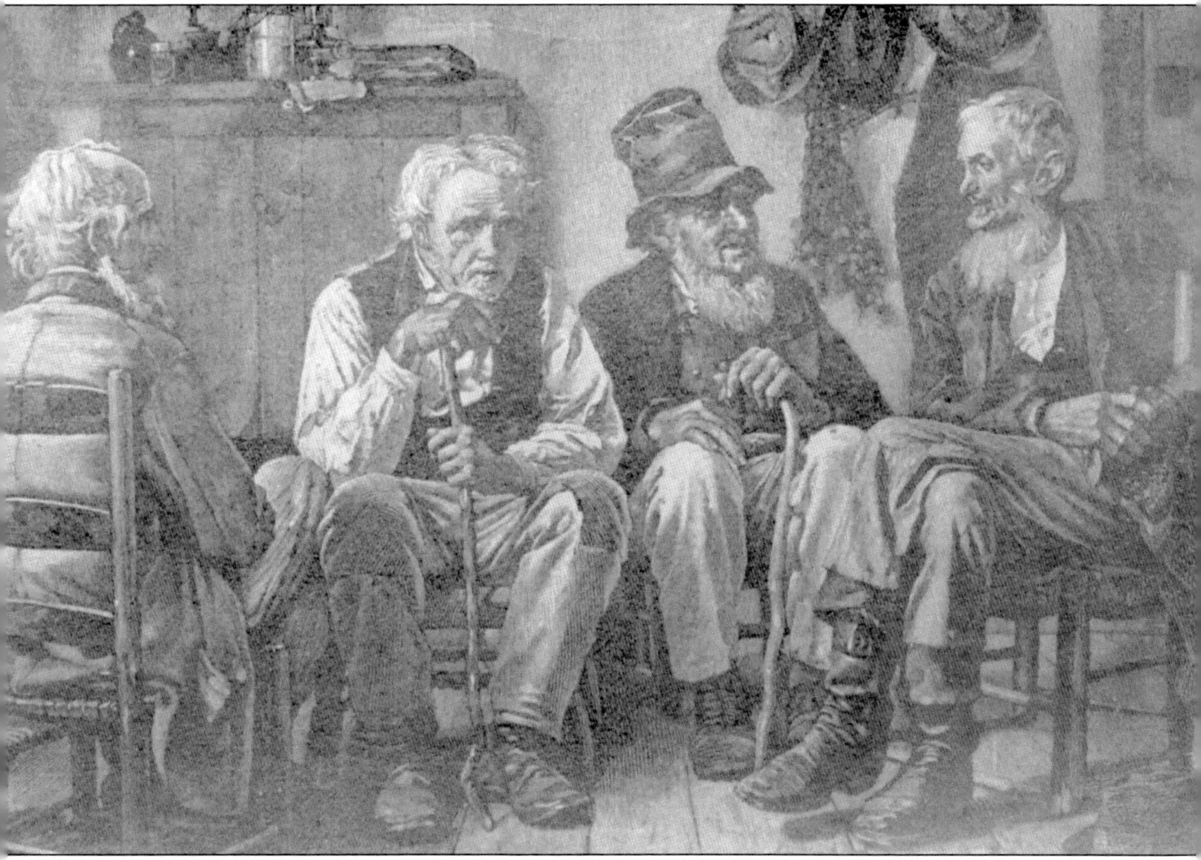

These four men were sometimes called "the grand old men of Neversink." Otto Hillig, renowned Liberty photographer, took the photograph, but the original artist is unidentified. The men are, from left to right, Higbe Everett, Sam Barnes, "Fade" Countryman, and Jim Curry. (Robert Curry family.)

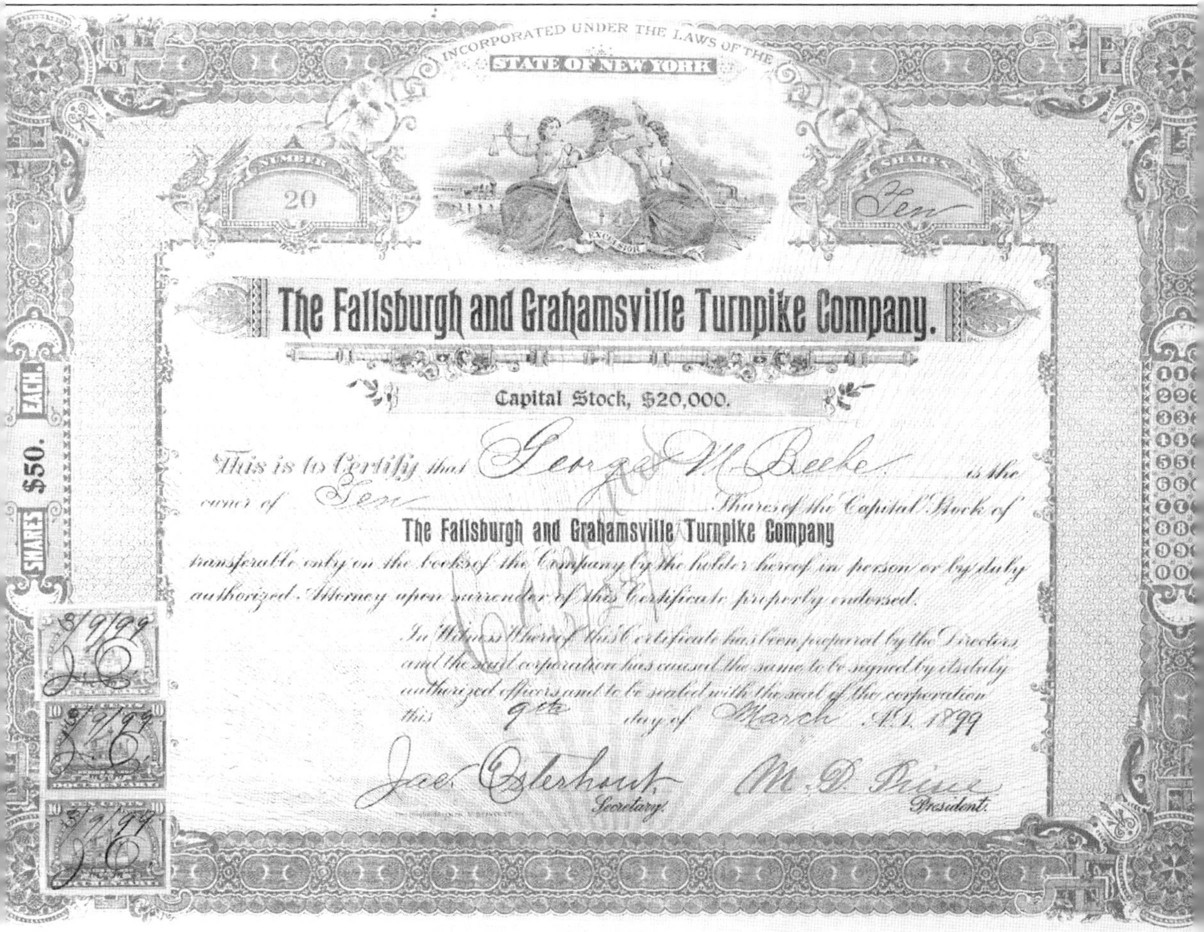

The Fallsburgh and Grahamsville Turnpike was organized in 1899. George B. Reynolds helped create the project by assisting in the location of the road and organization of the company. The turnpike was a plank road. Eventually, it was sold to the town and ceased to be a company.

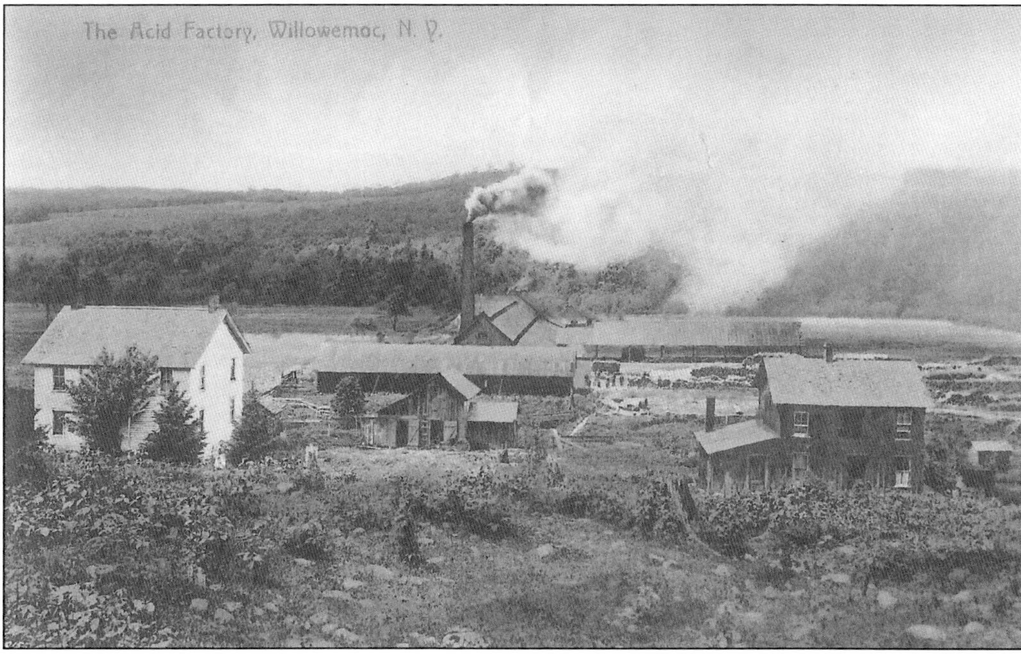

The beauty of the Willowemoc Creek was often eulogized by poets, including Alfred Billings Street (1811–1881), who grew up in Monticello and practiced law there before moving to Albany. The acid factory that sprang up along the Willowemoc did much damage to those pristine waters. All that remains are memories, a few photographs such as this one, and the acid factory's chimney.

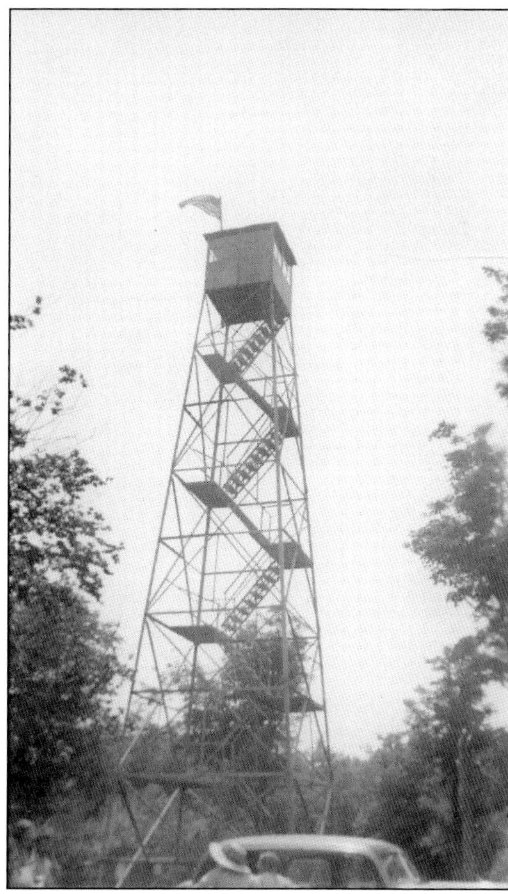

The Red Hill Fire Tower was sometimes called Moon Hill Conservation Tower. Built in 1920, it has Historic Landmark status. Ed Schultz was the first observer, from 1920 to 1938.

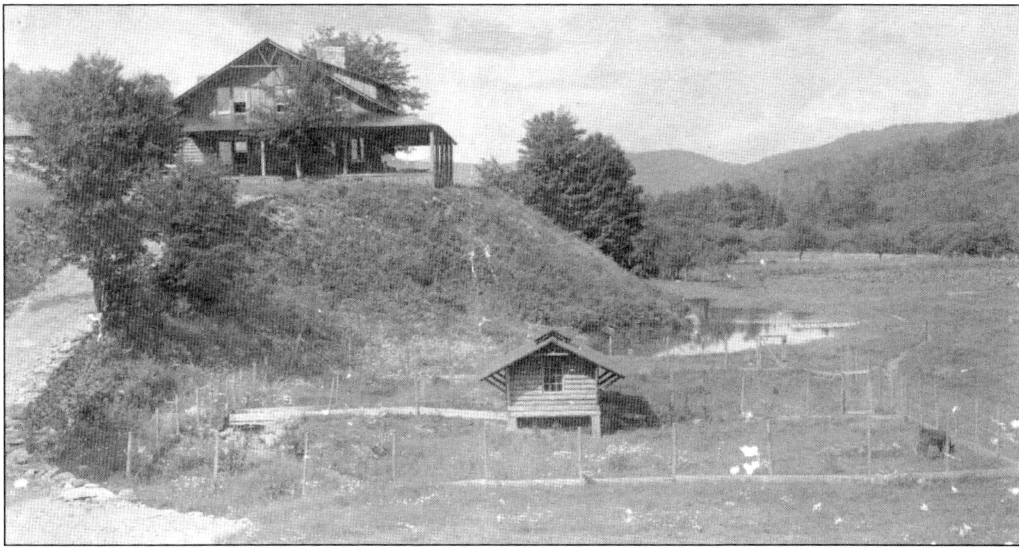

Wintoon Lodge was a early lodge built by Clarence Roof. It was constructed between 1885 and 1886 and was located on Frost Valley Road. Clarence Roof was one of a number of prominent people who bought large tracks of land along the Upper Neversink or the West Branch. The Roof property was increased by land purchases until there were over 3,000 acres in their holdings.

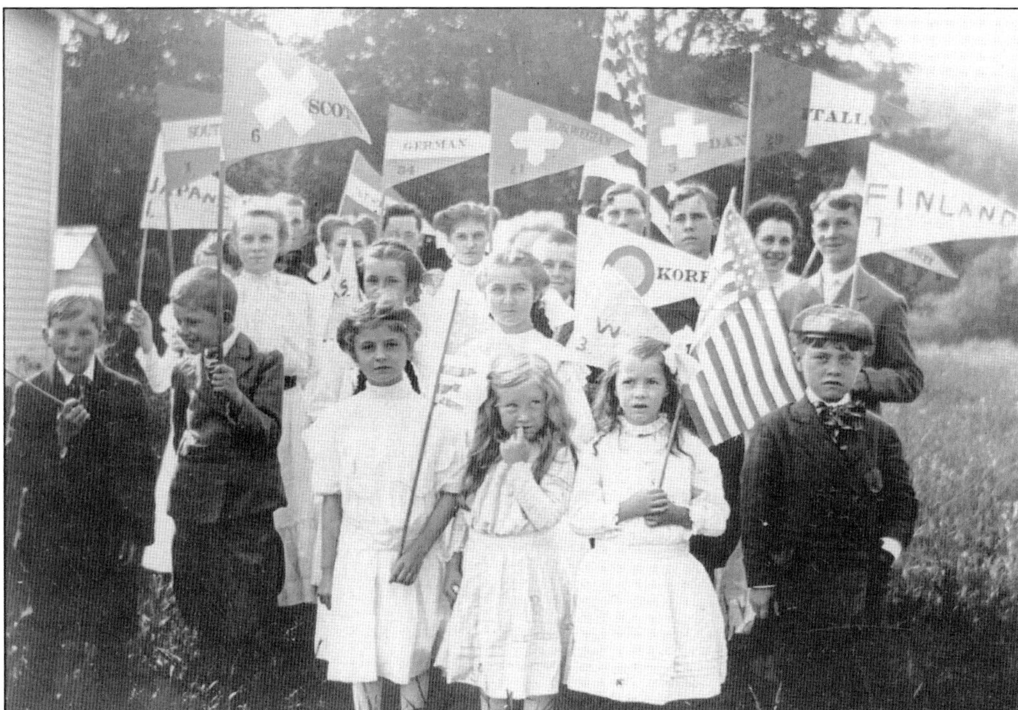

This photograph taken by Emma Erts shows Children's Day in June 1909 at the Methodist Episcopal Church in Claryville. The church is long gone. Those in the group include Mable Vanaken, Verda O'Dell, Emily Moore, Clarence Knight, Bernie Moore, Edna Vanaken, Floreen Bivins, Lulu Murray, Harrison Briggs, Pearl Taylor, Mattie Brundage, Harold "Pete" Hasbrouck, Clarence Hornbeck, Abbie Irwin, and Percy Bunton.

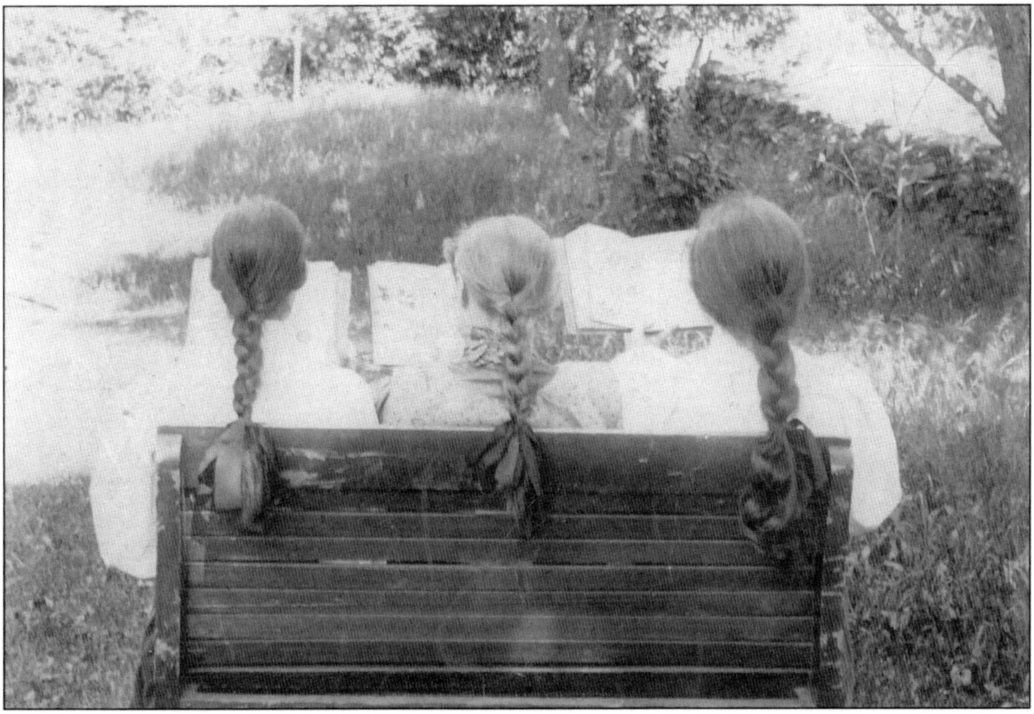

Eva, Mary and Harriet Smith of Eureka sat for this photograph about 1905. Whether called braids, plaits, or pigtails, this hairstyle certainly kept the hair quite tidy.

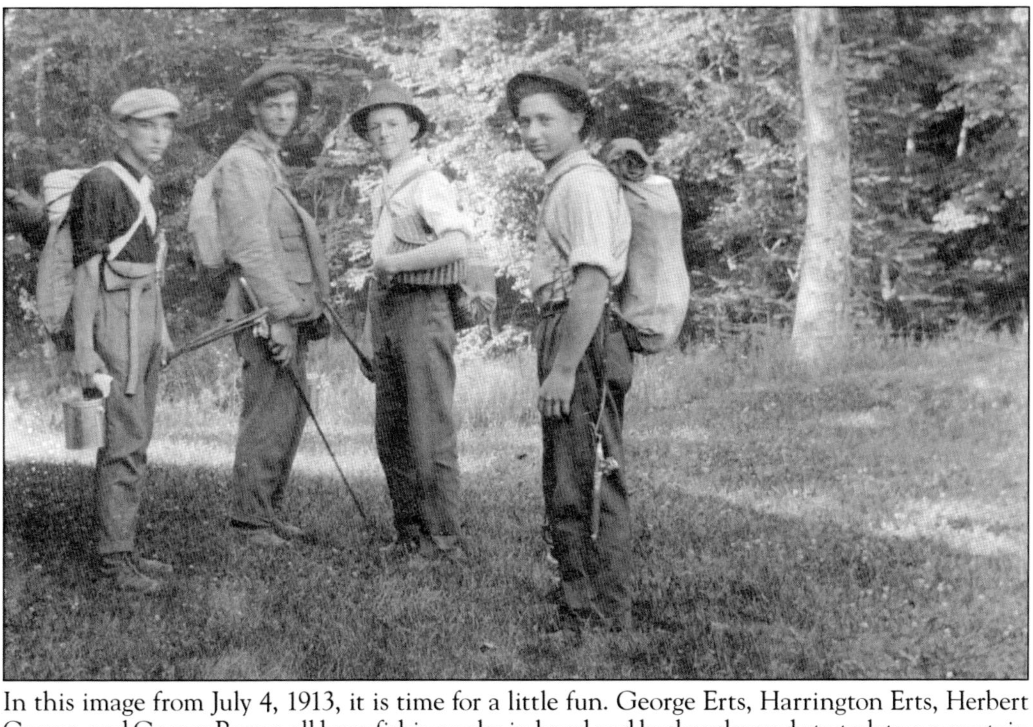

In this image from July 4, 1913, it is time for a little fun. George Erts, Harrington Erts, Herbert George, and George Brown all have fishing poles in hand and backpacks ready to trek to a mountain stream and set up camp. Their food will surely include their catch. (Erts/DuBois Collection.)

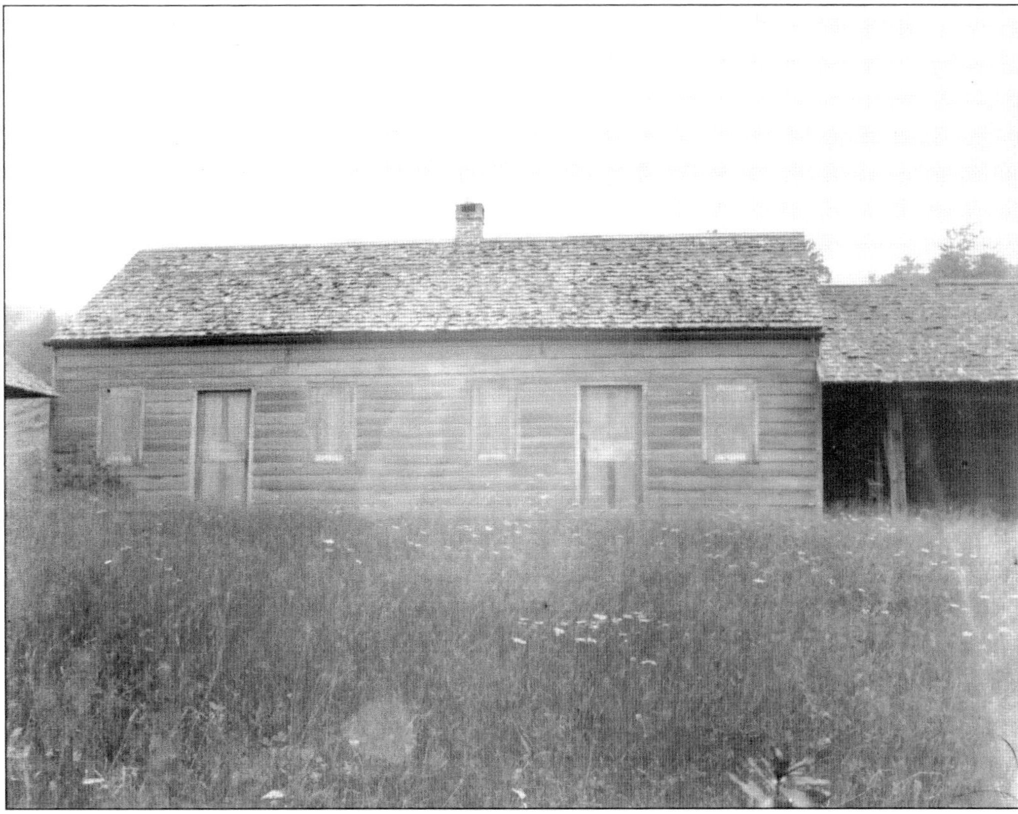

The Quaker Meeting House at Grahamsville was built in 1838. It was listed in the National Register of Historic Places in 2010. (Raymond Erath Collection.)

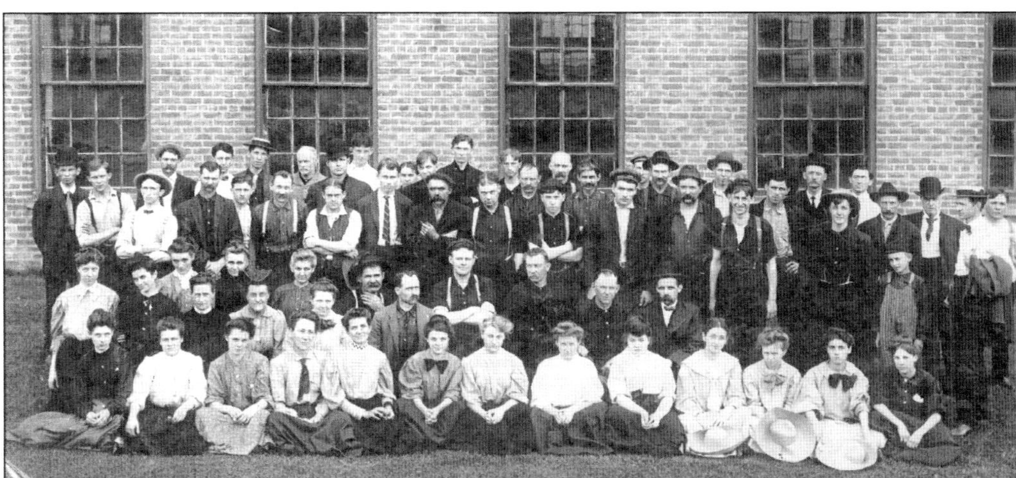

The Grahamsville Knife Factory was powered by water from the Chestnut Creek. Pictured here are workers in the factory. Knives produced at the factory and stamped "Grahamsville" are very collectible. The factory was destroyed by fire.

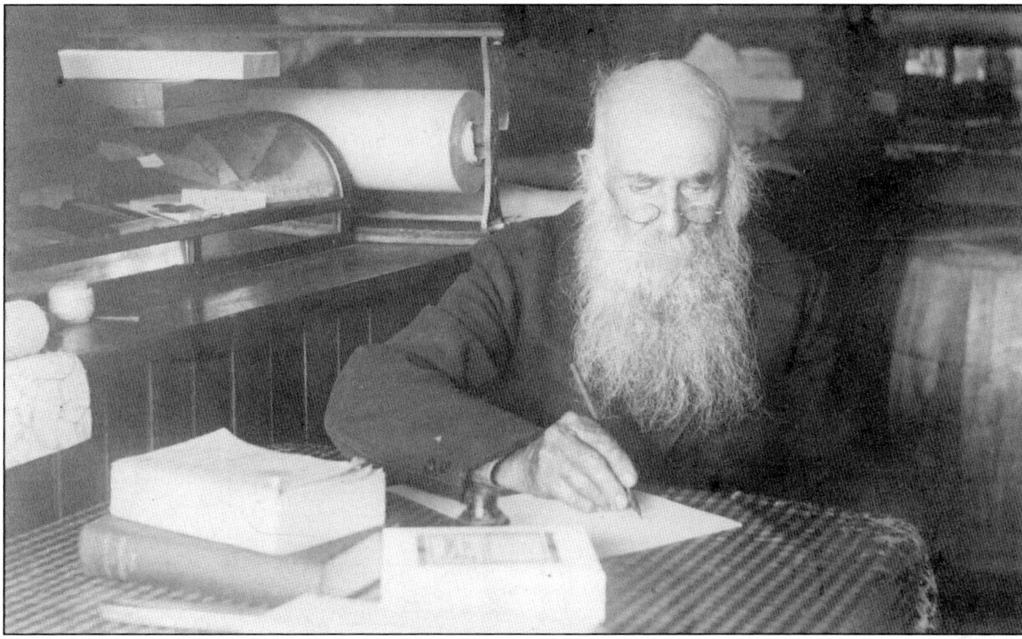

Albert VanDover was an illustrious man who was well known for walking a long distance to Shandaken, New York, to get permission to start the first school in what is now known as the town of Denning. That first school was located on Red Hill, near where VanDover lived. After that, many more one-room schools sprung up in the area.

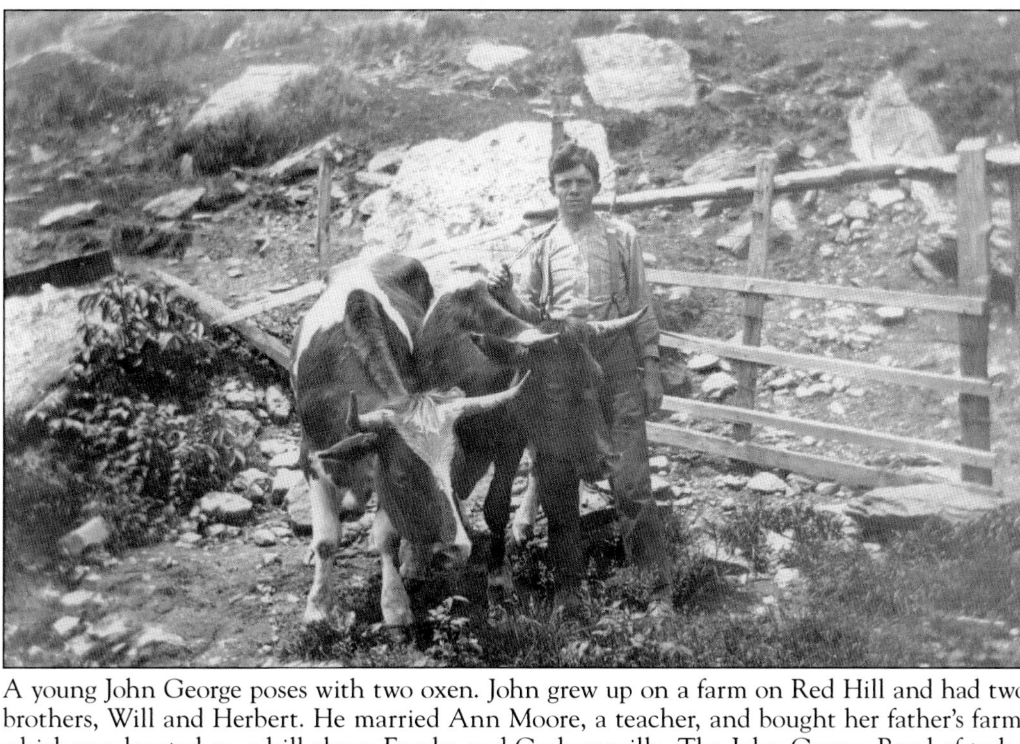

A young John George poses with two oxen. John grew up on a farm on Red Hill and had two brothers, Will and Herbert. He married Ann Moore, a teacher, and bought her father's farm, which was located on a hill above Eureka and Grahamsville. The John George Road of today goes directly up to this property and looks out over the Rondout Reservoir.

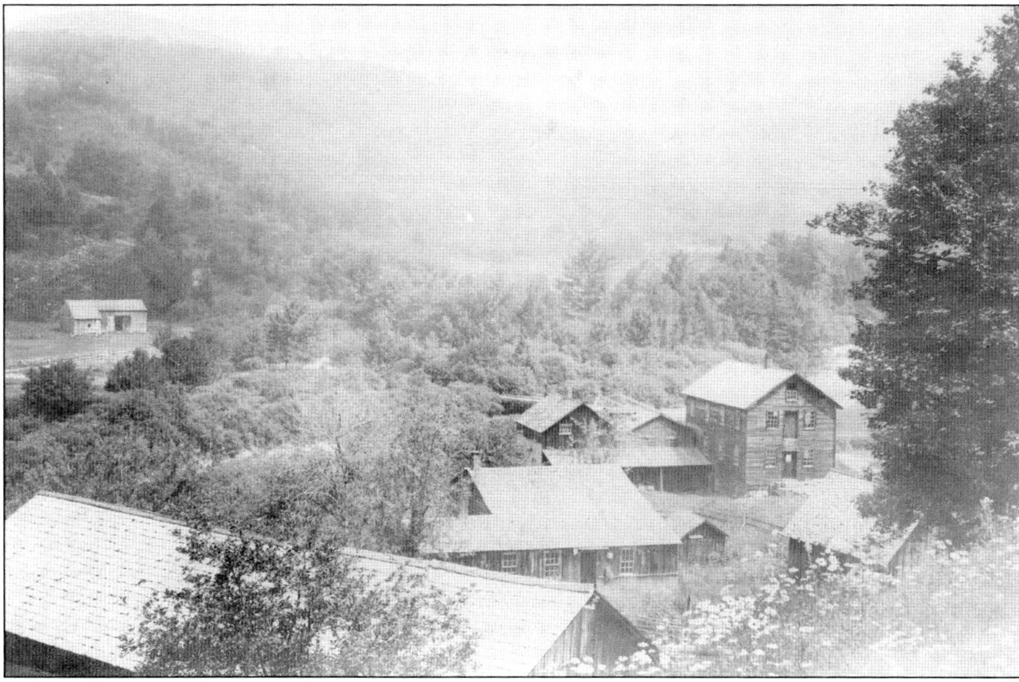

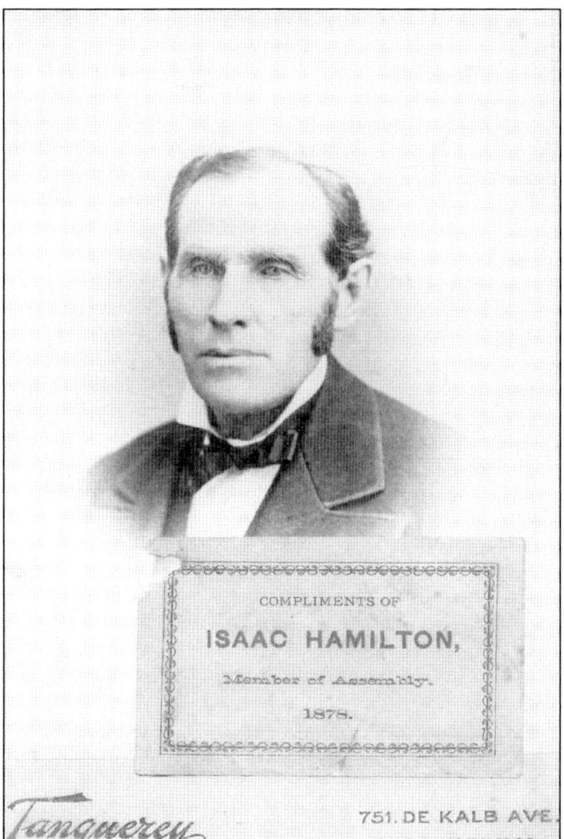

Jesse Hamilton's mill was located in Ladleton along the East Branch of the Upper Neversink. This photograph was taken in 1891. Ladleton got its name from the mill located there that made wooden ladles, bowls, scoops, and more.

Issac Hamilton of Ladleton had this photograph taken in Brooklyn. He handed it out to constituents while he was an assemblyman in Albany.

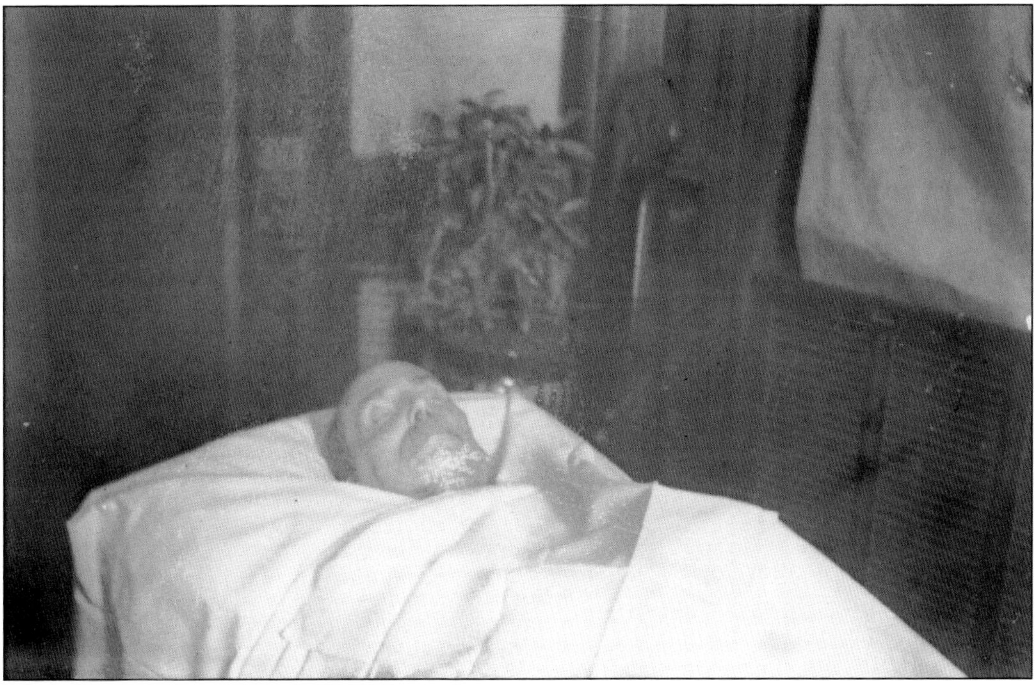

In rural America, it was not uncommon to photograph a deceased person. Funeral homes were not yet popular, and the individual would be laid out, most usually in a parlor. So was it in the Grahamsville area. Just a decade later, there would be two funeral homes right in Grahamsville. (Raymond Erath Collection.)

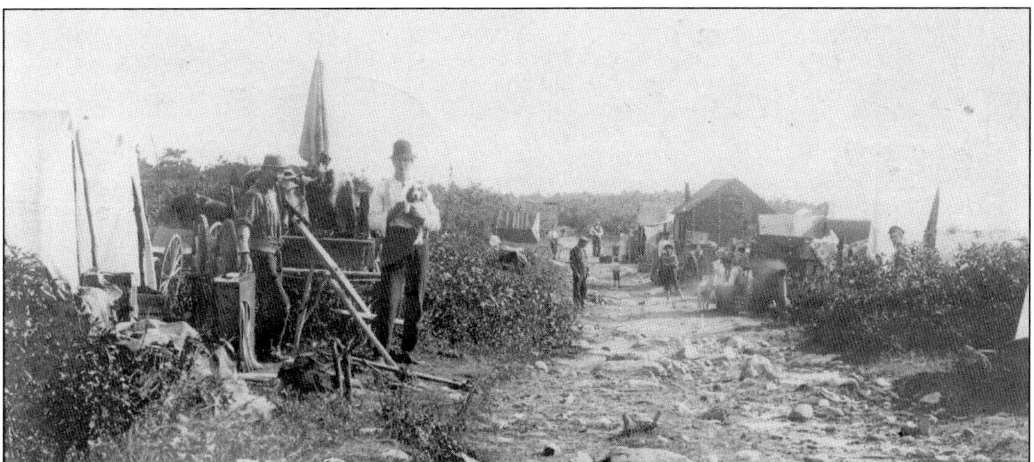

This 1906 image of the Berry Pickers Camp was sent to Maude in Grahamsville from nearby Ellenville, New York. These pickers may have been picking wild huckleberries or blueberries in the Sam's Point area of the Shawangunks. An interesting read about this topic is *The Huckleberry Pickers* by Marc B. Fried. (June Tillson collection.)

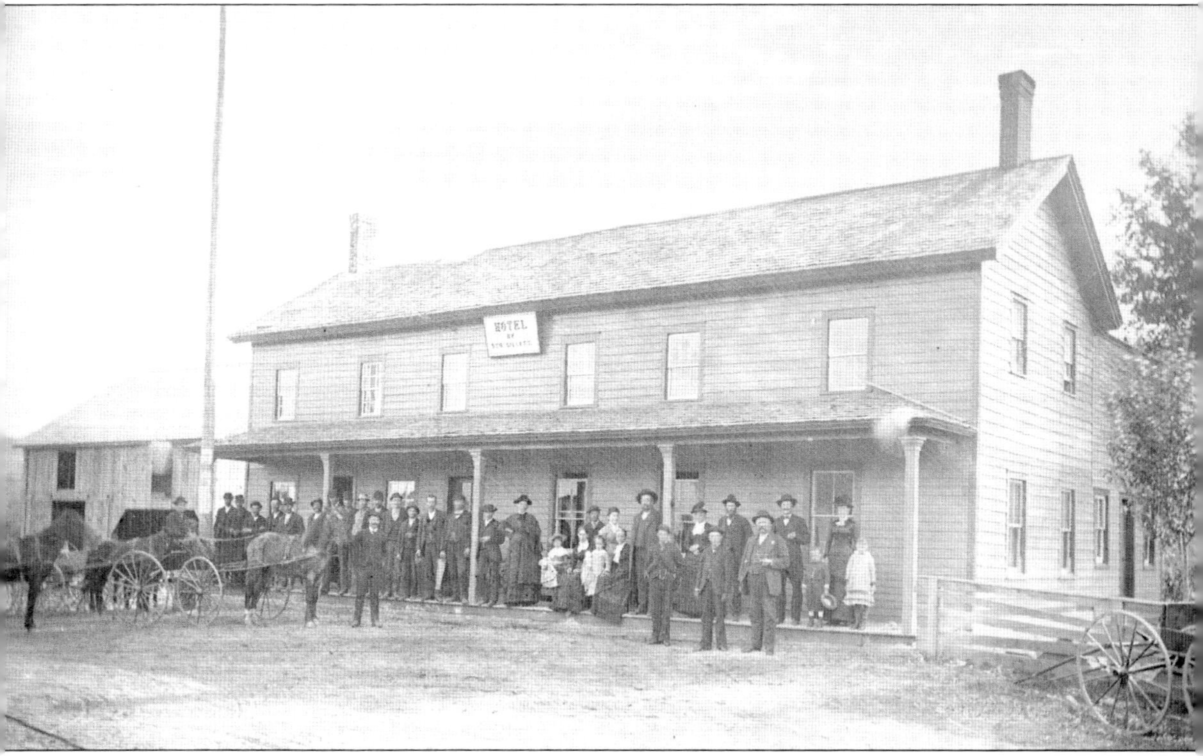

The sign reads "Hotel by Ben Gillett." Note that the road is all dirt; it must have been quite dusty when the horse and buggy started to roll. A handwritten caption on the back identifies many individuals in the photograph, including Charlie Eastman and his two sons, Arnie and Elwood; "Aunt Hat" and "Uncle John" VanBenschoten, "Uncle Henry" and "Aunt Phoebe" Lawrence, "Grandpa" and "Ma" Gillette, Hattie (with doll), Dr. Phoebe and a granddaughter, "I'm back" Oscar Grant, Ward Dunham, Eugene Benson, Mell Brannen, and Uncle Bruce (in the wagon). In Grahamsville today, the post office sits on the site where the hotel was.

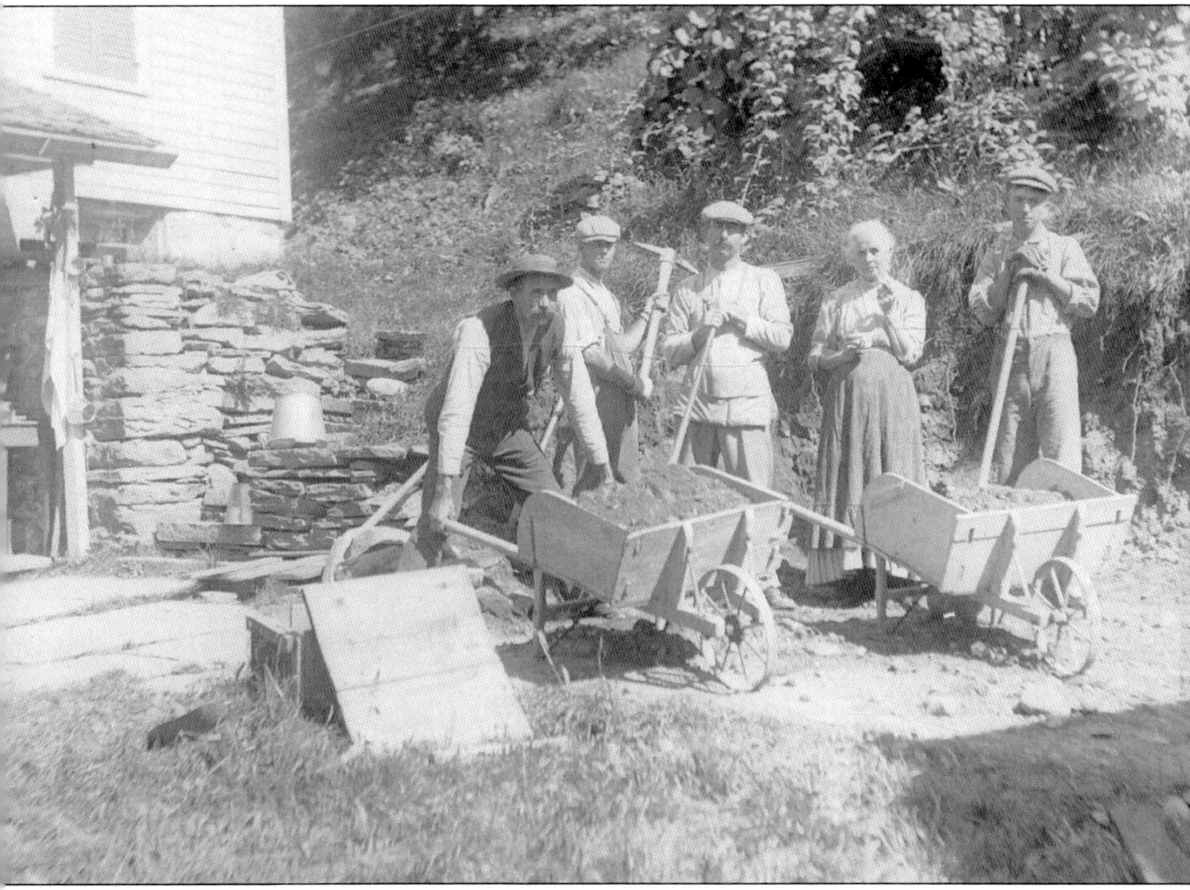

One cannot help but wonder what these industrious folks were doing as they stopped and posed for the photographer. Where are they bound with their wheelbarrows full of dirt and picks and shovels in hand? Identified in the photograph are Mose I., Emmett Walter, "Grandpa" Donaldson, "Great Grandma" Donaldson, and Ward Dierfelter. At one time, this house had a picket fence that was covered with hops vines. (Virginia Caldwell Bishop Collection.)

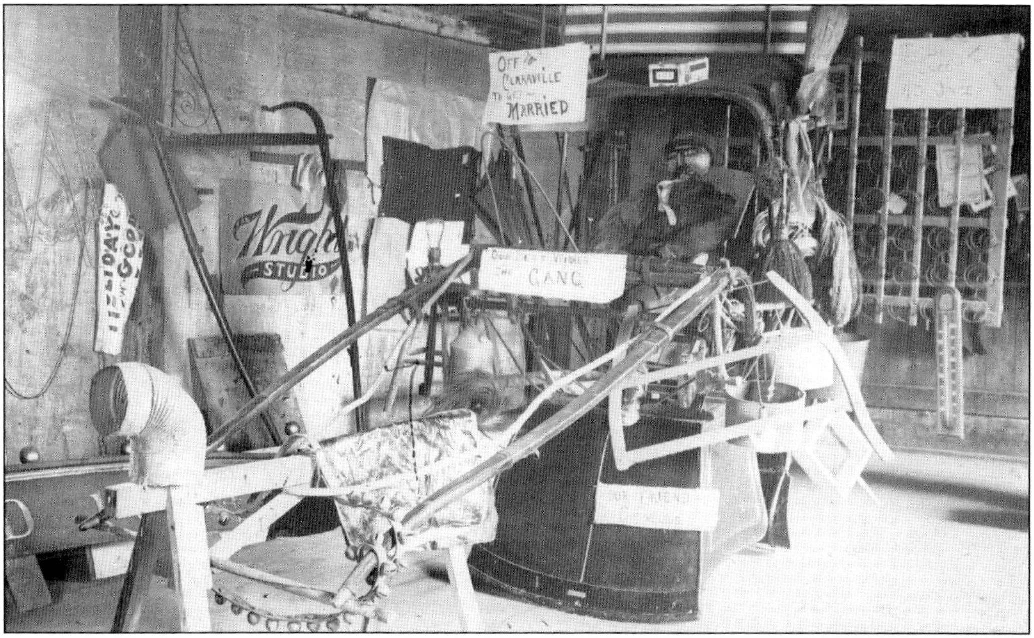

"Off to Claraville to get married" and "our best wishes" from "the gang" are messages of good cheer to Cornelius Hornbeck and Ora Hall. The caption on the back of the photograph says, "His paint shop decorated up while they were away on honeymoon." Claraville became Claryville and remains so to this very day. (Erts/DuBois collection.)

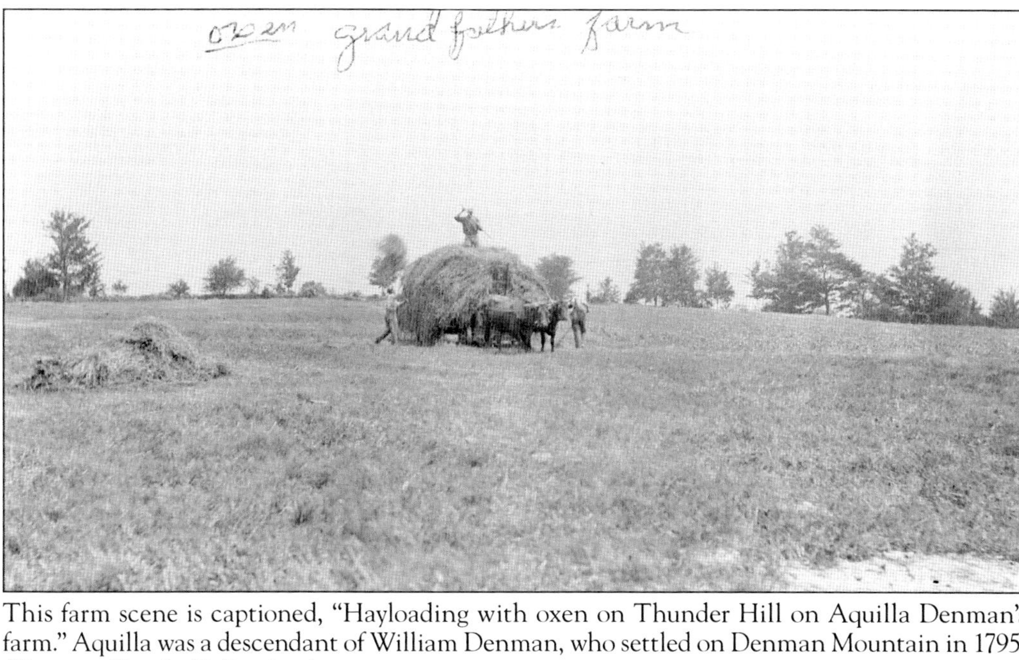

This farm scene is captioned, "Hayloading with oxen on Thunder Hill on Aquilla Denman's farm." Aquilla was a descendant of William Denman, who settled on Denman Mountain in 1795. (Denman Family Collection.)

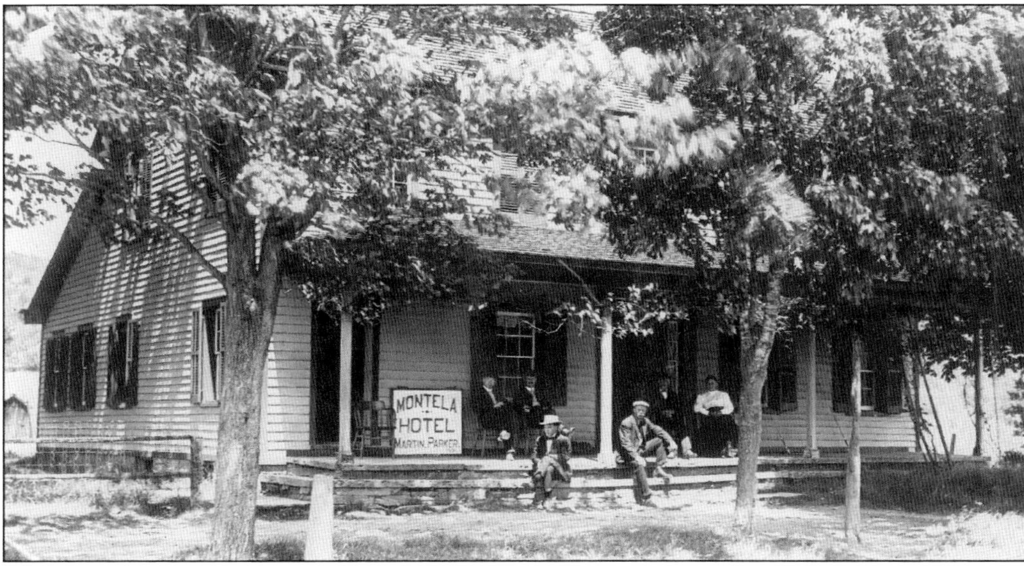

Martin Parker was proprietor of the Montela Hotel. This image has a very sad caption on the back that reads, "Under Rondout Reservoir." This could truly be said of every home, church, school, business, and cemetery in the valley, which originally held the three communities of Eureka, Montela, and Lackawack. A report of rowdy behavior after spending a day at the Montela Hotel was apparently newsworthy enough when it appeared in a news story in a Kingston newspaper prior to the taking of the Montela Hotel and other properties for the reservoir.

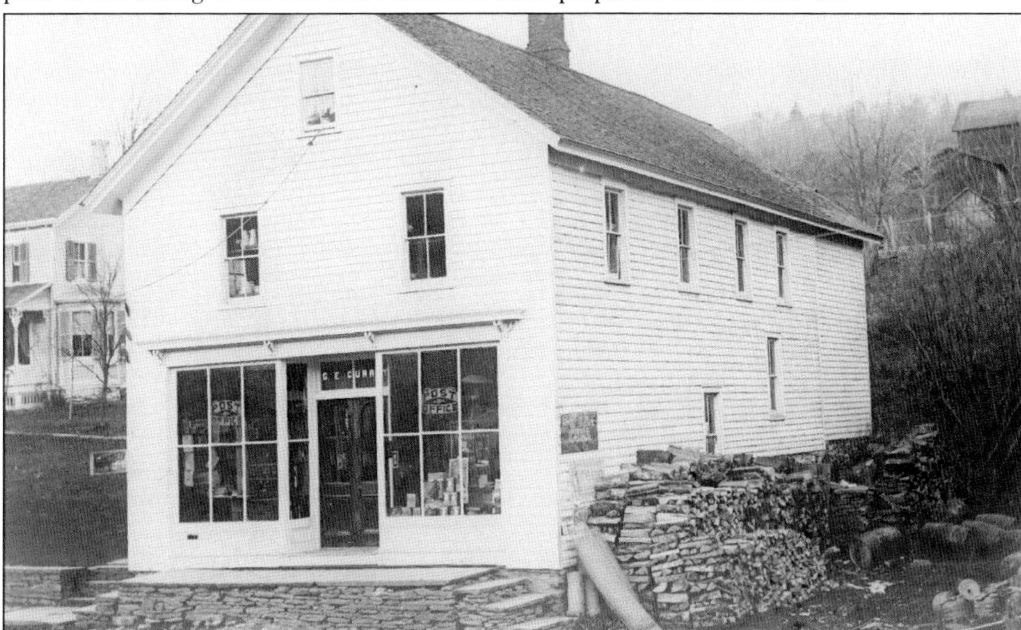

The Grahamsville Post Office was located in this building in 1905. G.F. Curry was the proprietor. The stacks of firewood next to the structure were necessary to keep the old potbellied stove fired up to heat the building. There would have been hard labor involved in splitting all that wood by hand. Visible in the background to the left is a home that still stands today. (Virginia Caldwell Bishop Collection.)

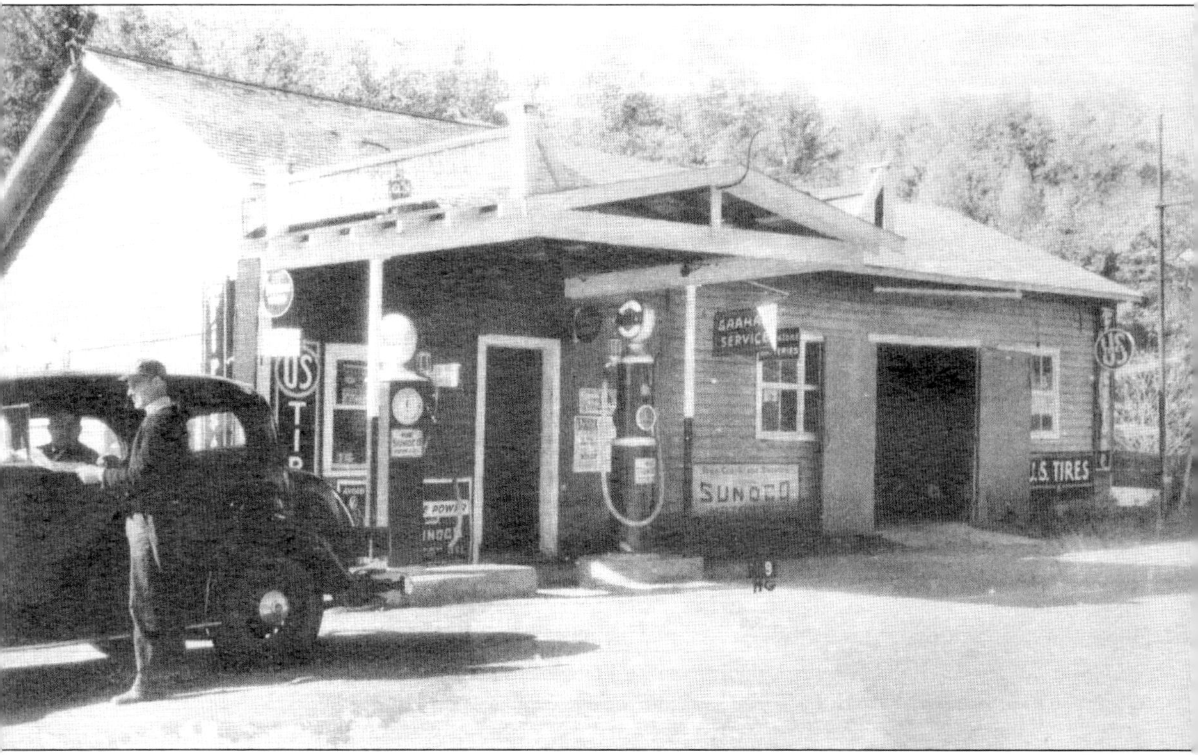

Dayton's Garage in Eureka moved up to Grahamsville when the water came and inundated the area for the Rondout Reservoir. Proprietor Lee Dayton pumped the gas for his customers, as did all rural gas stations in those days. This advertising card is addressed to Mr. Leslie H. Sagendorf of Eureka, New York. It took a penny stamp to mail.

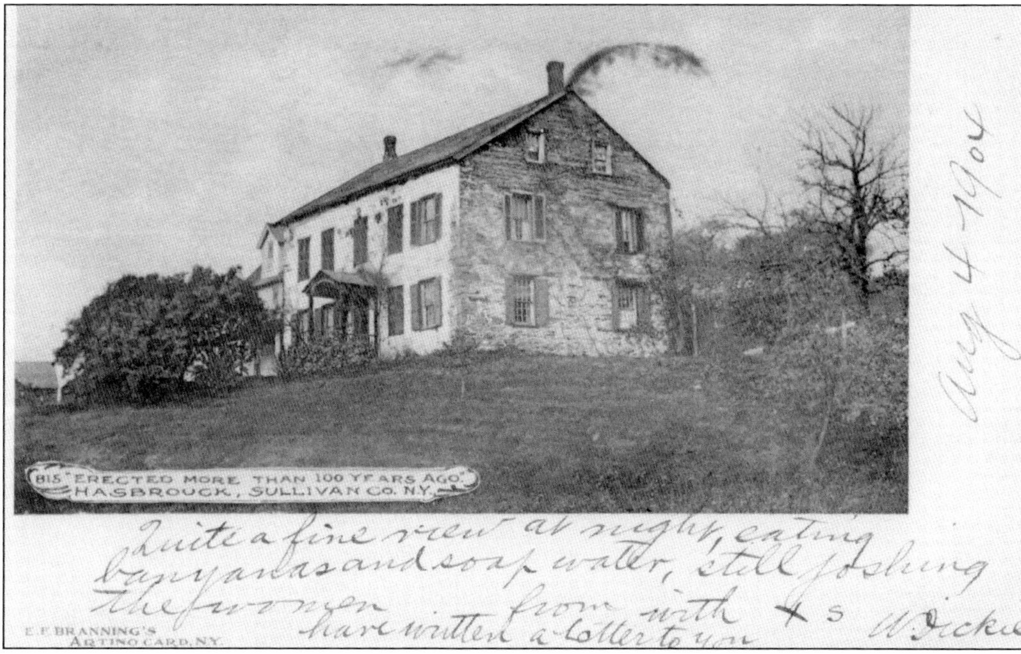

The Old Stone House at Hasbrouck stands as strong and tall today as it did in 1904. It is well cared for by a group of concerned citizens from the area. Hasbrouck was part of the town of Neversink until the 1820s, when the town of Fallsburg was created by the New York State Legislature.

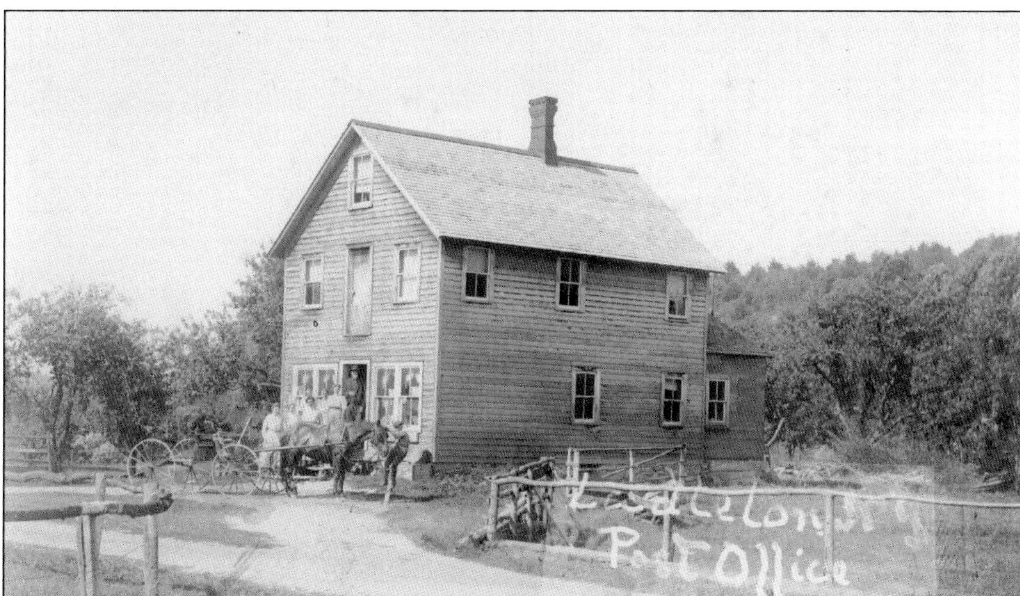

Ladleton's post office was located in a private home, as were many small post offices in early days. A note on the back of this image designates this as the home of "Aunt Sarah." The Ladleton Post Office was established in 1894 and discontinued in 1956. The Claryville Fire Company burned this building in 1965.

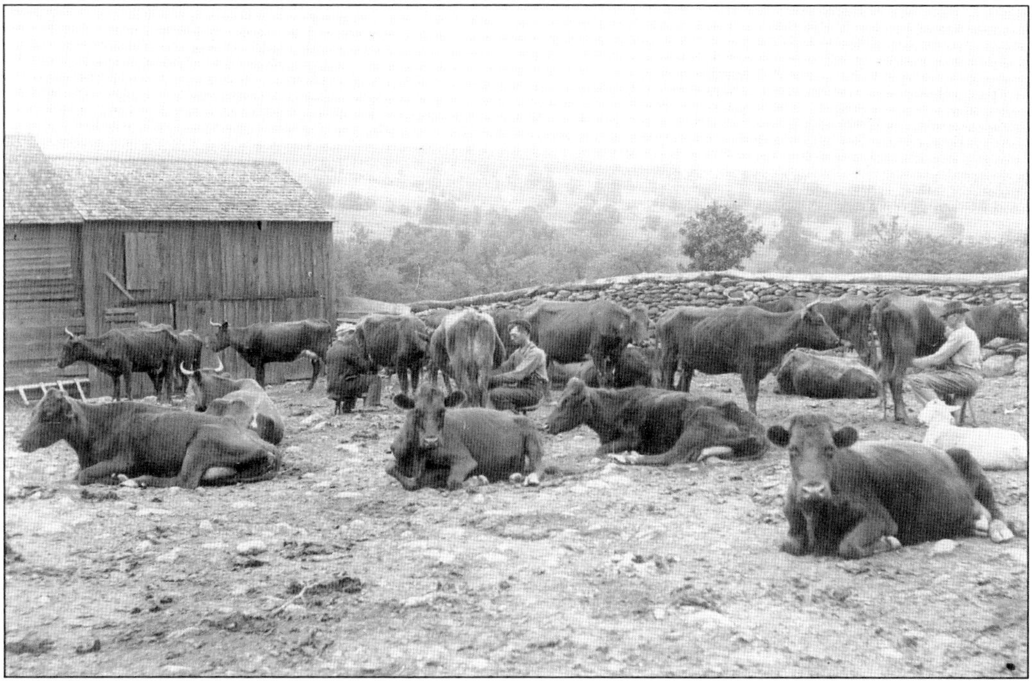

Modern-day farmers would shake their heads to see three men milking cows in a barnyard like this. Otto Hillig of Liberty, New York, took this photograph. Note the sheep lying peacefully in the group.

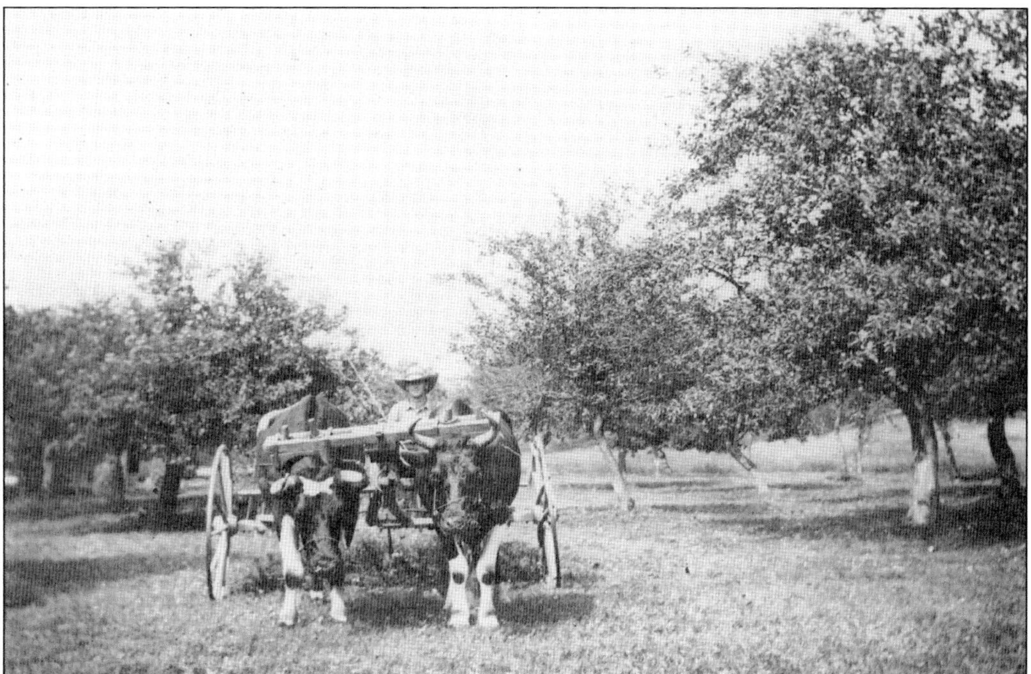

Frank Dulaff is driving this team of oxen and pulling what looks like a hay rake behind. The photograph is dated 1911.

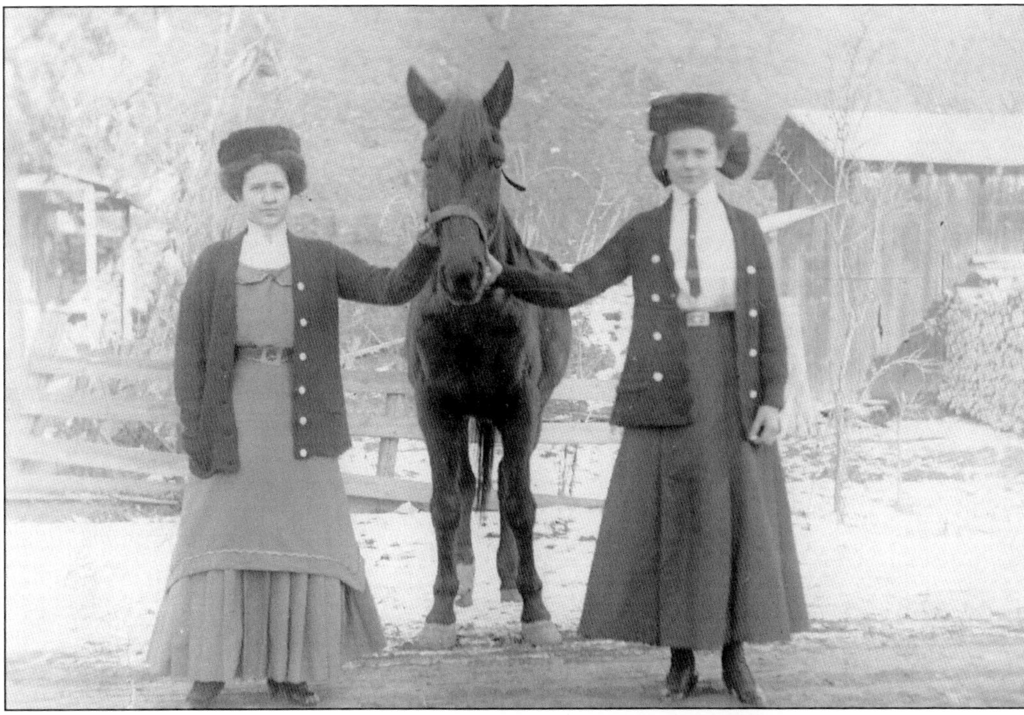

From left to right, sisters Theda and Laura Kortright stand proudly with a favorite horse. The early 1900s was a time for much photograph taking in Grahamsville and elsewhere. (Virginia Caldwell Bishop Collection.)

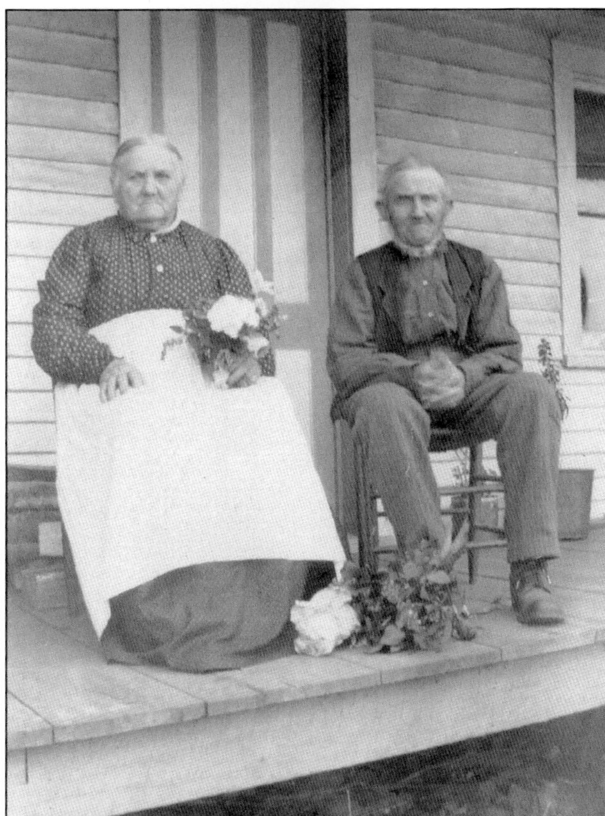

Mr. and Mrs. Henry George of Red Hill are pictured on their golden wedding anniversary. Henry George's father came to this country from Germany in the mid-1800s with other family members. (Helen Erts DuBois Collection.)

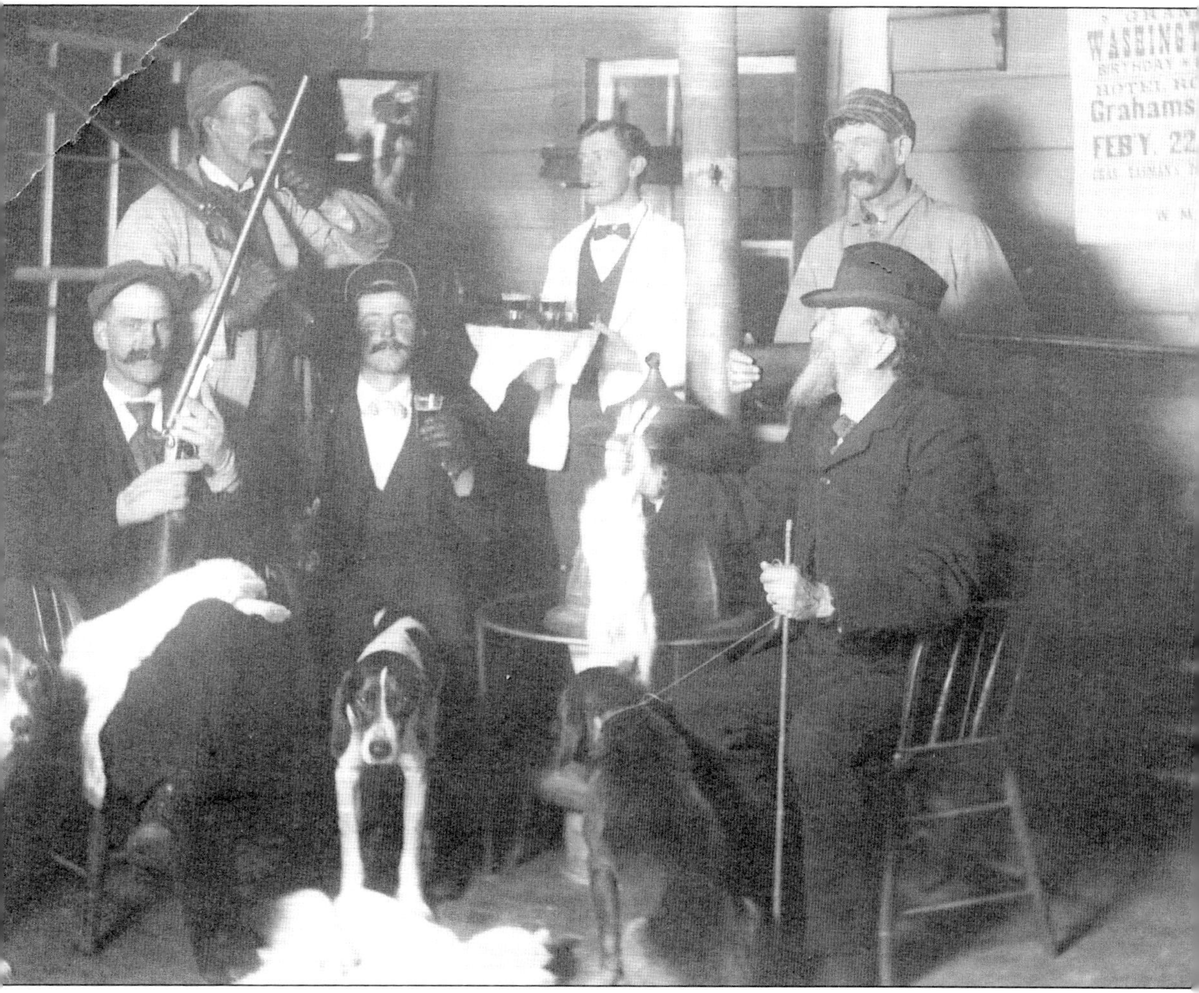

Rabbits seem to be the prey of the day for the interesting group pictured here. The Neversink historian's office has Hotel Roosa documents that place the hotel in Grahamsville with W.M. Roosa as proprietor and date as February 7, 1894. This photograph was in a frame and mat vintage early 1900s. The poster shows the date as 1898. It is the thought of some local history buffs that the location for this photograph was what was later known as the Gillette Hotel. (Robert Curry collection.)

Two

Schools and Churches

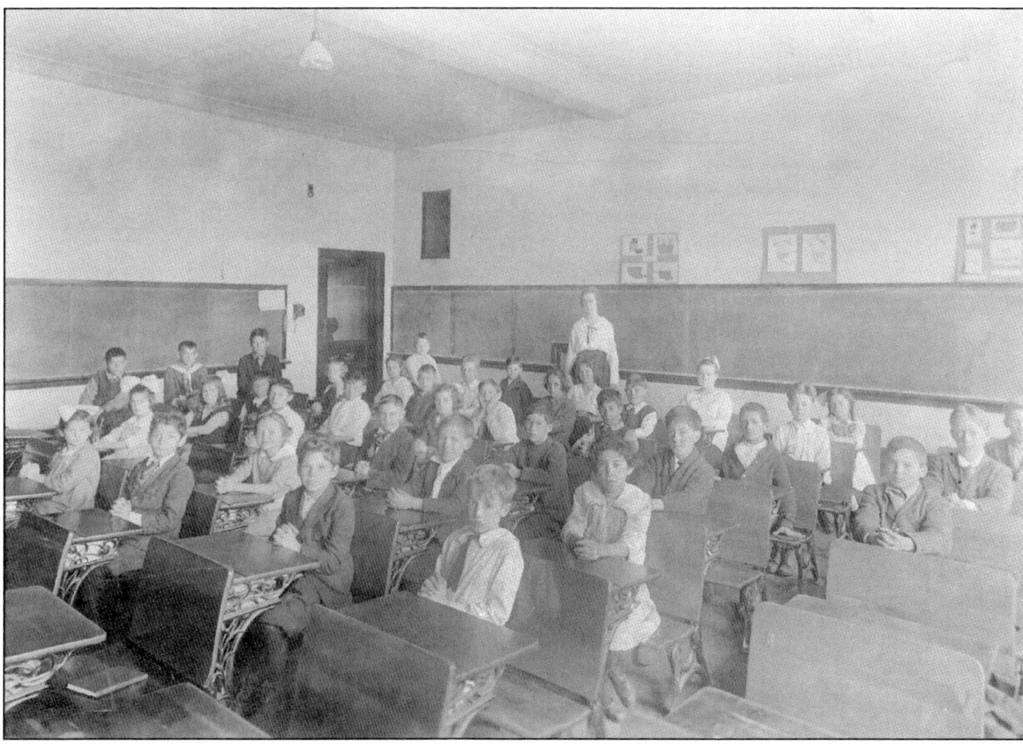

This interior shot is of a multiple-grade classroom. It is probably one room of the Grahamsville two-room school. In Grahamsville, the first four grades were on one side and grades five through eight were on the other side. Youngsters might attend a one-room school in their immediate vicinity and then get sent to a two-room school. The desks are wood and wrought iron, typical of the day. This is a big class for the teacher having to instruct all different subjects to four different grades.

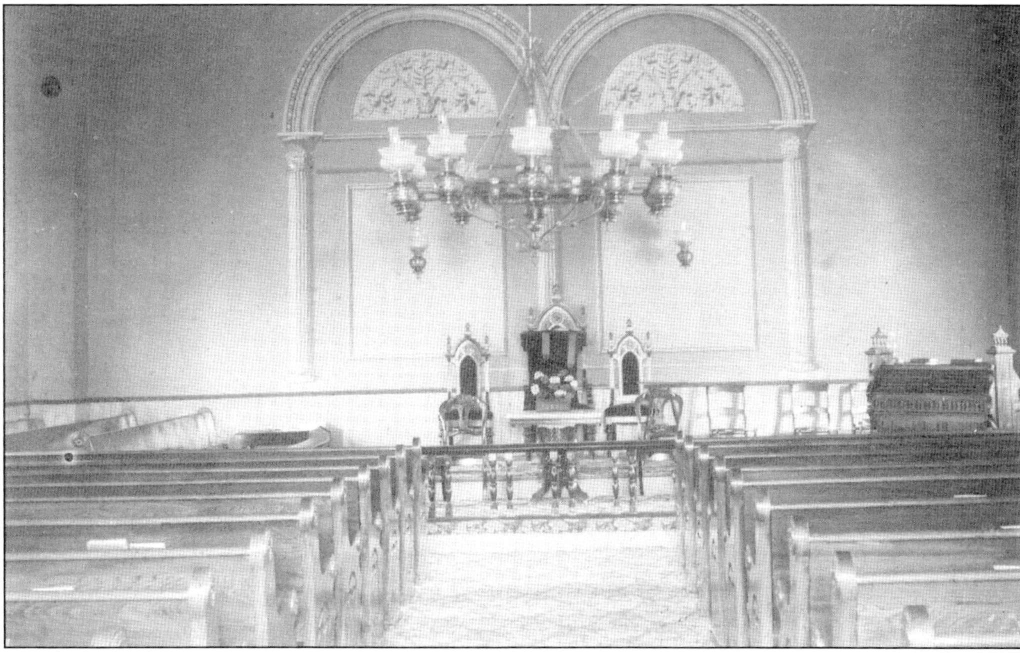

Here is the interior of the Grahamsville Methodist Church, photographed sometime between 1905 and 1915. It is rare to see the interiors of rural churches from this time period, so this image is a treat. The hanging chandelier is made for kerosene lighting. The church still stands today and is well attended. The pews are the same.

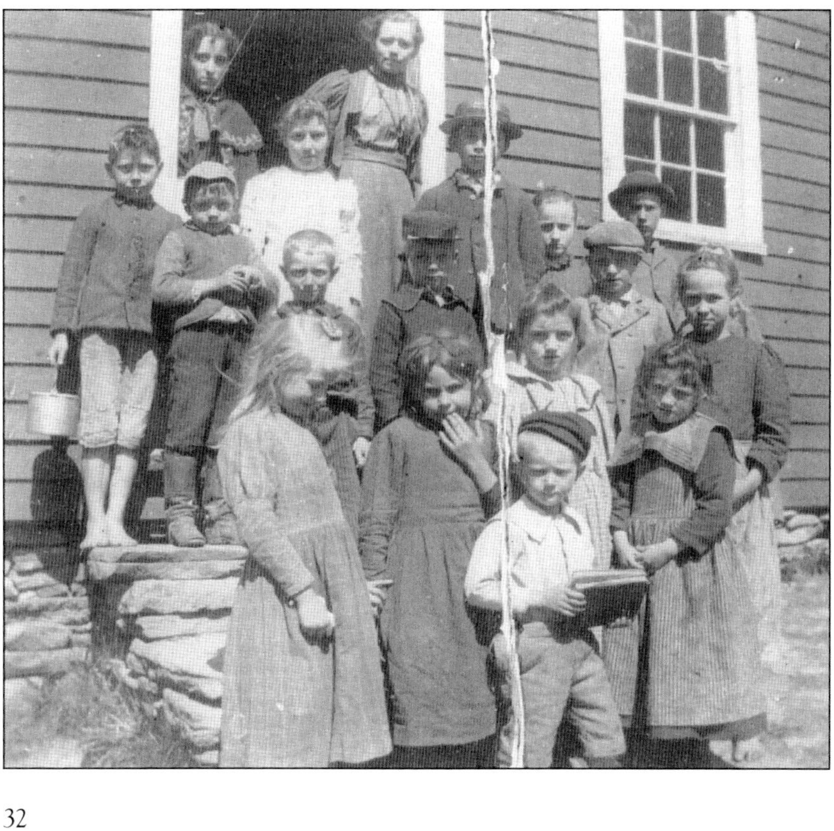

This is the class of Belle Marshall at South Hill School for the academic year beginning September 12, 1898, and ending May 29, 1899.

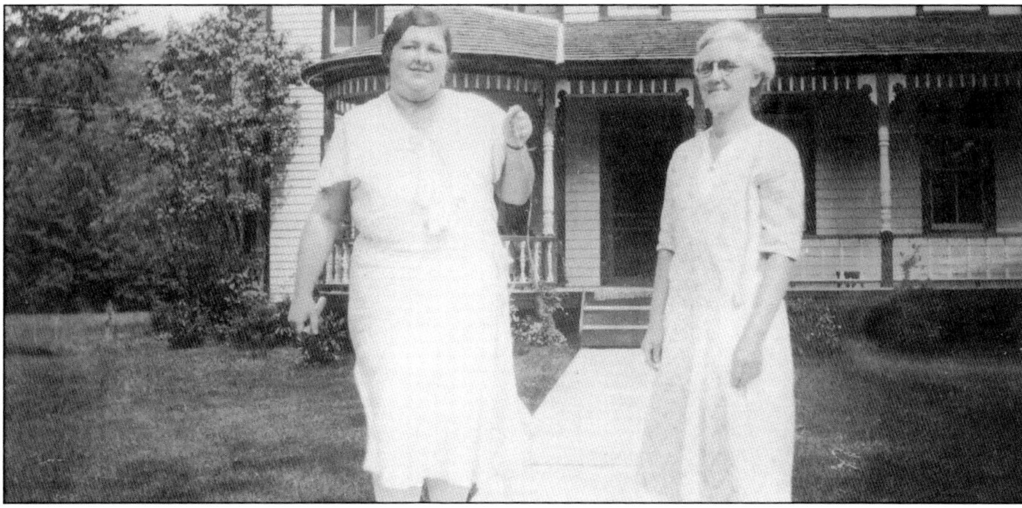

Madelene Hornbeck (left) and Ethel Currey (right) stand in front of Ethel's residence in Claryville. The date of the photograph is not known. (Nancy Cross Collection.)

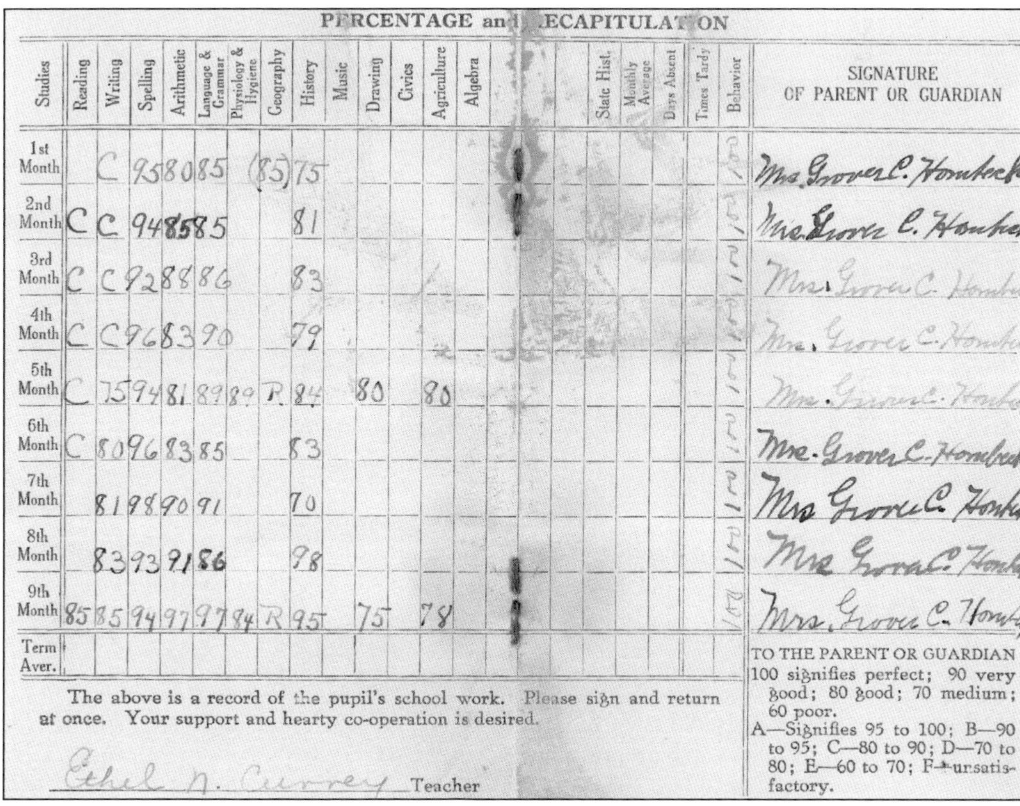

PERCENTAGE and RECAPITULATION

Studies	Reading	Writing	Spelling	Arithmetic	Language & Grammar	Physiology & Hygiene	Geography	History	Music	Drawing	Civics	Agriculture	Algebra	State Hist.	Monthly Average	Days Absent	Times Tardy	Behavior	SIGNATURE OF PARENT OR GUARDIAN
1st Month		C	95	80	85		(85)	75										[illegible]	Mrs. Grover C. Hornbeck
2nd Month	C	C	94	85	85			81										[illegible]	Mrs. Grover C. Hornbeck
3rd Month	C	C	92	88	86			83										[illegible]	Mrs. Grover C. Hornbeck
4th Month	C	C	96	83	90			79										[illegible]	Mrs. Grover C. Hornbeck
5th Month	C	75	94	81	89	89	R	84		80		80						[illegible]	Mrs. Grover C. Hornbeck
6th Month	C	80	96	83	85			83										[illegible]	Mrs. Grover C. Hornbeck
7th Month		81	98	90	91			70										[illegible]	Mrs Grover C. Hornbeck
8th Month		83	93	91	86			98										[illegible]	Mrs Grover C. Hornbeck
9th Month	85	85	94	97	97	84	R	95		75		78						[illegible]	Mrs. Grover C. Hornbeck
Term Aver.																			

The above is a record of the pupil's school work. Please sign and return at once. Your support and hearty co-operation is desired.

Ethel A. Currey Teacher

TO THE PARENT OR GUARDIAN
100 signifies perfect; 90 very good; 80 good; 70 medium; 60 poor.
A—Signifies 95 to 100; B—90 to 95; C—80 to 90; D—70 to 80; E—60 to 70; F—unsatisfactory.

Here is the pupil's monthly report for Madelene Hornbeck, dated September 1924. Hornbeck was in the seventh grade at the Grahamsville two-room school with Ethel Currey as her teacher. "Madge," as she later was known, grew up to be a teacher herself. She ended up working at the Grahamsville School she had attended, as well as at other local schools. Teachers and students alike honored and respected her because of her teaching capabilities. She was married to Ralph Adams. (Nancy Cross Collection.)

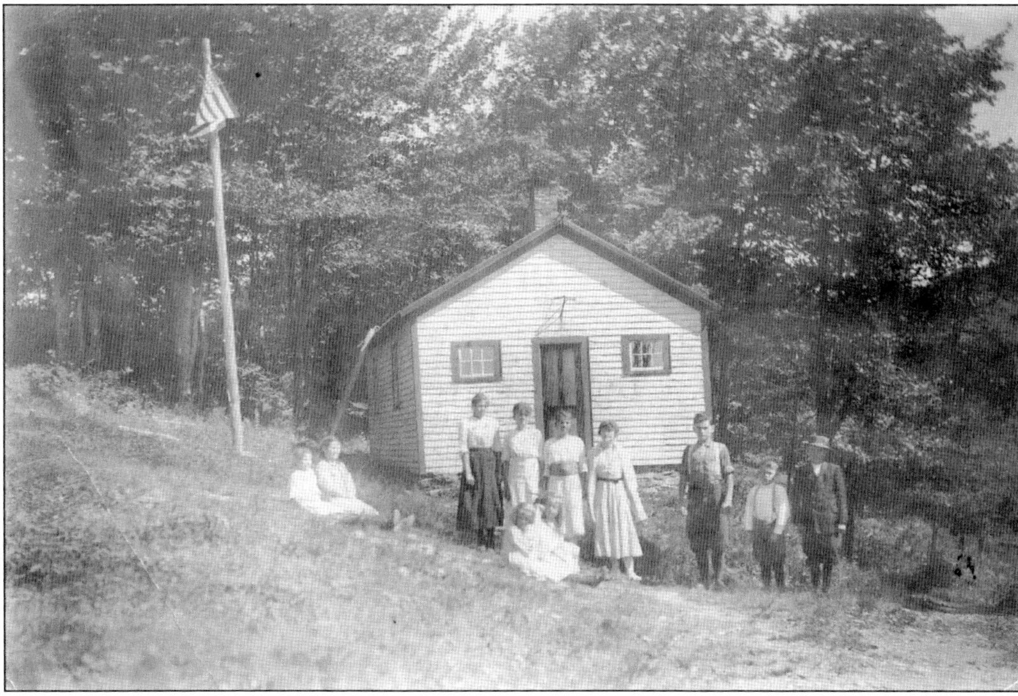

The Red Hill School was the first school to open in what became the town of Denning. This photograph was taken by Albert V. Porter of Ellenville, New York. The story is legend; Denning was part of the town of Shandaken, Ulster County, in those days, and two local residents walked over the mountain to Shandaken proper to get permission to open the school.

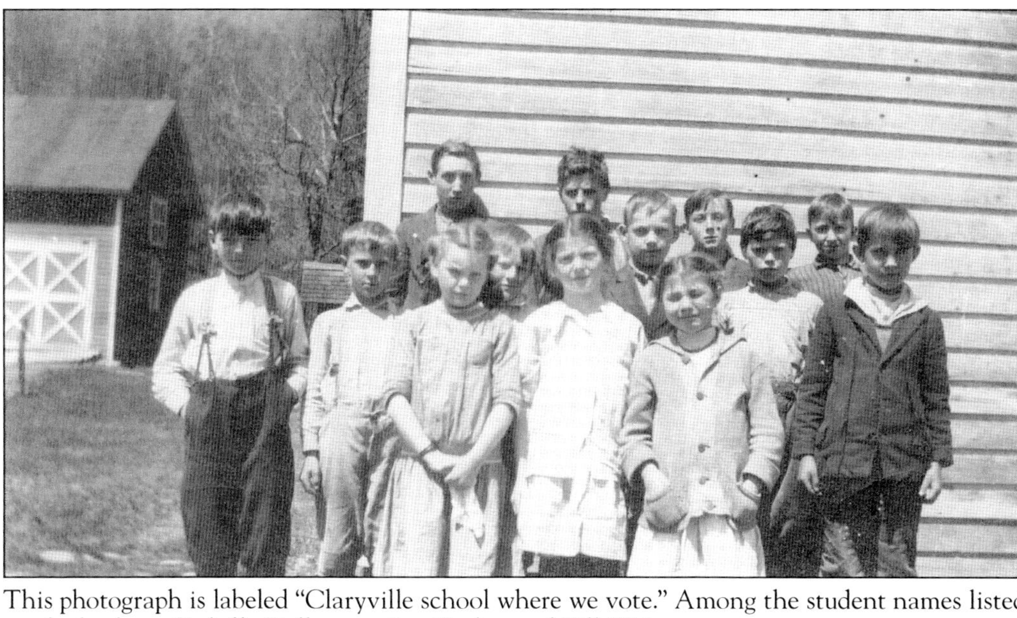

This photograph is labeled "Claryville school where we vote." Among the student names listed on the back are Dulaffs, Dolloways, Bea Kothe, and Bill Waizman.

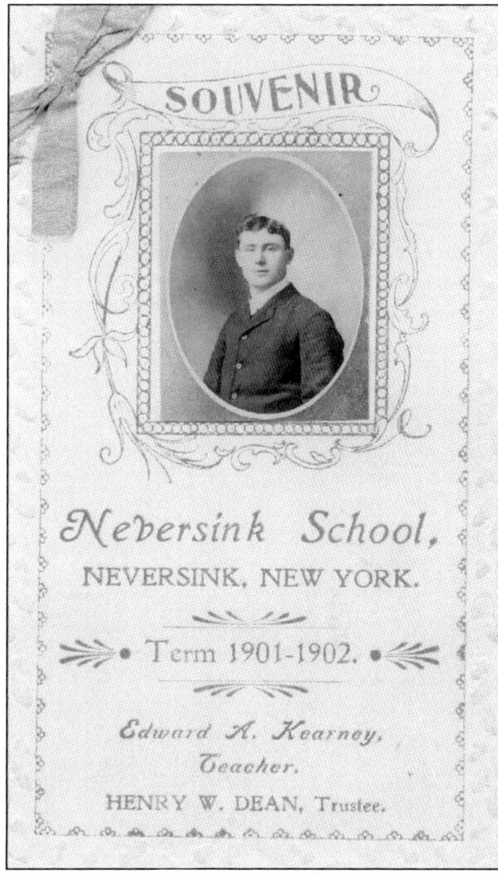

This is a souvenir booklet of the 1901–1902 Neversink School academic year. The school was located in village of Neversink, now under the reservoir of the same name. In those days, Neversink was more commonly known as Neversink Flats. Teachers often handed these souvenirs out to their students at the end of the school year. (Virginia Caldwell Bishop Collection.)

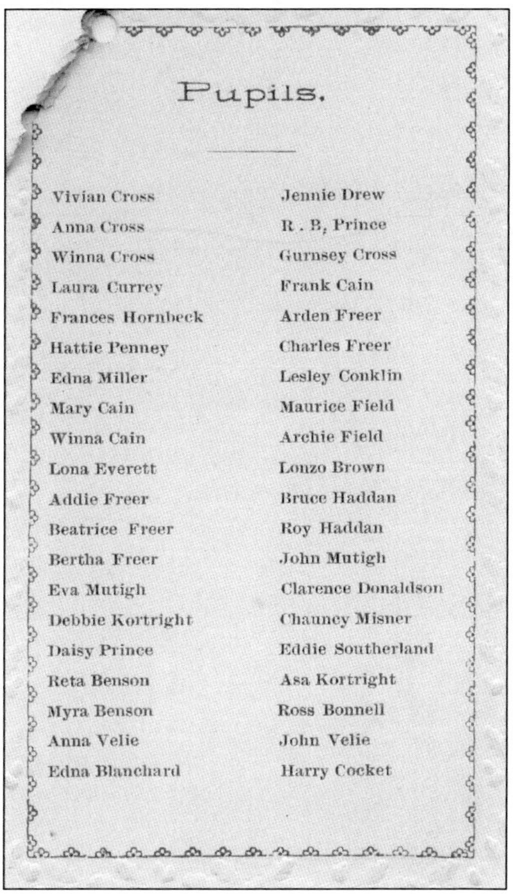
Pupils.

Vivian Cross	Jennie Drew
Anna Cross	R. B. Prince
Winna Cross	Gurnsey Cross
Laura Currey	Frank Cain
Frances Hornbeck	Arden Freer
Hattie Penney	Charles Freer
Edna Miller	Lesley Conklin
Mary Cain	Maurice Field
Winna Cain	Archie Field
Lona Everett	Lonzo Brown
Addie Freer	Bruce Haddan
Beatrice Freer	Roy Haddan
Bertha Freer	John Mutigh
Eva Mutigh	Clarence Donaldson
Debbie Kortright	Chauncey Misner
Daisy Prince	Eddie Southerland
Reta Benson	Asa Kortright
Myra Benson	Ross Bonnell
Anna Velie	John Velie
Edna Blanchard	Harry Cocket

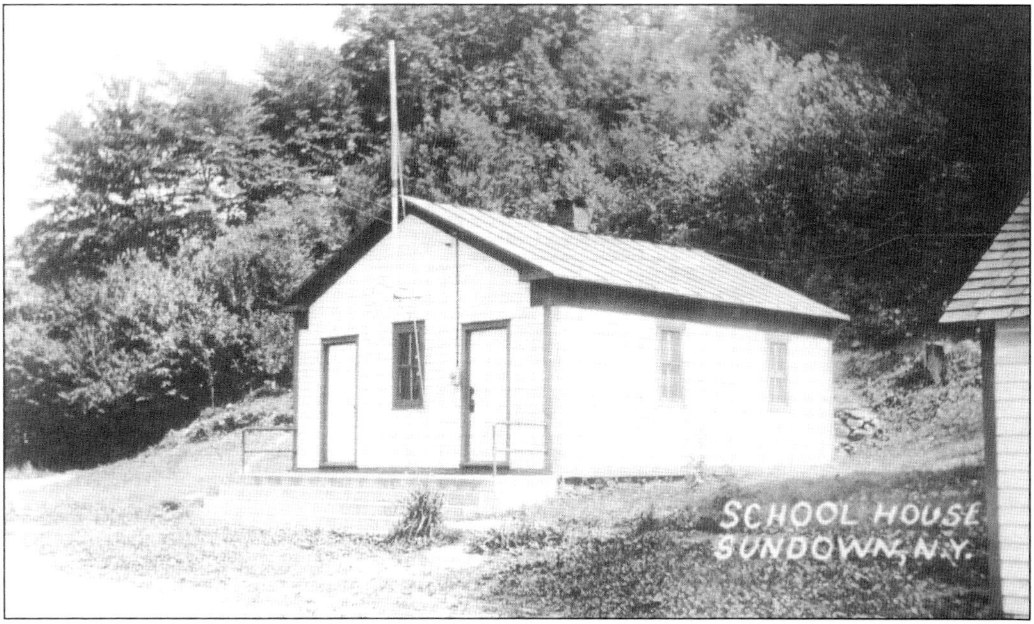

The Sundown schoolhouse is pictured here around 1905. Visible are the separate doors for boys and girls. Interestingly, the schoolhouse is located across the road and very near to the Sundown Methodist Church. Today, this building is the nucleus for a private home.

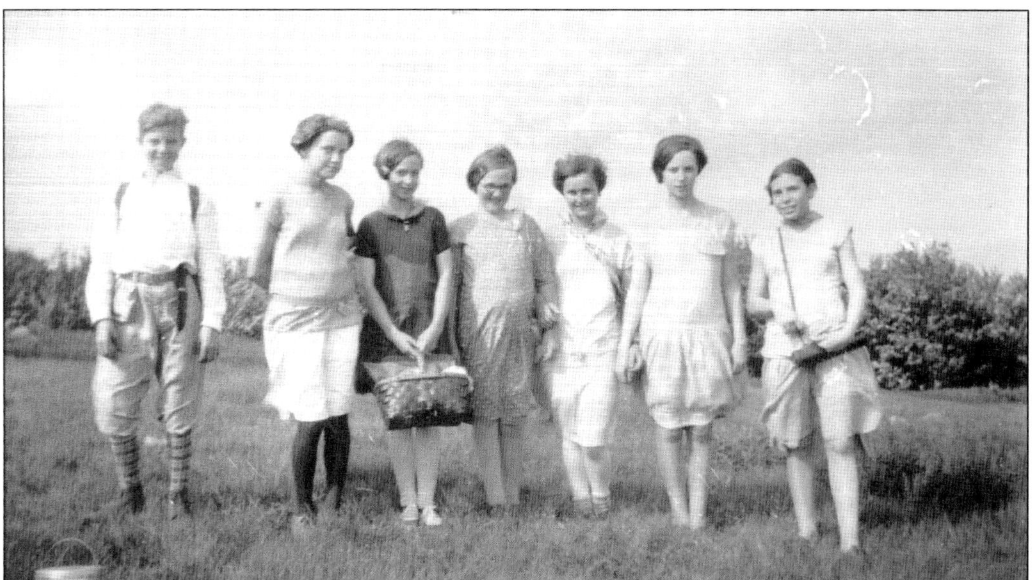
This Lows Corners school picnic on Red Hill took place around the 1920s. Students picnicking included members of the Hamilton, Low, and Wright families.

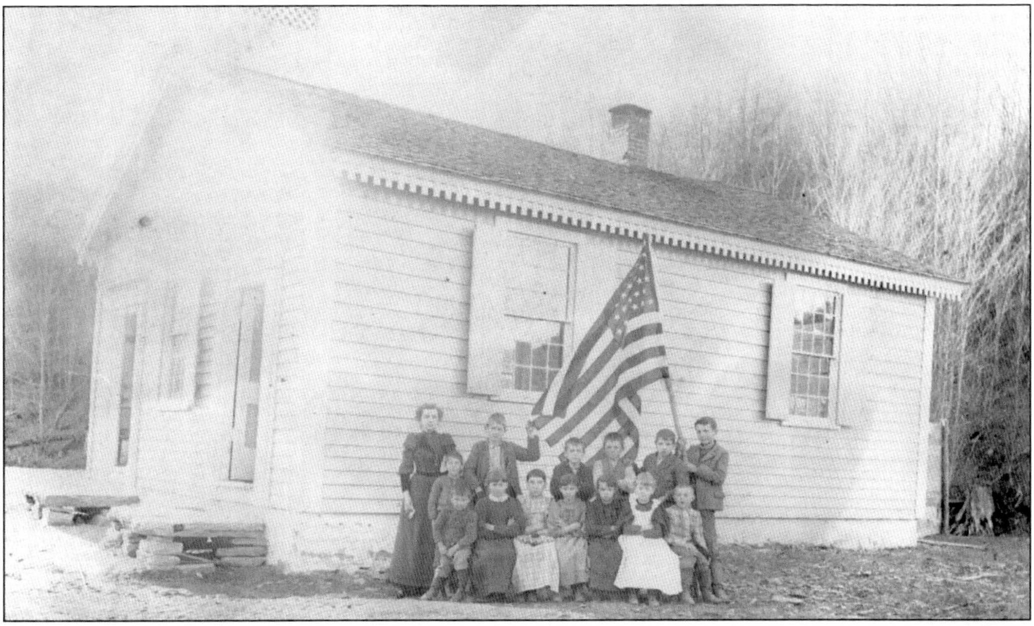

This photograph shows the Denning schoolhouse, with William George holding the flagpole, in 1896. Note the two doors—one was for boys, the other for girls. The flag is waving proudly for this group of boys and girls at District No. 4, Denning, New York. It is reported that the school burned about 1930 and was rebuilt in the same place. The photograph was taken by Ticefeldt of Chichester, Ulster County.

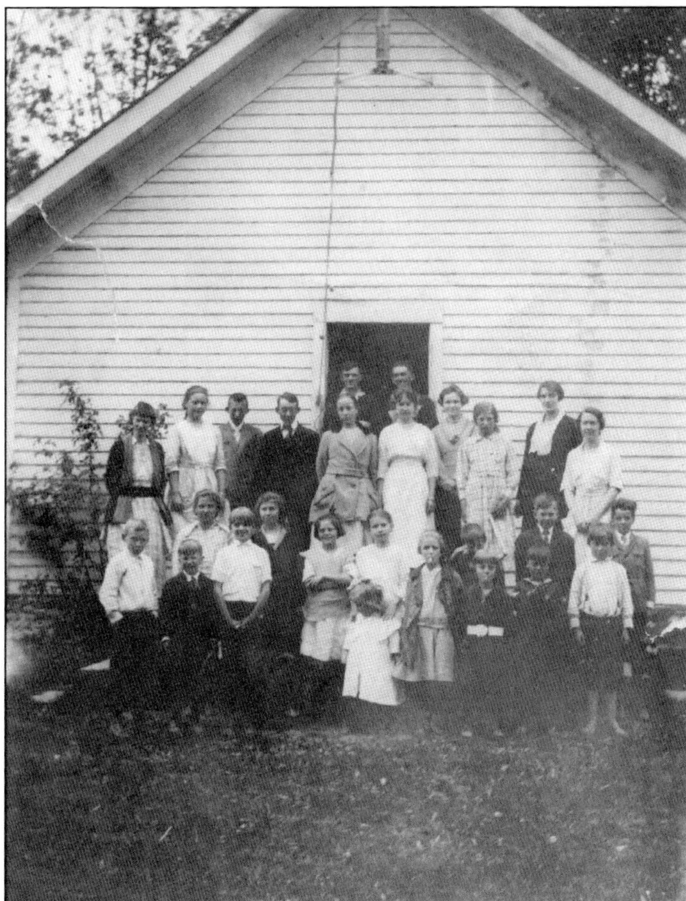

This photograph is labeled simply "Claryville School—Teacher Mabel TerBush Slater." (Andrew DuBois Collection.)

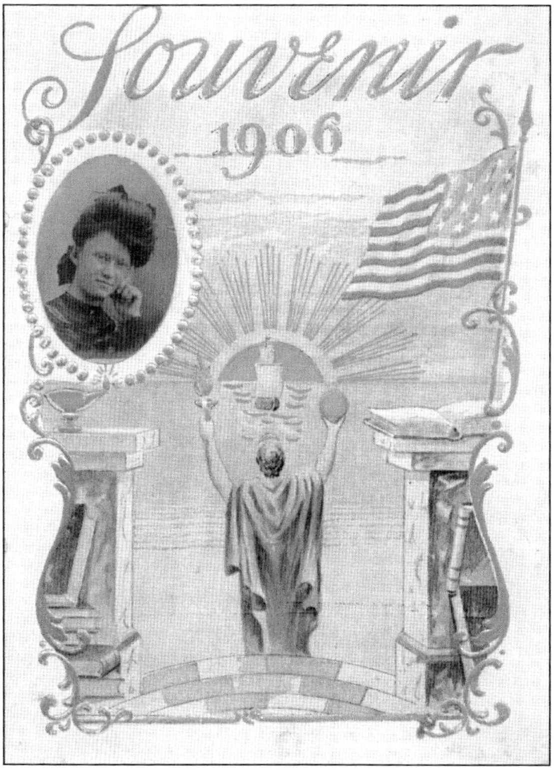

This is the School District No. 12 Upper South Hill School souvenir booklet from 1906. The cover shows a photograph of teacher Leeta Oneill. The school had 21 pupils enrolled. P.D. Sheeley was trustee; B. Porter, collector; and M. Divine, clerk.

SOUTH HILL

PUBLIC SCHOOL

District No. 12

Neversink Tp.. Sullivan Co., New York.

LEETA ONEILL, Teacher

PUPILS

Wallace Sheeley	Helen Low
Irwin Edwards	Grace Sheeley
Stoddard Porter	Beulah Sheeley
Henry Sturgis	Mary Low
Dannie Sturgis	Bertha Low
Francis Low	Gussie Miller
Graham Sheeley	Louise Edwards
Mack Sheeley	Pearl Sheeley
Samuel Divine	Caroline Divine
Harold Hill	Harold Sturgis

Myrtle Low

P. D. Sheeley,	Trustee
B. Porter,	Collector
M. Divine,	Clerk

The souvenir booklet has a delightful verse on the inner pages titled "The Close of School."

These students of South Hill School are pictured in 1904 with teacher Anna Groo. Gussie Miller stands in the background to the left, and in the row of girls are, from left to right, Pearl Sheley, Mary Low, Beulah Sheley, Grace Sheley, Helen Low, Anna Groo, and Myrtle Groo. The row of boys includes Joseph Rampe, Wallace Sheley, Irwin Edwards, Stoddard Porter (face hidden, one leg showing), Graham Sheley, and Mark Sheley.

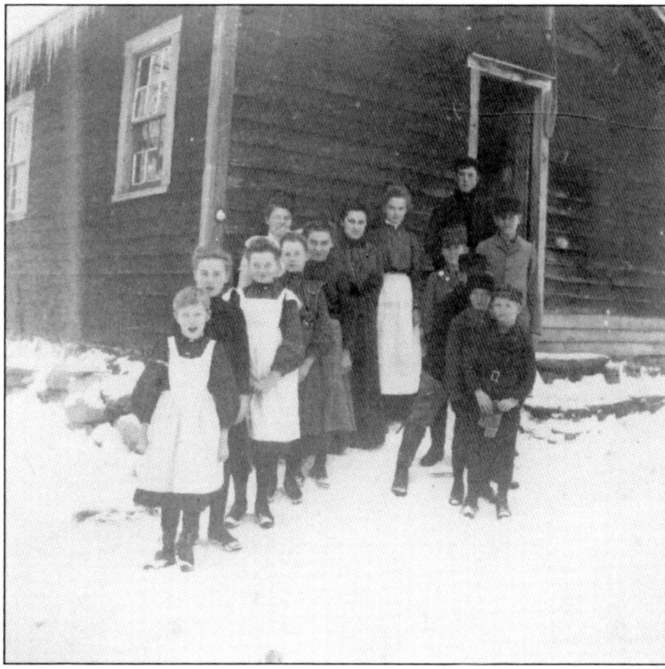

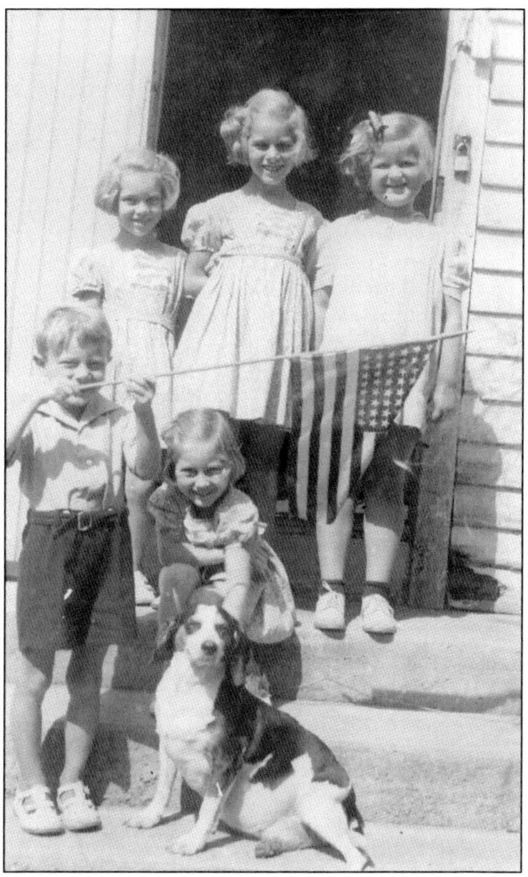

First, there was just a single student in this one-room school on South Hill. Then Charlotte, Phyllis, Marilyn, and Phil joined Carol in school. The Coombe family was staying on South Hill while their home in Ridgewood, New Jersey, was being built. Evelyn Hill Huntsberger was the teacher from 1939 to 1941. This may have been Flag Day as indicated by the students proudly holding the American flag. Flag Day was not a legal holiday but was widely celebrated in schools.

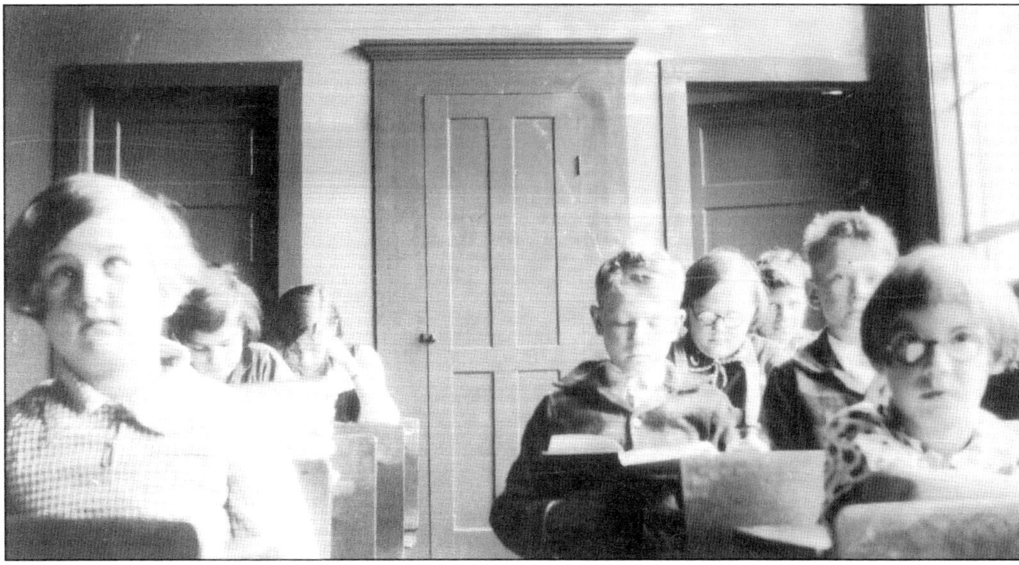

The Lows Corners School was located up from the Baptist church, same side of the Sundown-Grahamsville Road. Inez George Gridley was teacher the year this photograph was taken. She lists the students on the left as Catherine Burch, Florence H. and Marian Wright. On the right they are Loretta Low in the front seat, Roy Burch, Ethel Low, Edward Hamilton and Georgia Burch.

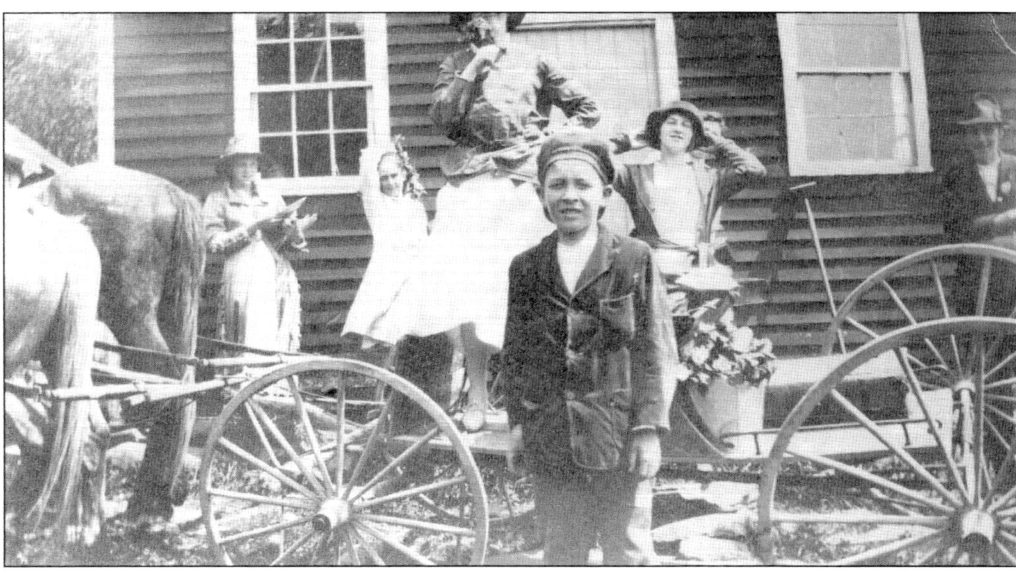

This is the last day of school at Greenville about 1918. The caption on the back reports that "Linda drove Tom and Daisy with the buckboard to pick Ruth up on the last day of school at Greenville. Later Linda taught at the same school in 1924."

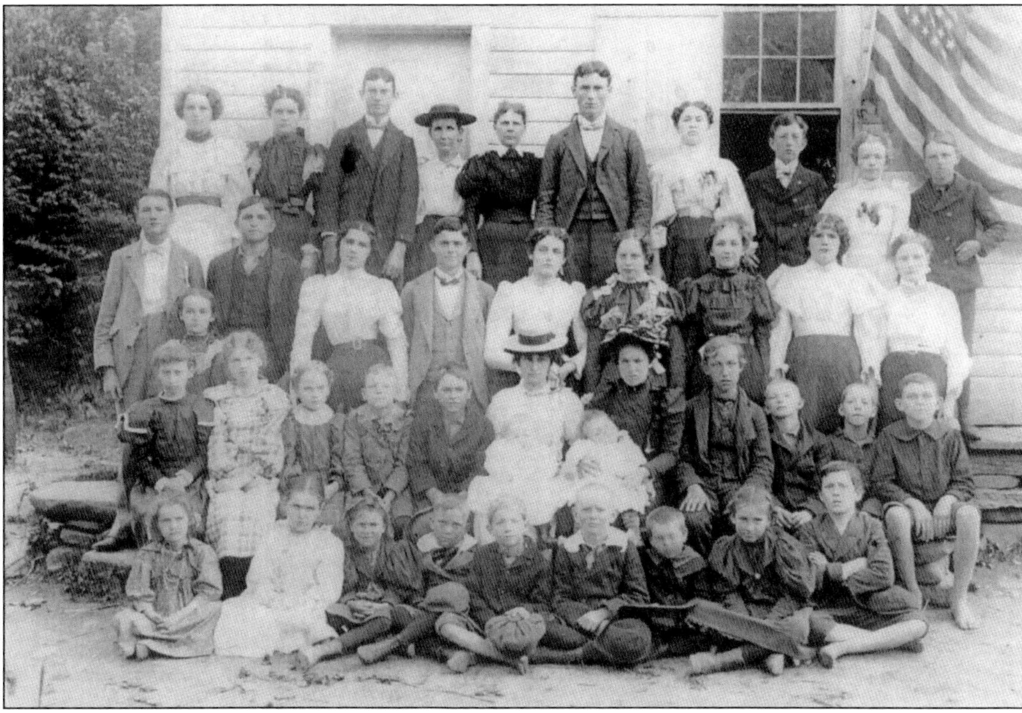

Edward Kearney taught the Unionville School during the 1897–1898 school year. Pupils that year included Grace Slater, Maud Gillett, Ethel Headden, Grace Coger, Nellie Hornbeck, Helen Low, Pearl Carney, Florence Wright, Mable Curry, Mary Charter, Charles Curry, Hugh Galbraith, Archie Teller, Israel Slater, Frederick Wright, John Wright, Oliver Brought, Theron Charter, Elsie Slater, Inda Teller, Nora Coger, Myrtle Hornbeck, Maud Brought, Bessie Curry, Sarah Carney, Addie Wright, Lula Townson, Frank Brundage, Vernon Pierce, Austin Teller, Ira Coger, Wilbur Wright, Wilber Carney, Albert Wright, May Miller, Eve Moore, Hattie Coger, Grace Hornbeck, Myrtle Low, Nellie Curry, Pearl Wright, Phebe Shurley, Julia Charter, Earl Brundage, William Galbraith, Rance Teller, Russell Hornbeck, Lewis Wright, Randall Headen, Pierce Shurley, John Brought, and Cecil Corkins.

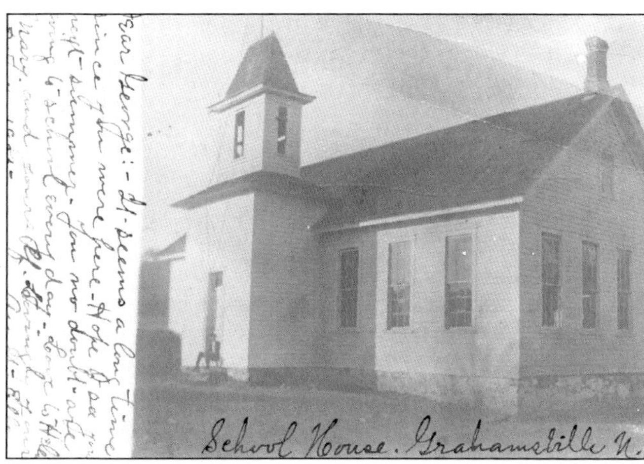

This is the two-room school at Grahamsville that was attended by generations of local children. As the era of one- and two-room schools was coming to an end, this school and the land around it became the site of the new central school. Tri-Valley Central School first opened in the 1940s and housed kindergarten through high school. Prior to the opening, local students were bused to high school in either Ellenville or Liberty. (Addy Collection.)

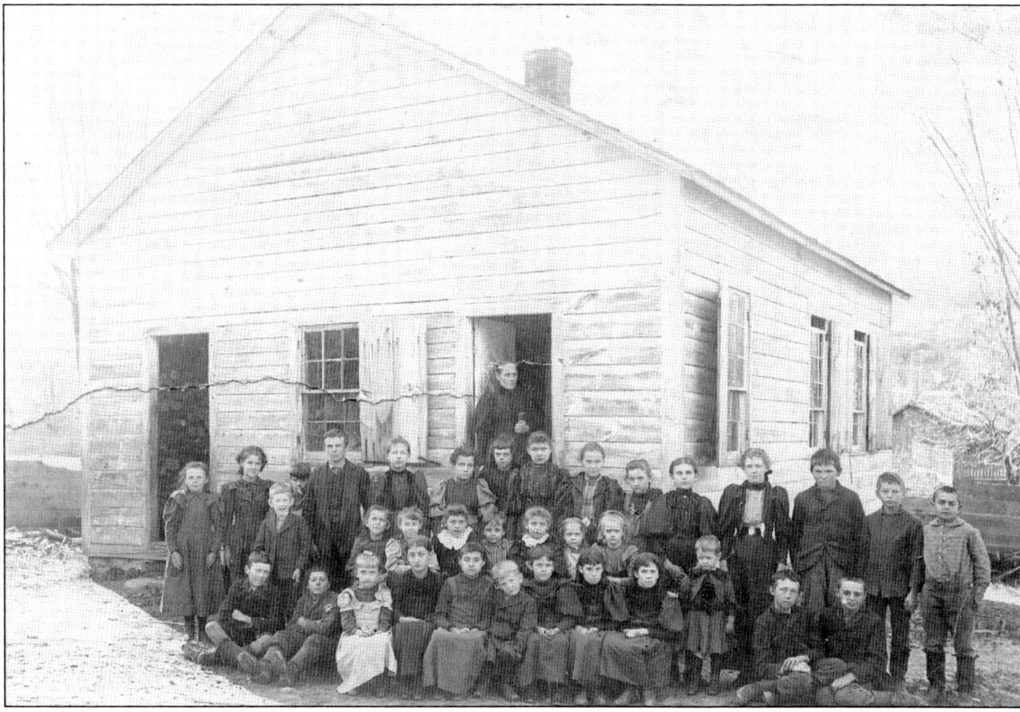

Here is the Eureka School with Nancy Moore as teacher, pictured around 1895. It is reported that photographer Ticefeldt of Chichester would ride horseback to the different schools to take photographs.

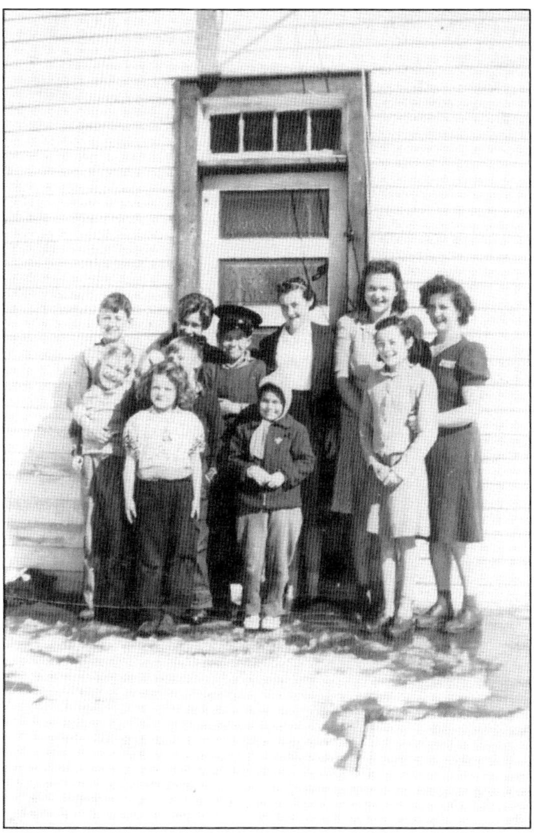

This is DeWittville School in the town of Denning c. 1942. Inez Gridley, the teacher, stands to the right wearing bobby sox. When the school closed, it was converted to the Denning Town Hall.

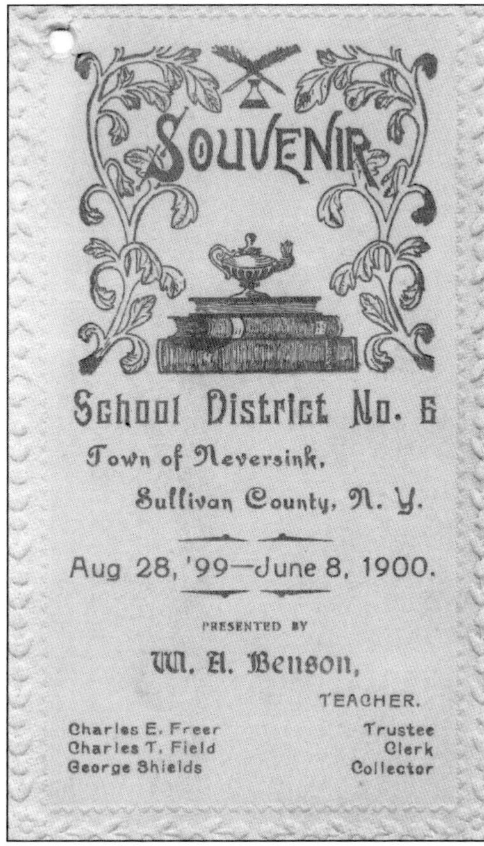

SOUVENIR

School District No. 6

Town of Neversink,

Sullivan County, N. Y.

Aug 28, '99—June 8, 1900.

PRESENTED BY

W. A. Benson,

TEACHER.

Charles E. Freer	Trustee
Charles T. Field	Clerk
George Shields	Collector

These are pages one and two of the Town of Neversink School District No. 6 souvenir booklet given out to students at the end of year by their teacher. The pages were usually tied together with a ribbon. (Virginia Caldwell Bishop Collection).

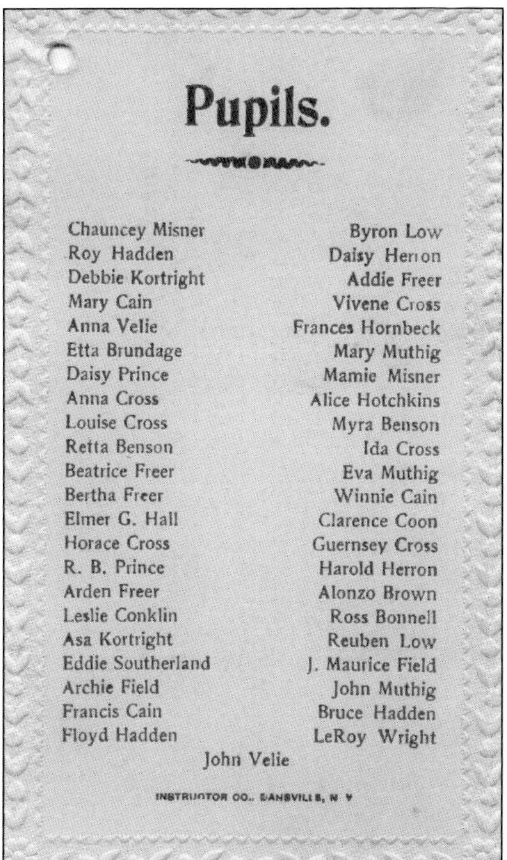

Pupils.

Chauncey Misner	Byron Low
Roy Hadden	Daisy Herron
Debbie Kortright	Addie Freer
Mary Cain	Vivene Cross
Anna Velie	Frances Hornbeck
Etta Brundage	Mary Muthig
Daisy Prince	Mamie Misner
Anna Cross	Alice Hotchkins
Louise Cross	Myra Benson
Retta Benson	Ida Cross
Beatrice Freer	Eva Muthig
Bertha Freer	Winnie Cain
Elmer G. Hall	Clarence Coon
Horace Cross	Guernsey Cross
R. B. Prince	Harold Herron
Arden Freer	Alonzo Brown
Leslie Conklin	Ross Bonnell
Asa Kortright	Reuben Low
Eddie Southerland	J. Maurice Field
Archie Field	John Muthig
Francis Cain	Bruce Hadden
Floyd Hadden	LeRoy Wright

John Velie

INSTRUCTOR CO., DANSVILLE, N. Y.

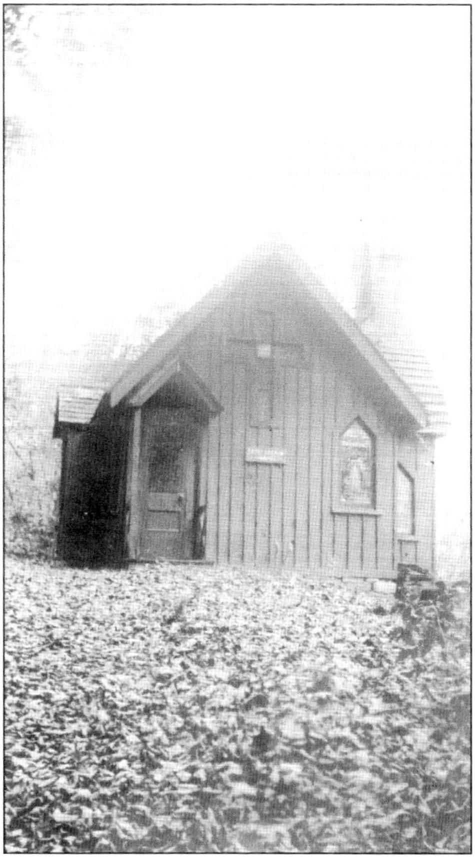

The Little Chapel at Peekamoose was located near Peekamoose Lake. It was built prior to 1900 by a Peekamoose Club member, and it is reported that local folks attended services there on Sundays.

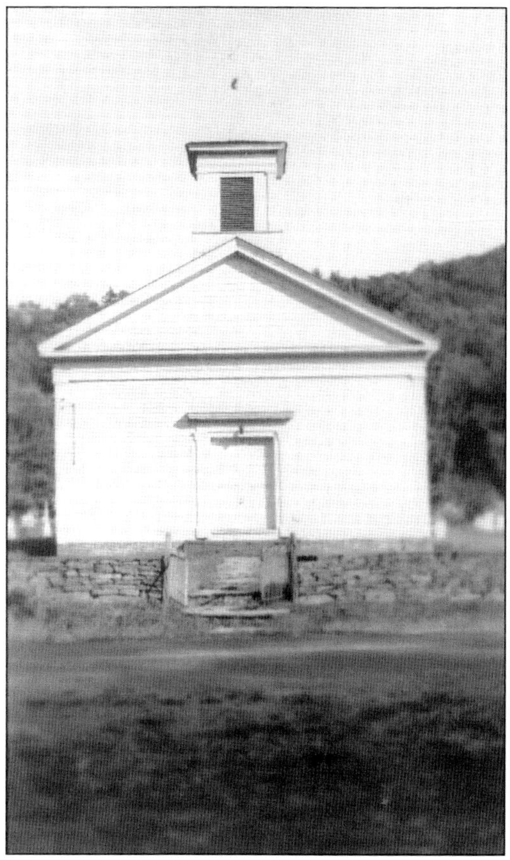

Claryville originally had a Methodist church and a Dutch Reformed church, but the Methodist church did not survive. This rather austere photograph of the Dutch Reformed church was probably taken around 1920. Tombstones from the local cemetery, which began in 1848, can be seen in the background. There are a number of Civil War veterans buried here. Written church and cemetery records are available for research. The Divine Cemetery, the pioneer burial ground of the area, was located in nearby Halls Mills. The Divine Cemetery was last used in 1863. It was flooded many times by the Neversink River, and there are no signs left of it and no written records known. Family bibles and other records will give the best information about anyone buried there.

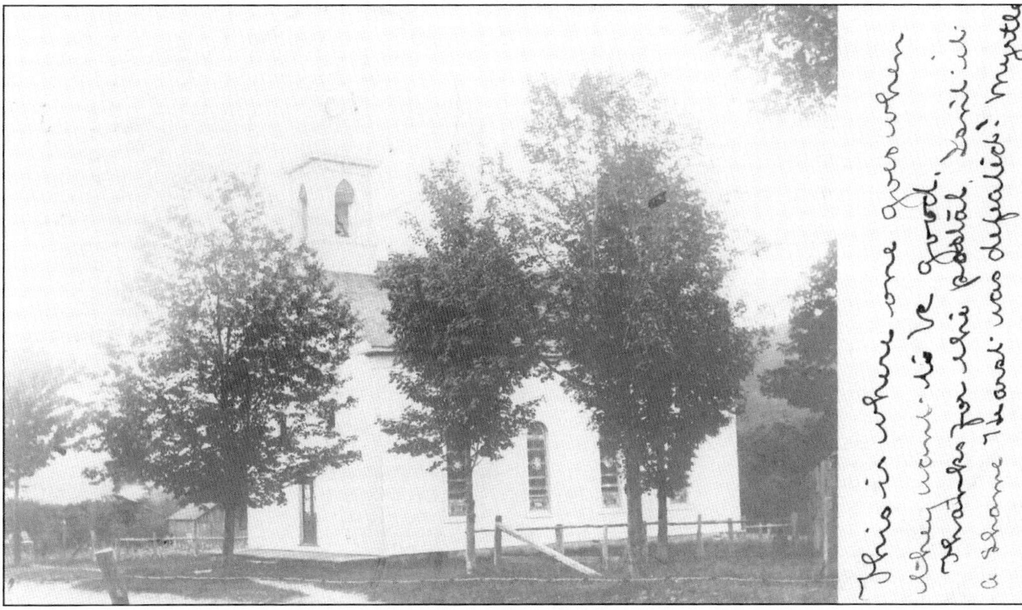

This 1909 real-photo postcard shows the Dutch Reformed church in Grahamsville. The message reads, "This is where one goes when they want to be good. Thanks for the postal. Isn't it a shame Hearst was defeated!" and is signed "Myrtle." The Grahamsville Rural Cemetery can be found on three sides of the church, which is located on New York State Route 55 across from the Tri-Valley Central School. The cemetery was started in 1874. Around 1939, with the building of the Rondout Reservoir, 840 bodies were relocated there from the Porter Burial Grounds and the Sheley Burial Grounds.

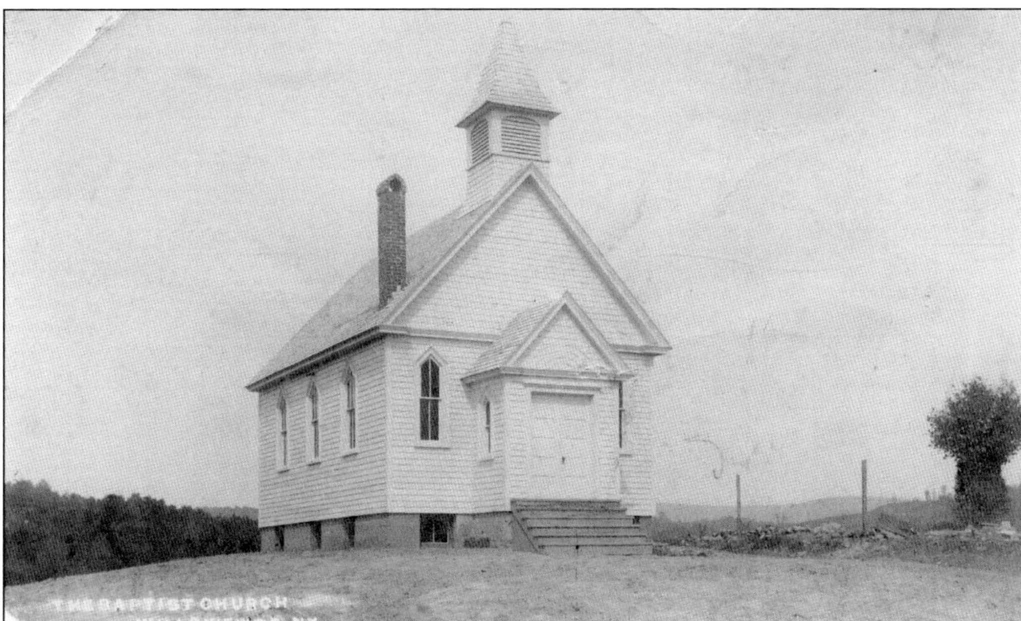

The Baptist Church of Willowemoc no longer has a congregation. However, the church remains standing to this very day, a beacon reflecting the strength of spirit of this small community that rests on the banks of the Willowemoc Creek. The legendary Indian burial ground is reported to be nearby.

SIXTY-SIXTH

ANNIVERSARY

Lows Corners Baptist Church

NOVEMBER FIRST, SECOND, THIRD, FOURTH

1935

OFFICIALLY ORGANIZED NOVEMBER 11th, 1869

REV. HENRY ALFKE, Pastor
RAYMOND GEORGE, Clerk
ABRAM LOW, Treasurer

DEACONS

BENNETT MANY, JOHN I. BROOKS, SHERMAN GOCKEL, RAYMOND GEORGE

TRUSTEES

JOHN H. BROOKS, LOWELL FURMAN, HERMAN TER BUSH

This bulletin was printed in 1935 for the 66th anniversary of the Lows Corners Baptist Church. The back page is headlined "Worthy of Note." The Baptists' missionary Malissa Aldrich went to Burma. Ministers sent out in service were Rev. Leonard Aldrich, Rev. Cyrus Aldrich, and Rev. Sidney Aldrich. Local preachers were Lyman Hornbeck and Otis Snyder. The congregation's first baptisms were Rebecca Porter and Aurilla Benson, both July 7, 1869, and Nathaniel Aldrich, September 5, 1869. A footnote tells the reader that "George Smith of Eureka is the great-grandson of Erastus Smith, in whose home, adjoining our present place of worship, the Church was organized, and Daniel Smith, the father of Erastus Smith was a Captain in the Revolutionary Army."

THE CHARTER MEMBERS

OF

THE LOWS CORNERS BAPTIST CHURCH

LODUSKA BARKLY	ERASTUS SMITH
LORILLA VAN WAGENER	AMANDA SMITH
NELSON DUNNIVAN	NATHAN SPENCER
BETSEY DUNNIVAN	PHOEBE SPENCER
ELISABETH TOWNSEND	JOHN OSTERHOUDT
CLARISSA TOWNSEND	MARIAH OSTERHOUDT
ISAAC BROOKS	SARAH OSTERHOUDT
HANNAH BROOKS	HENRY ALDRICH
JOANNA BROOKS	EMILY ALDRICH
CHARLOTTE BROOKS	ELLEN ALDRICH
MARY McCONNEL	MINERVA ALDRICH
CARMILE McCONNEL	CATHARINE FURMAN
CLARISSA McCONNEL	CLARY GRISWOLD
MARY AMELIA McCONNEL	ISAAC ALDRICH
BERNICIA McCONNEL	DELILA ALDRICH
AMY McCONNEL	PETER ALDRICH
HENRY INGRAHAM	JOHN P. ALDRICH
MANASSA INGRAHAM	AMARILLA ALDRICH
ALMEDA INGRAHAM	TRYPHENA HALL
LOUISSA INGRAHAM	ALFIETTA ALDRICH

ARIETTA ALDRICH

The three oldest members now living, JOANNA SWARTWOUT, MINERVA TER BUSH, nee ALDRICH and JOHN HENRY BROOKS.

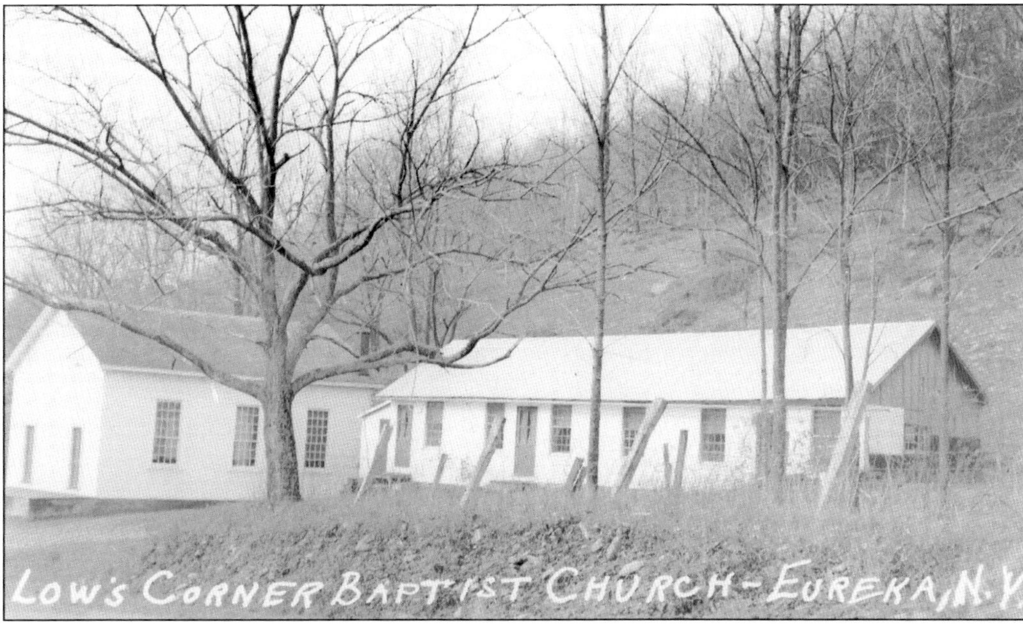

The Lows Corners Baptist Church still stands today but no longer serves a congregation. Organized in 1869, it served over 150 in its heyday. The church permanently closed several years ago when attendance dwindled to fewer than five people. The former church and its social hall are located along the road between Grahamsville and Sundown. Its mailing address was originally Eureka, but that post office closed when plans were finalized for the building of the Rondout Reservoir. (Virginia Caldwell Bishop Collection.)

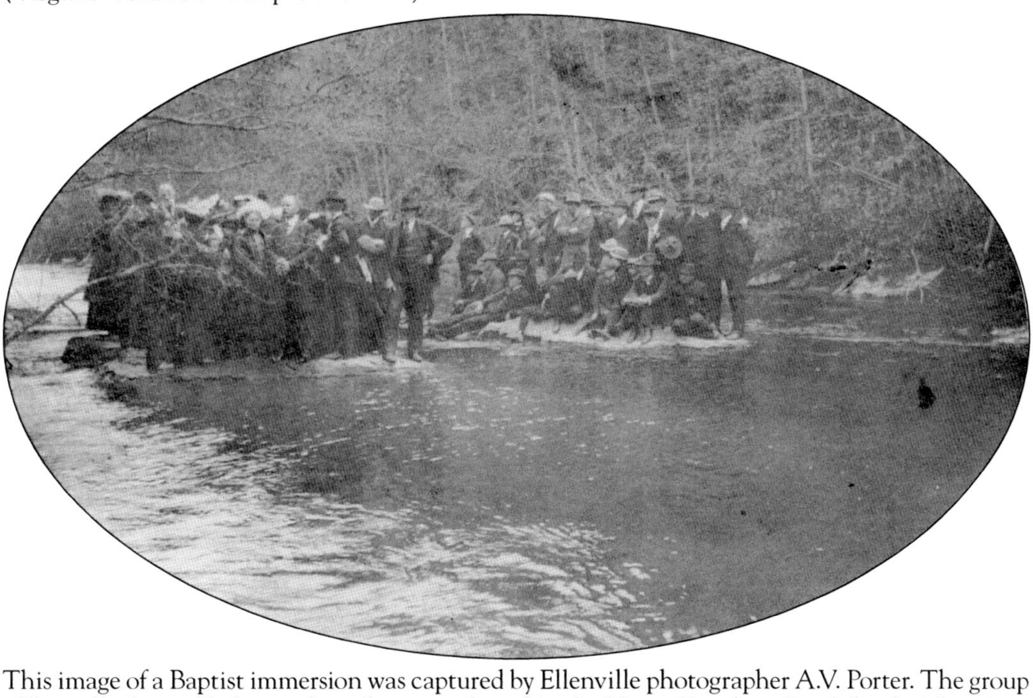

This image of a Baptist immersion was captured by Ellenville photographer A.V. Porter. The group of formally dressed ladies and gentlemen gathered in the Upper Rondout Creek for their baptism. The time period is around the early 1900s. (Virginia Caldwell Bishop Collection.)

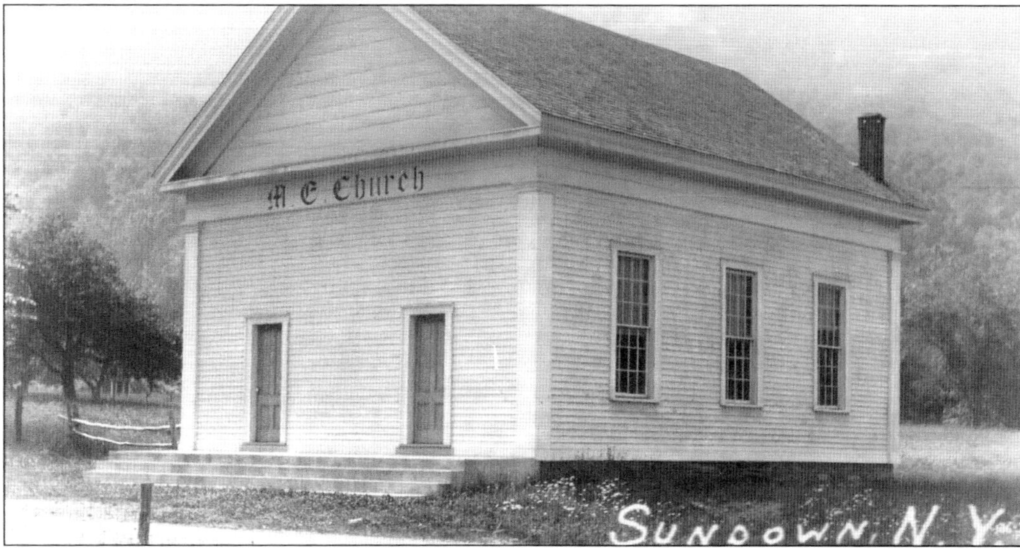

This Methodist Episcopal Church at Sundown was organized in 1856 with 33 members, according to Hamilton Child in his 1871–1872 *Gazetteer*. Longtime resident Esther George stated that the church was informally divided into two parts. No dividing line was seen, but it was very real to the church attendees. The men entered through the left door, and the women went in through the right door. It seems the Sunday meeting was held in the afternoon and attended by both Methodists and some Baptists.

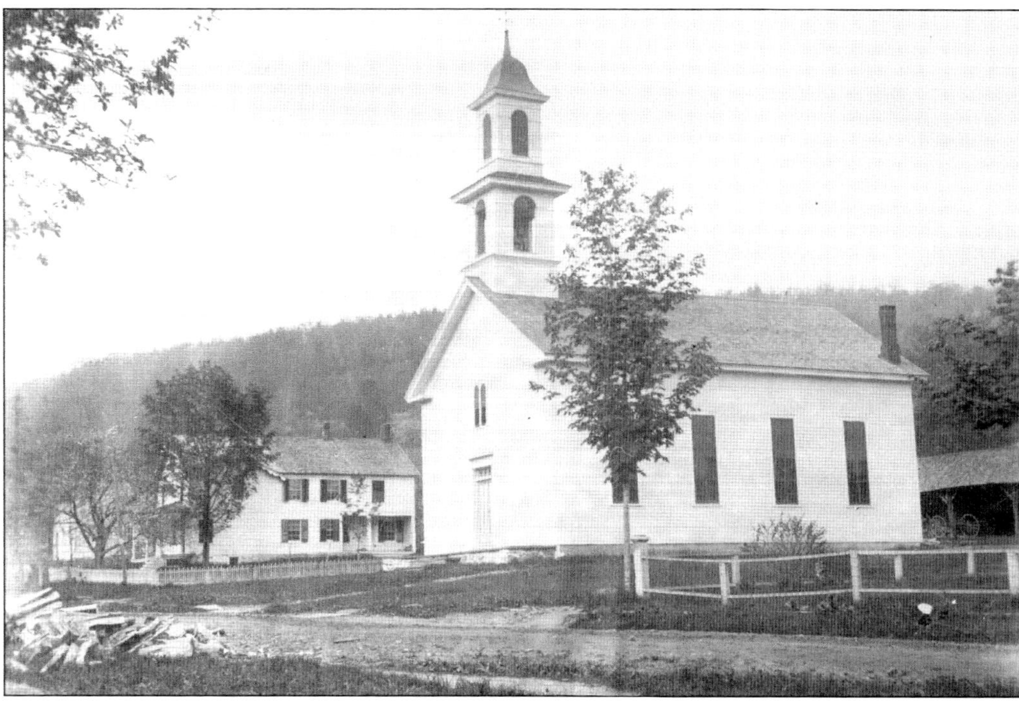

Take a close look at this vintage c. 1900 photograph of the Grahamsville Methodist Church. Behind the church, to the right, is a section of the carriage house. Across the road from the church is a pile of wood. The dirt road looks rather narrow considering that it later became New York State Route 55. A sidewalk is barely visible on the same side where the wood is piled.

Three

WATER

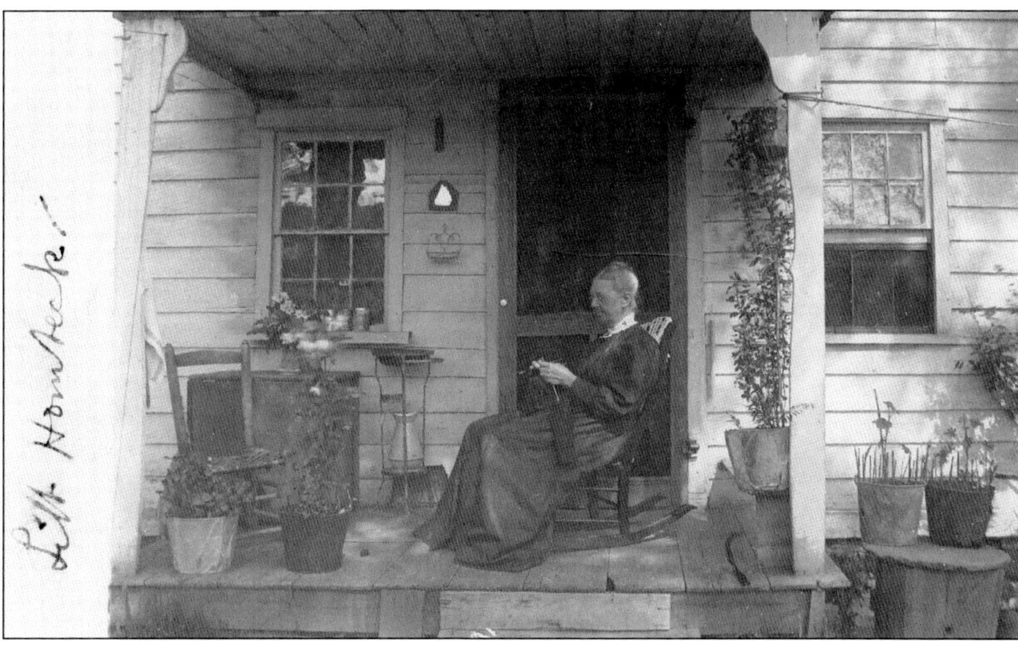

Elizabeth DuBois Hornbeck, great-grandmother of Raymond Hornbeck, rocks and knits in this photo postcard. A washbasin and ewer sit to the left of the door, ever ready for hand washing. There is a screen in the window to the right of the door, which helps keep insects out. The date of the photograph is probably around 1910. Elizabeth Hornbeck was married to Horace Hornbeck and was the mother of Chester Hornbeck. The family lived in Eureka and lost their property to New York City.

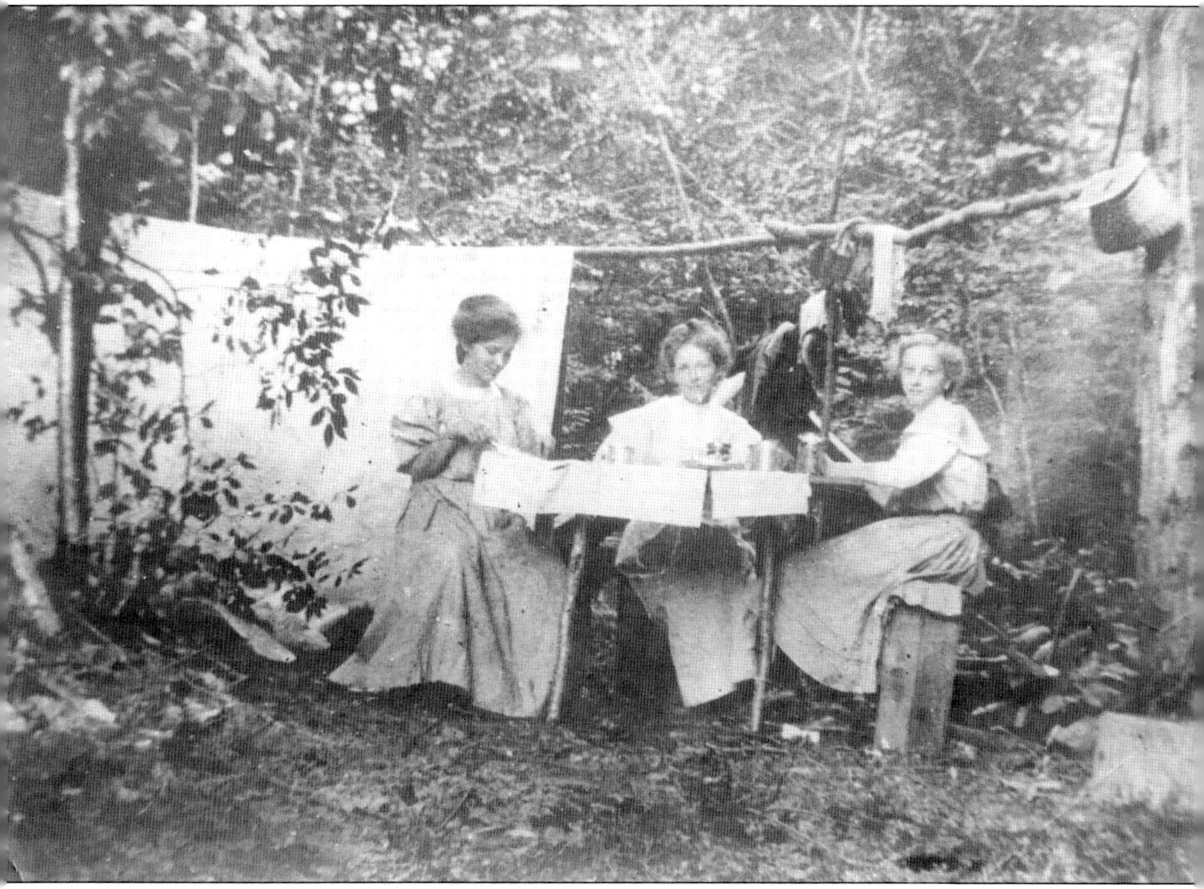

Here, sisters Nell, Eva, and Mary Smith do their camping and fishing on the Rondout. They have their campfire going, and smoke can be seen rising. They are wearing the long skirts typical of the day; the garb may have been cumbersome, but it would certainly keep the bugs away.

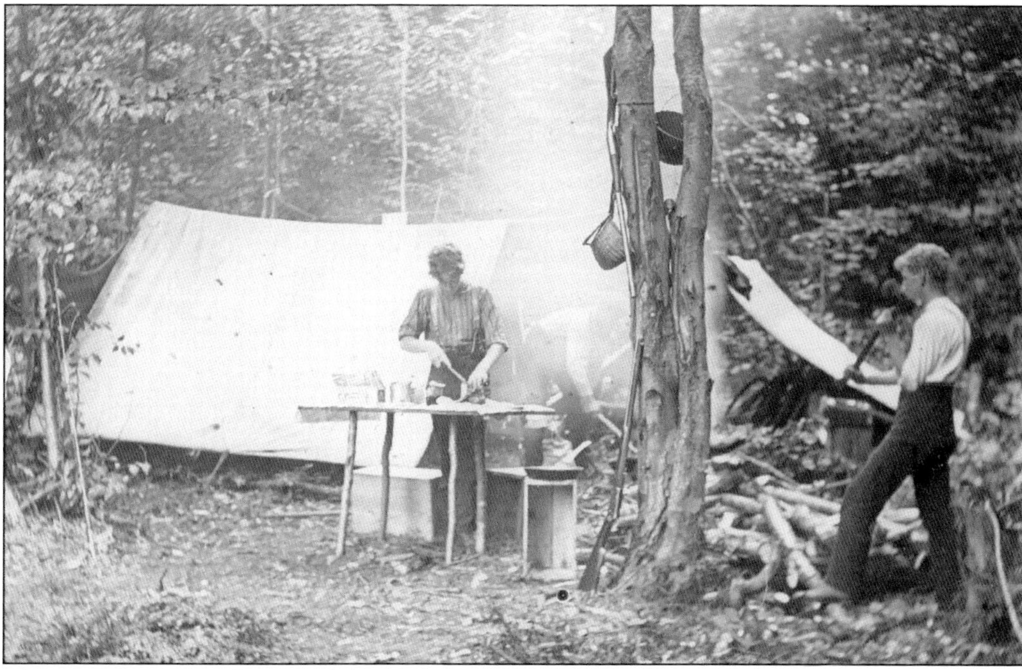

This is camping in style around the summer of 1907. An inscription on the back of the image says, "Art or George Smith on right." This image of "Camp Comfort Peekamoose," as it was called by the group camping, shows smoke rising from the campfire, a fishing creel hanging on the tree, and a rifle leaning against the tree trunk. This area is now part of the Sundown Wild Forest in the Catskill Forest Preserve. Campers, hunters, and hikers still enjoy the outdoors here.

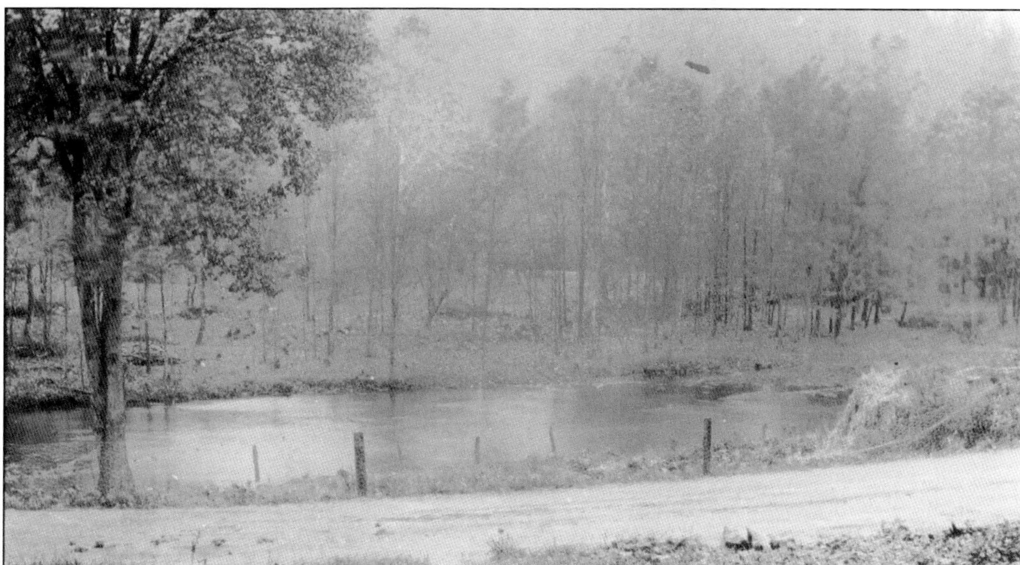

This view shows East Mountain in the background. The Upper Rondout Creek runs peacefully by with no sign of the disruption sometimes caused by a flooding stream. A penciled note on the back says "Kodak 1A, 10 seconds, Rainy Day." The shot was taken from the Andrew George home. Today, Andrew George's great-grandson Scott Grey has his house in almost the same location as Andrew George did in those days.

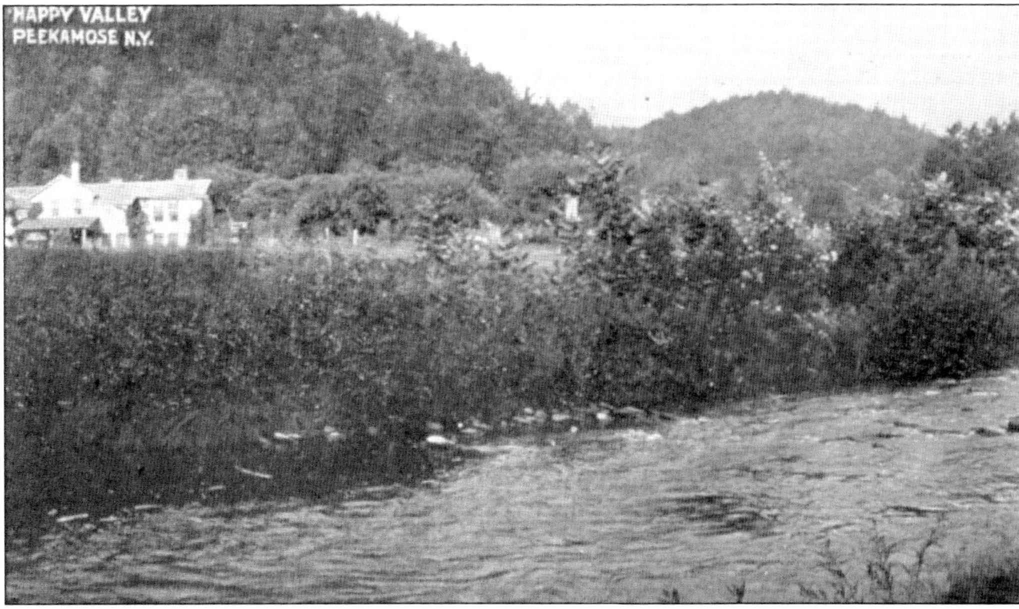

The Peekamoose Valley was often photographed. It was sometimes dubbed "Happy Valley" by those who did not have to eke out a living there. This photograph dates to sometime in the early 1900s. It may have been taken by Julian Dimock, who spent many hours in the area and often photographed it.

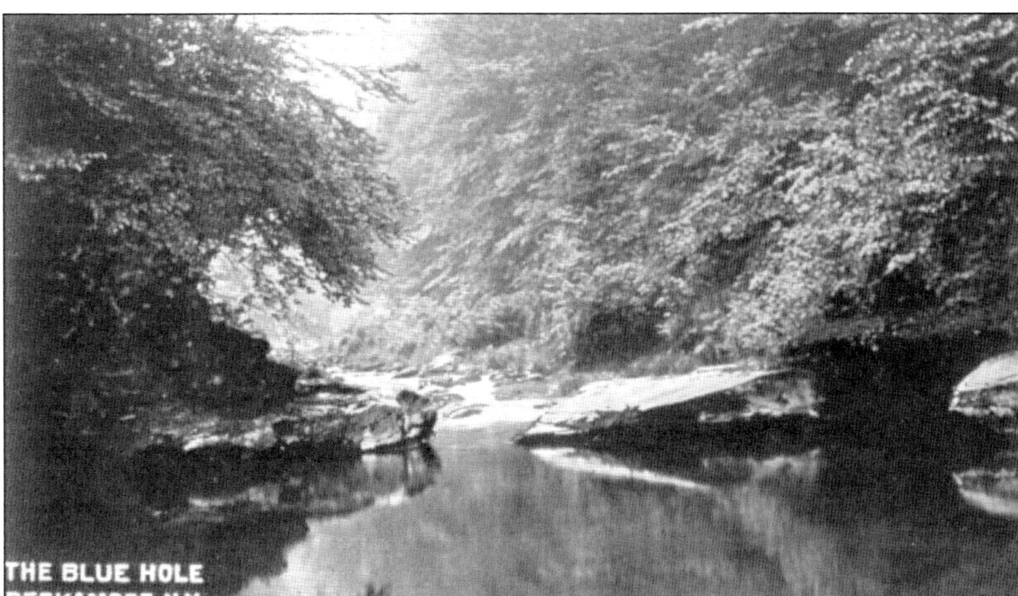

Blue Hole in Peekamoose was named one of America's Best Swimming Holes by *Travel & Leisure* in 2010. The story is that it was called "Blue Hole" because the water was so cold that the swimmer's skin turned blue.

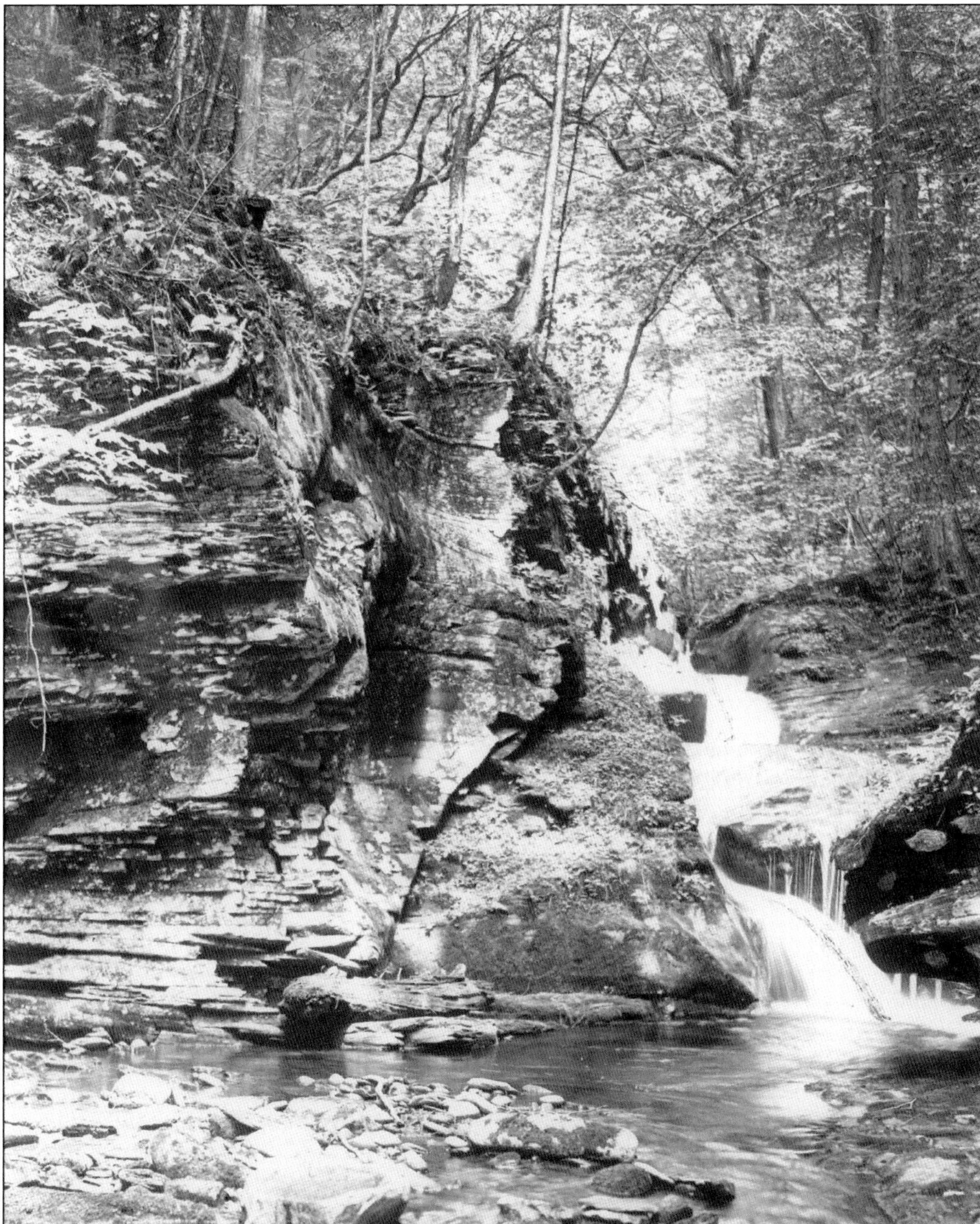

The Sawkill Falls was a very scenic falls that was often photographed and used on postcards. Water from the falls fed into the Upper Rondout Creek. Now, any water from the falls and the stream it is located on feeds into the Rondout Reservoir near where the community of Lackawack was located.

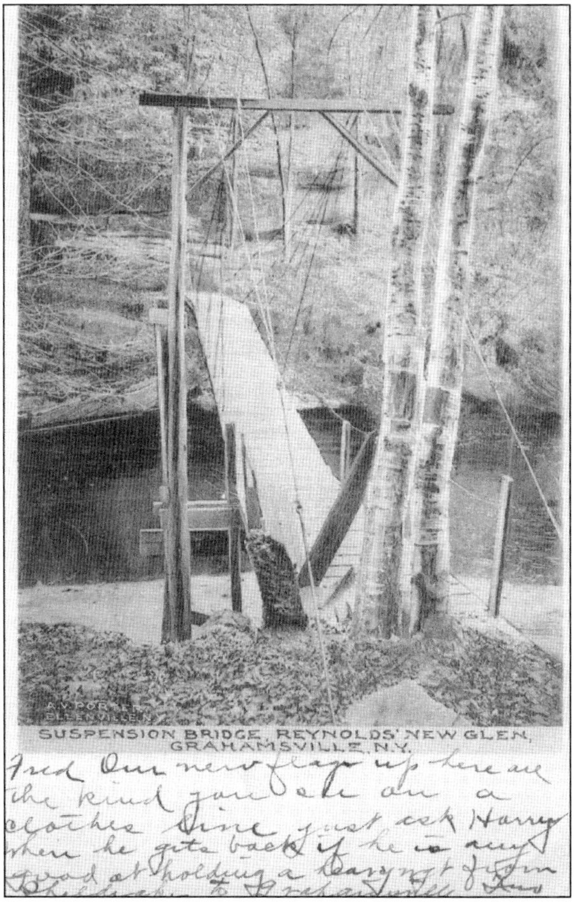

Postmarked Grahamsville, 1906, this is a detailed look at the suspension bridge at "Reynolds' New Glen." Photographer A.V. Porter snapped this shot.

Reynold's Glen is the site of this suspension bridge crossing the Chestnut Creek. This valley was once called the Chestnut Valley because there was a huge stand of chestnut trees. Older homes dating back to 1906, the year this photograph was taken, may have a chestnut floor or perhaps a piece of furniture made from local chestnut.

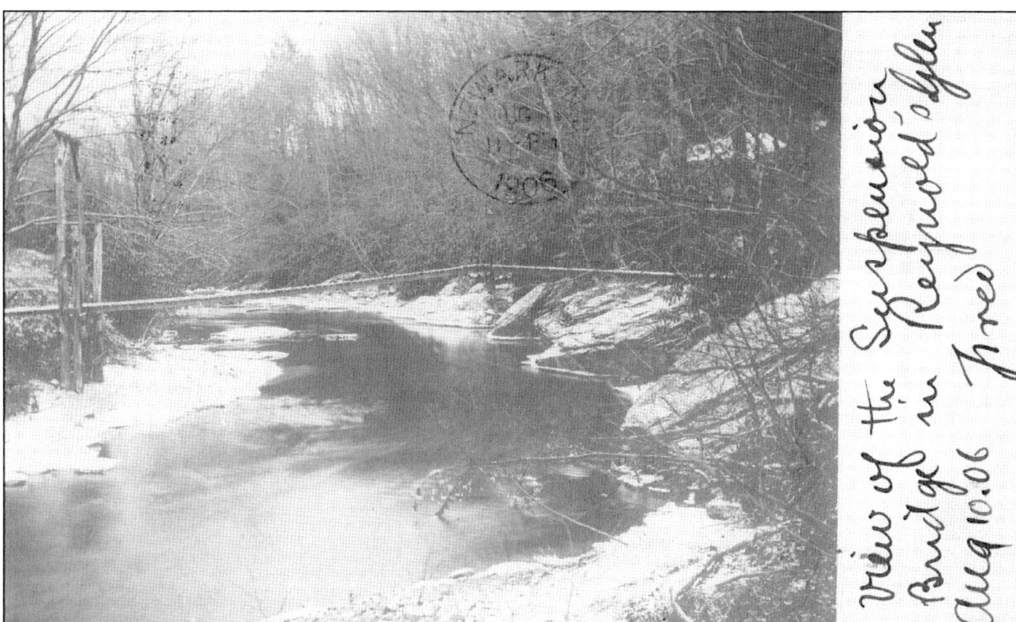

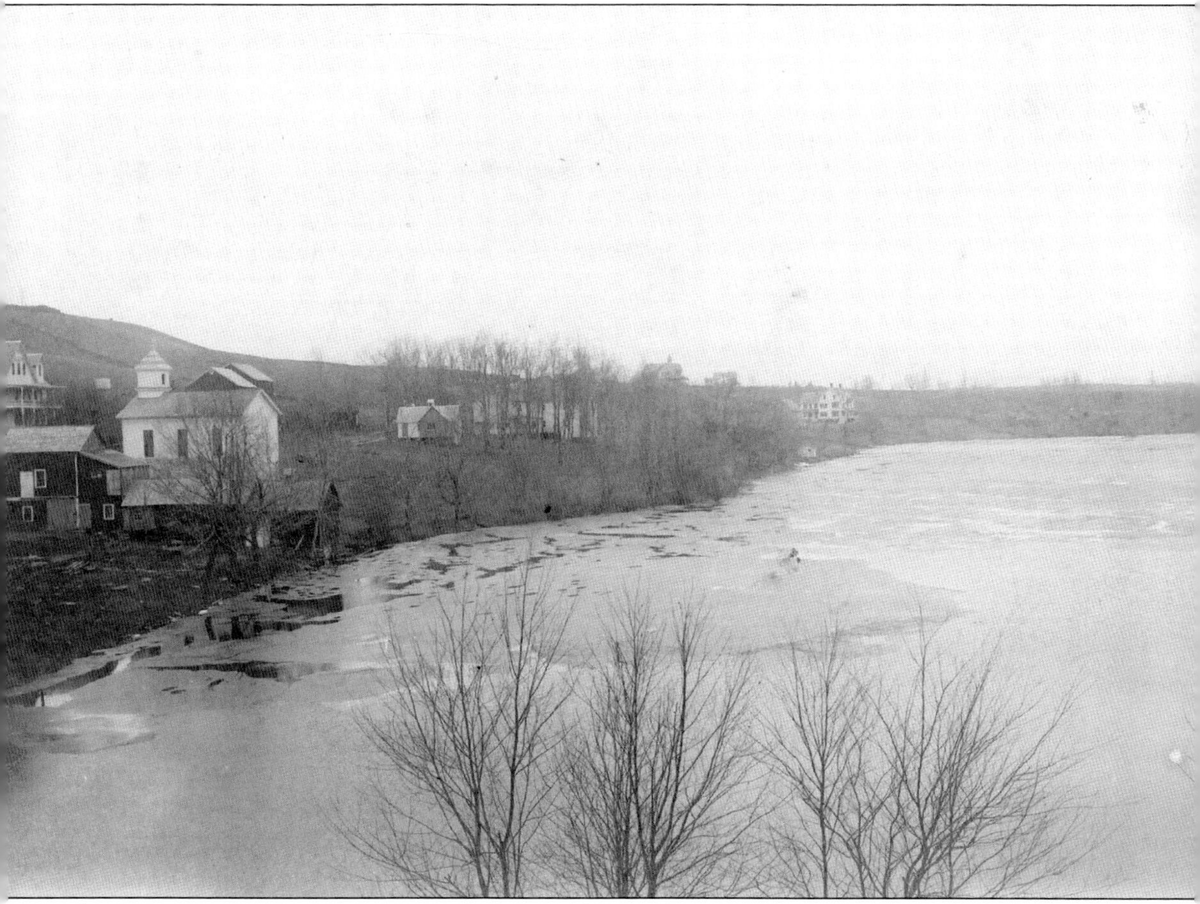

This is a portion of the Rondout Creek that was lost to the reservoir that helps supply New York City with water. Eureka, Montela, and Lackawack were all located along its banks before they were taken for the building of the Rondout Reservoir.

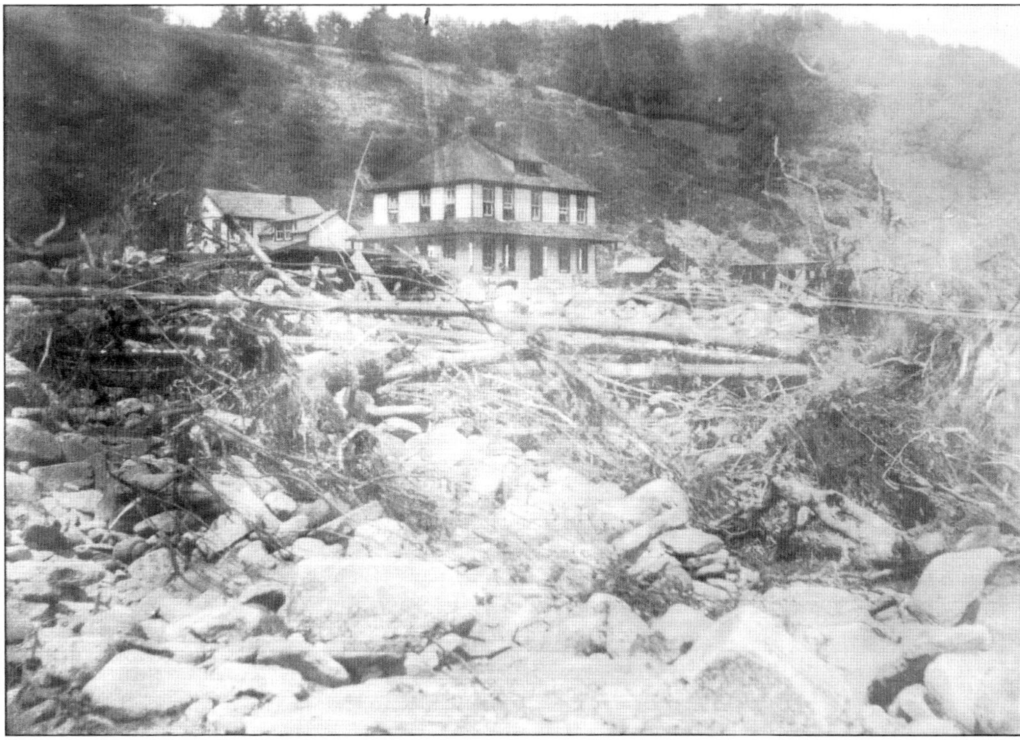

This photograph of Burl Burch's home, taken by George B. Reynolds, looks up Sugar Loaf Creek. A note on back says, "Caused by Little Rock Brook and Sugar Loaf Brook. All roads demolished with trees torn out by their roots and piled in every direction." The 1928 flood was not the first time floodwaters had raced down the Sugar Loaf. In 1878, the Methodist church came tumbling down during a bad flood. It was Burl Burch's mother who reported seeing it go downstream.

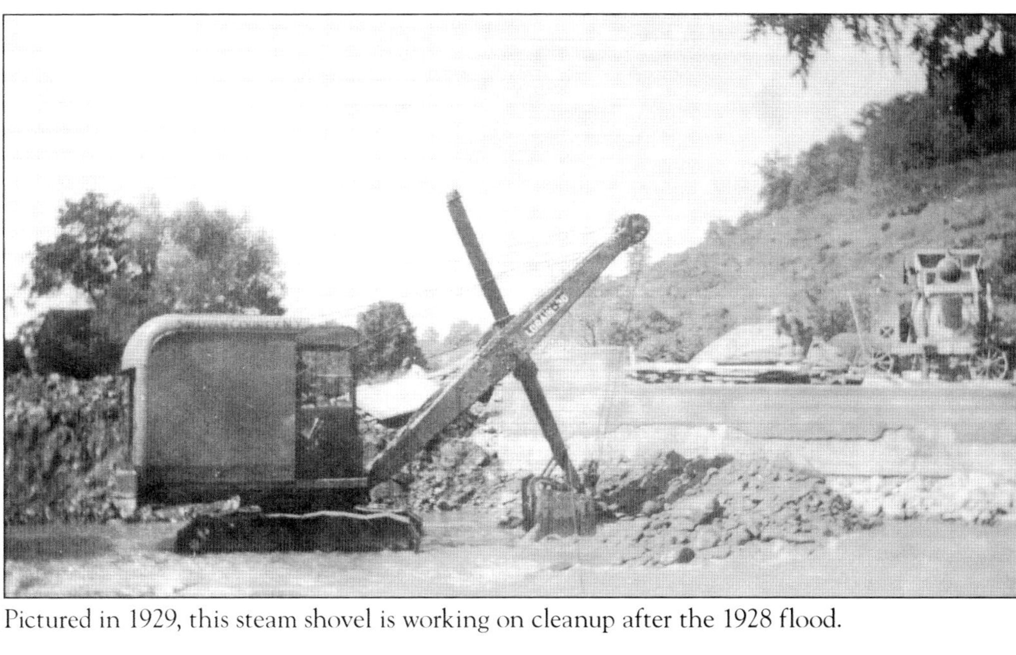

Pictured in 1929, this steam shovel is working on cleanup after the 1928 flood.

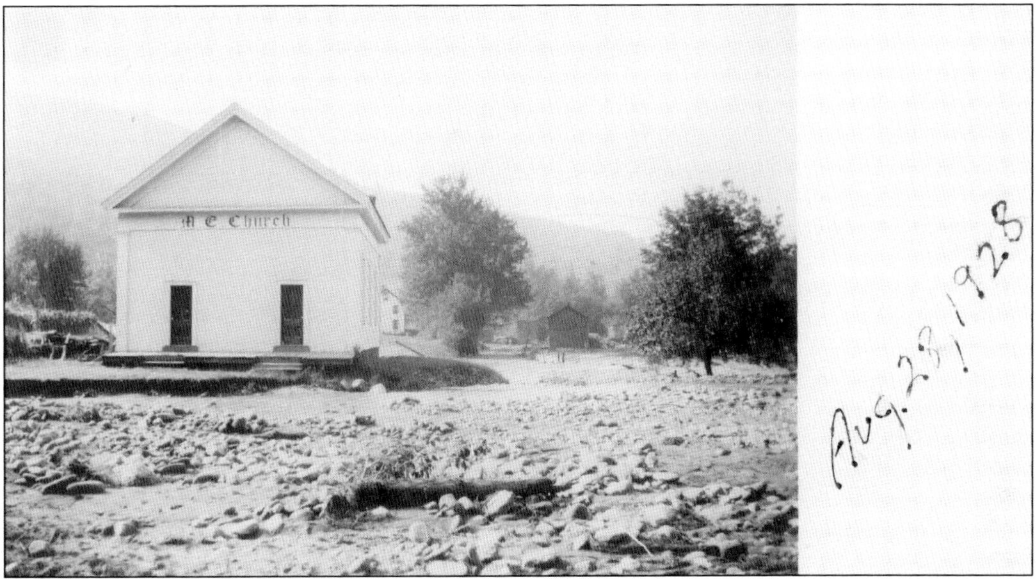

The Rondout Stream floodwaters left this Methodist Episcopal Church standing in the 1928 flood. (DuBois Collection)

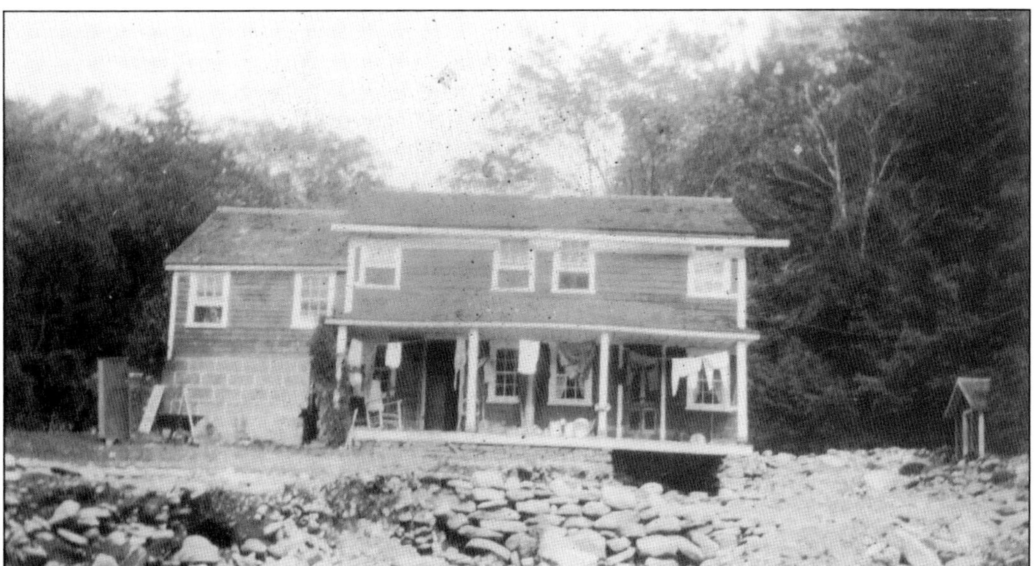

The back of this postcard reads, "A neighbor's house which suffered. Norman DuBois house after flood." The word "suffered" says it all.

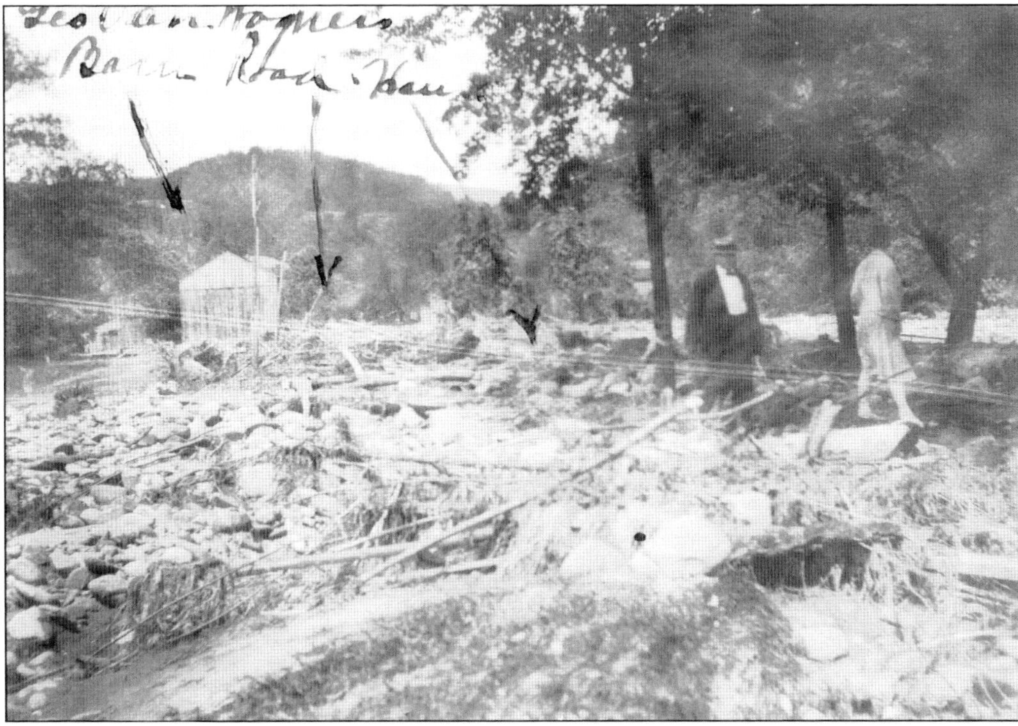

The caption reads, "Looking up Sugar Loaf Road from Abram Lows." The photograph shows a man and woman surveying the damage and dressed as though they had been to church. George Van Wagner's barn, road, and house are seen in the background. George B Reynolds, who took the photograph, wrote elsewhere about the flood, "Six bridges gone from the foot of the Red Hill road to Abram Low's and the road and stream almost beyond recognition."

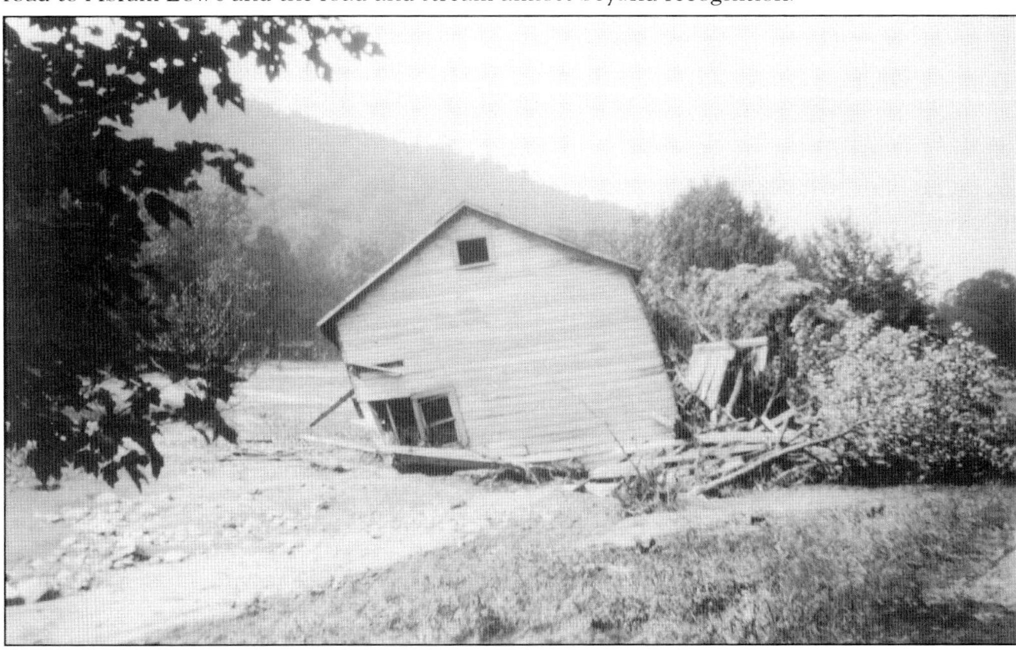

This image is labeled simply "1928 flood Loron Dean's Barn." (DuBois Collection.)

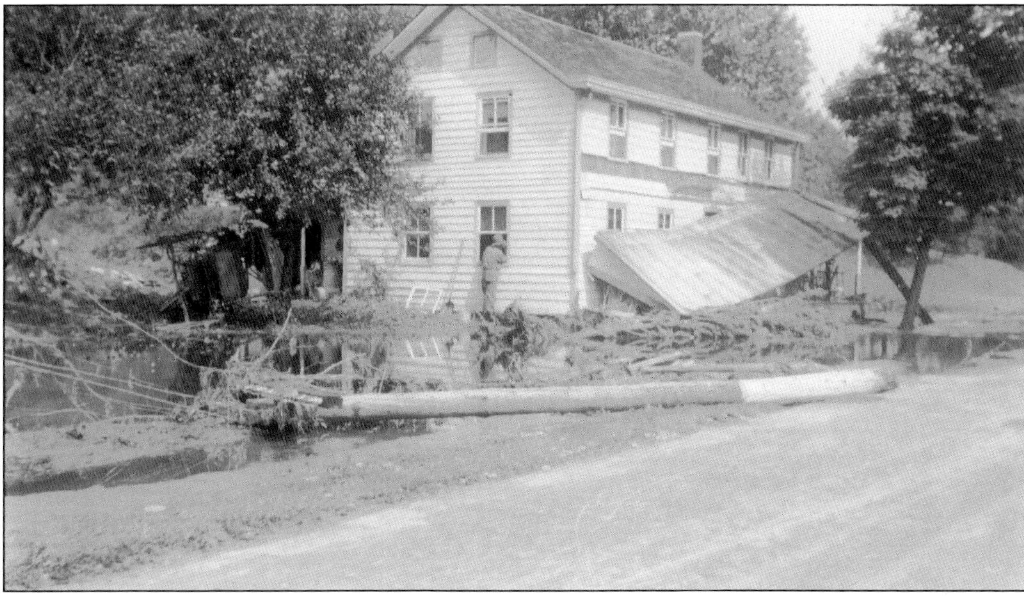

This picture of Melvin DuBois's house in Eureka was taken after the flood of 1928. Family snapshots like this were plentiful. The notes on the back of this George Reynolds photograph told of Leland Dayton's new five-passenger Studebaker sedan floating around until it struck this house and tore the porch off. Stories from that time told of the DuBois garage floating away and water rising nearly five feet over the first floor. It was also reported that DuBois took out seven one-horse wagon loads of dirt as he tried to restore his home. (TN.)

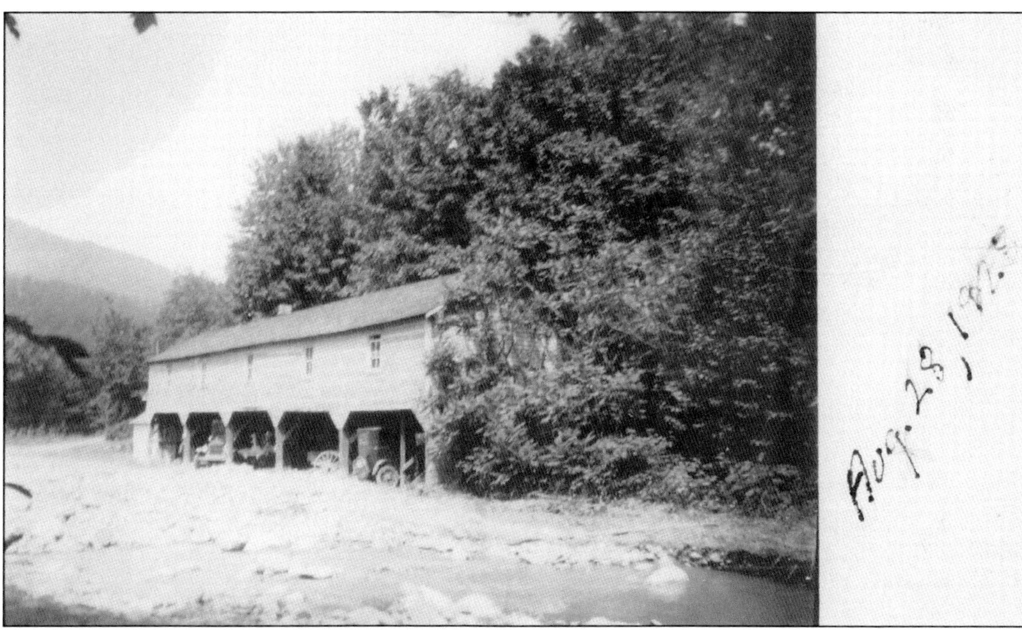

This photograph of the flood of 1928 shows a carriage house in transition, with both a horse-drawn carriage and an early automobile sharing quarters. It is dated August 28, 1928. (DuBois Collection.)

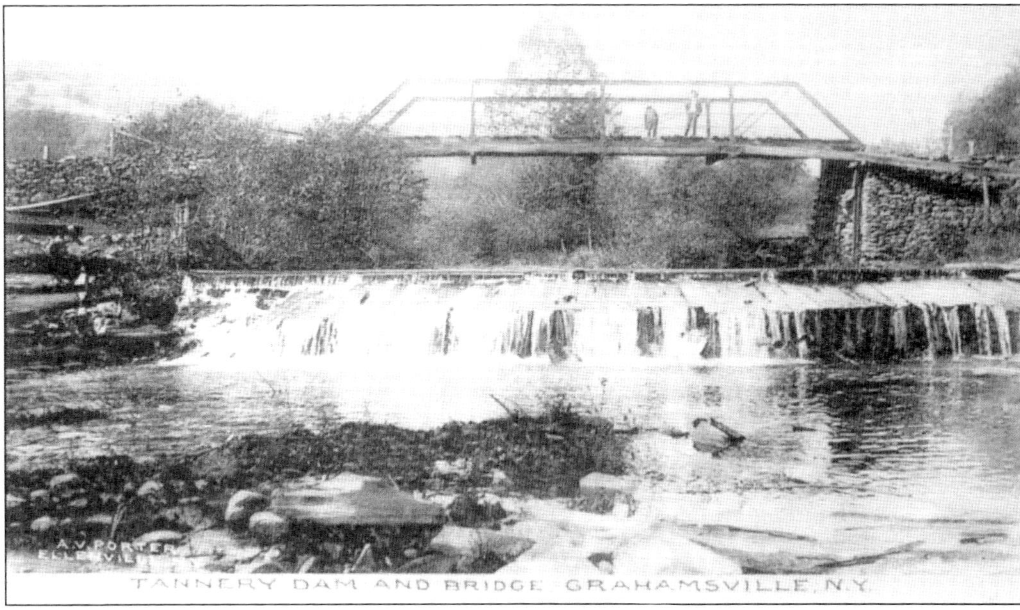

This scene shows an early iron bridge crossing the Chestnut Creek at Grahamsville. The Chestnut Creek feeds into the Rondout Reservoir. The c. 1905 photograph was taken by A.V. Porter of nearby Ellenville.

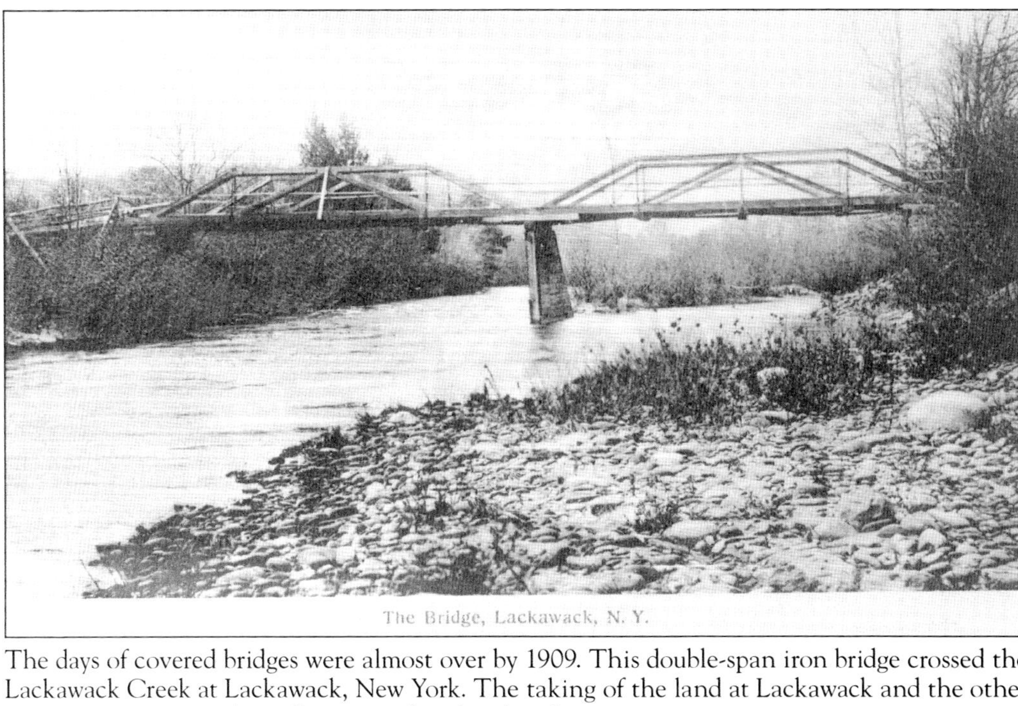

The days of covered bridges were almost over by 1909. This double-span iron bridge crossed the Lackawack Creek at Lackawack, New York. The taking of the land at Lackawack and the other two communities in the valley was only a few decades away.

Buttermilk Falls is another scenic spot in Peekamoose. This c. 1910 real-photo postcard shows the scenic falls. Photographers today still consider it an extraordinary spot. The Sundown Wild Forest covers approximately 30,000 acres; some of this is in Neversink, Sullivan County, and the rest is in Denning and other townships in Ulster County.

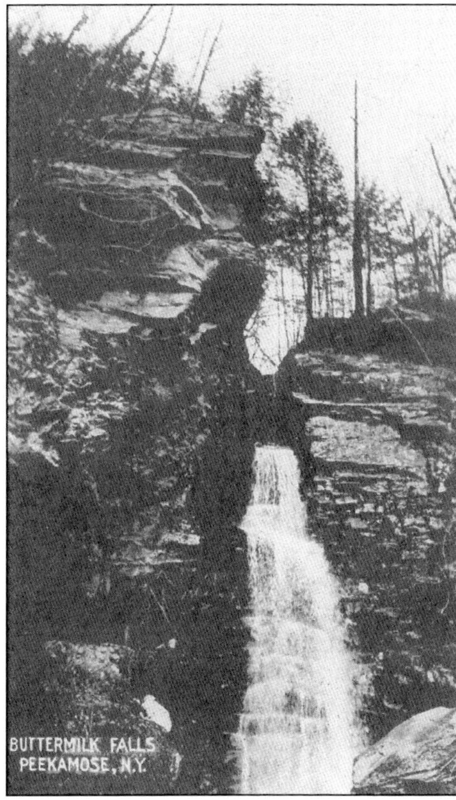

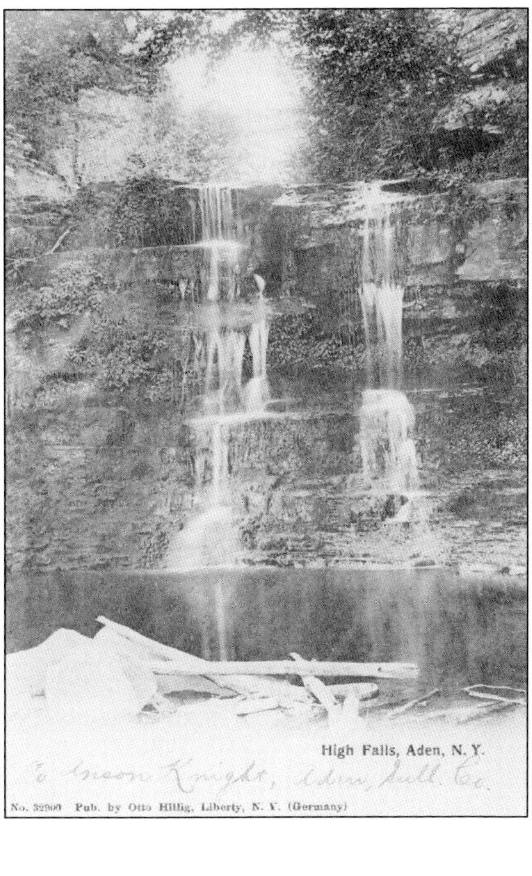

Otto Hillig snapped this photograph of the High Falls at Aden, New York. The year was 1908, and a summer guest from Brooklyn was staying with the Anson Knights in Aden.

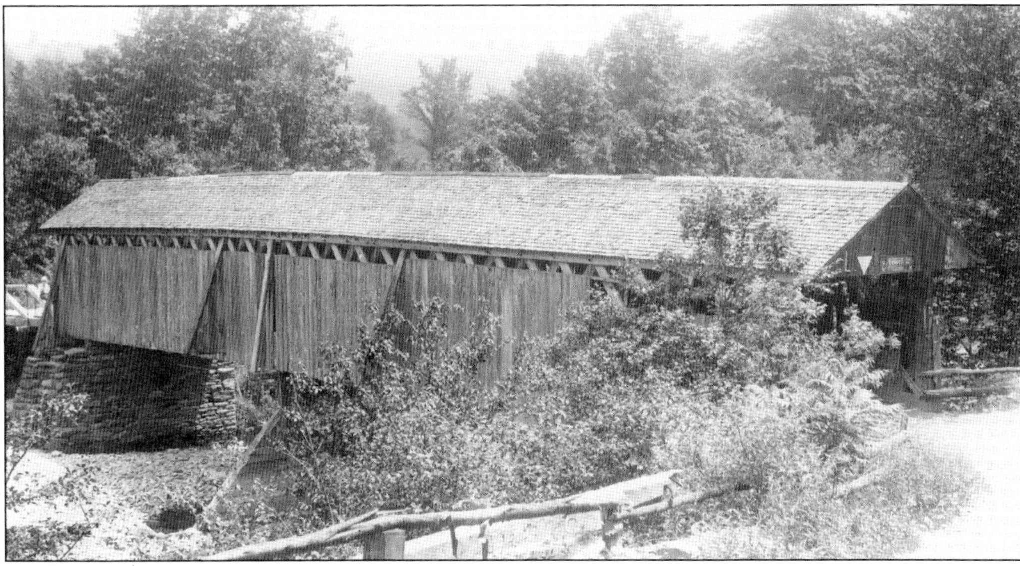

This covered bridge saw a lot of traffic in its day. Covered bridges in New York State are few and far between, and Neversink is fortunate to have two. The covered bridge at Halls Mills has been battered by storm and the turbulence of the Neversink River. It is still standing today; its stone piers are being replaced by concrete, but the structure itself remains intact. The Chestnut Creek Covered Bridge is a short-span covered bridge built to celebrate the bicentennial of the town of Neversink in 1978. Built to last by volunteers, it sees a lot of traffic each year thanks to events such as the beloved "Little World's Fair."

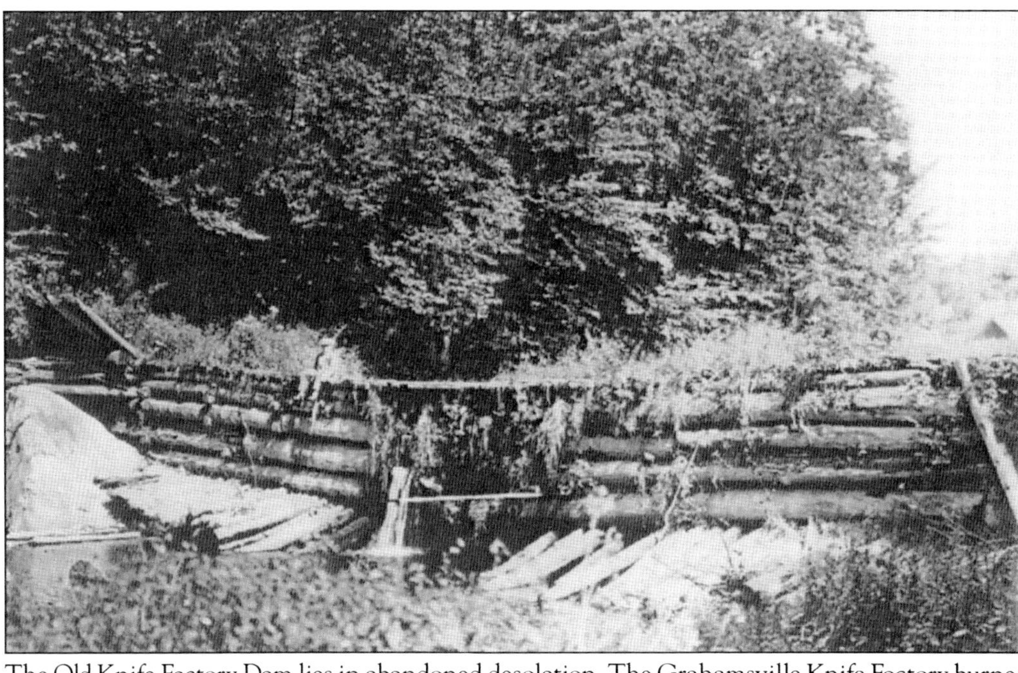

The Old Knife Factory Dam lies in abandoned desolation. The Grahamsville Knife Factory burned in 1907. The wheel that gave the knife factory waterpower used the Chestnut Creek for water. Prior to the knife factory, a gristmill had ground grain for local farmers in the same building. (Don Erath Collection.)

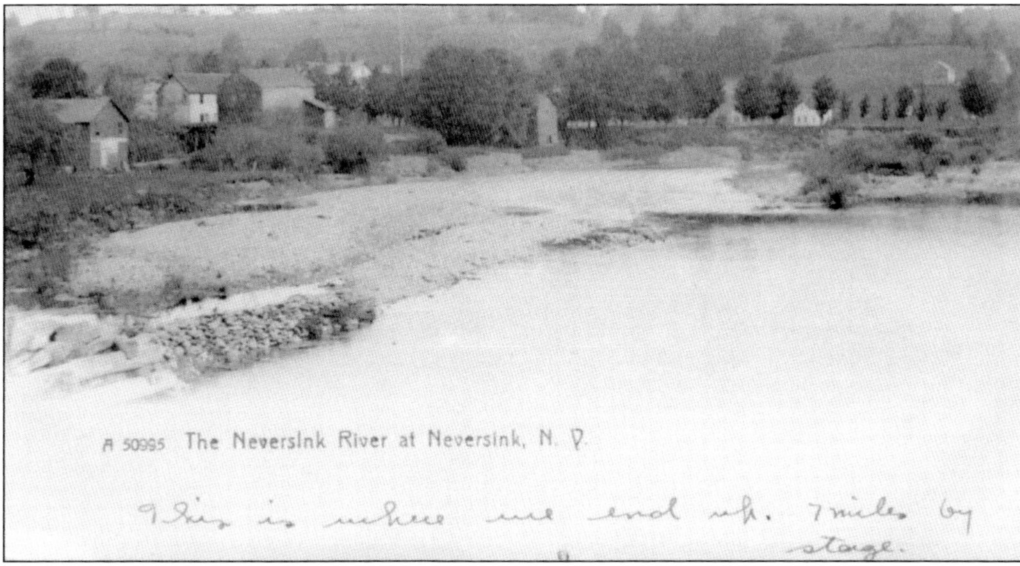

It is the year 1907, and this charming village was clustered on the Neversink River where the reservoir of the same name now rests. Recreational fishing and some boating are now allowed but no swimming. In 1907, summer visitors came up from the city on the train and then drove seven miles by stage or wagon to reach their destination. The locals always talked about the great swimming holes. A stripped-down version of Neversink was relocated on New York State Route 55, the highway between Grahamsville and Liberty. The location along a highway is simply not the same as being on the banks of the Neversink River. (Kurt Knuth Collection.)

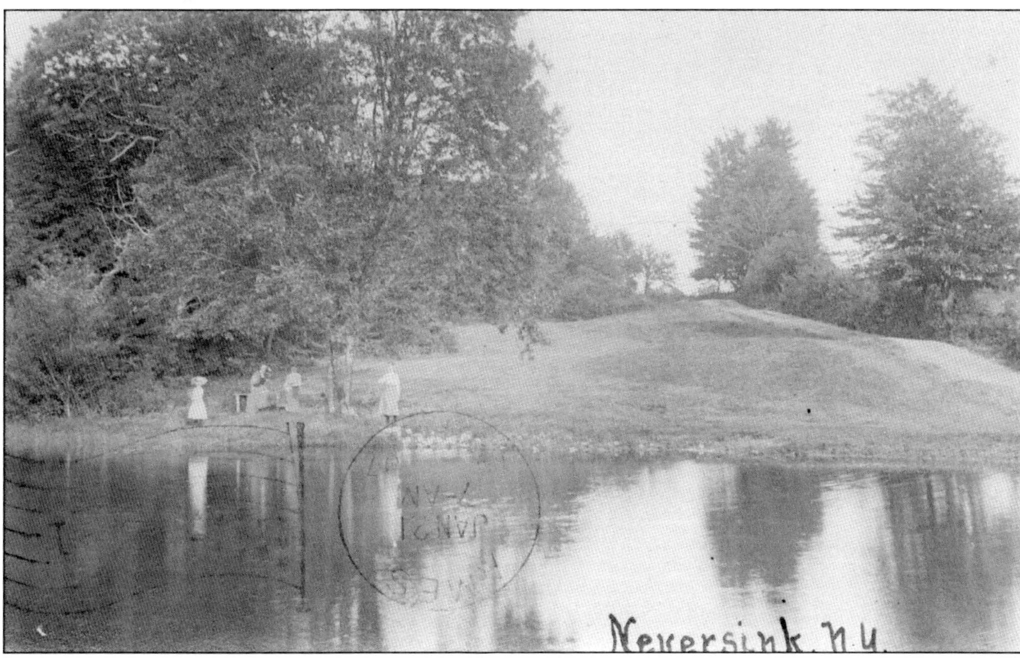

The serene group photographed on the far shore of the Neversink River helps lend understanding to why people traveled from Coney Island among other places to spend a few weeks or the entire summer in the Neversink area. This real-photo postcard was created and mailed between 1901 and 1907. (Donna Brooks Collection.)

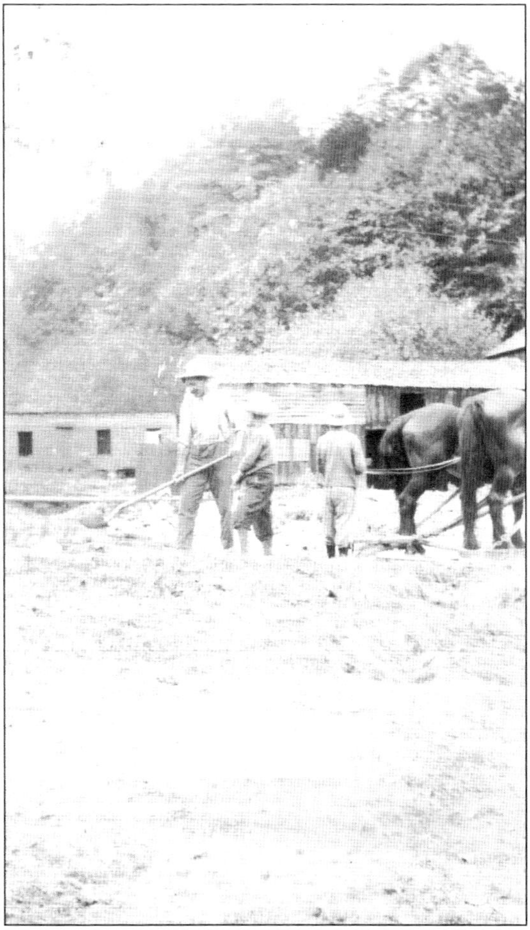

Here, flood cleanup is being done with a team of horses. Floods still occur in this section of the Rondout, and it still takes a long time for an area to recover from a flood.

These road workers are trying to mitigate the damage from the 1928 flood that devastated the Upper Rondout Valley. They have removed their hats so the person taking the snapshot can get a clear view of their faces. Documented floods here are part of the area's history and continue to this very day.

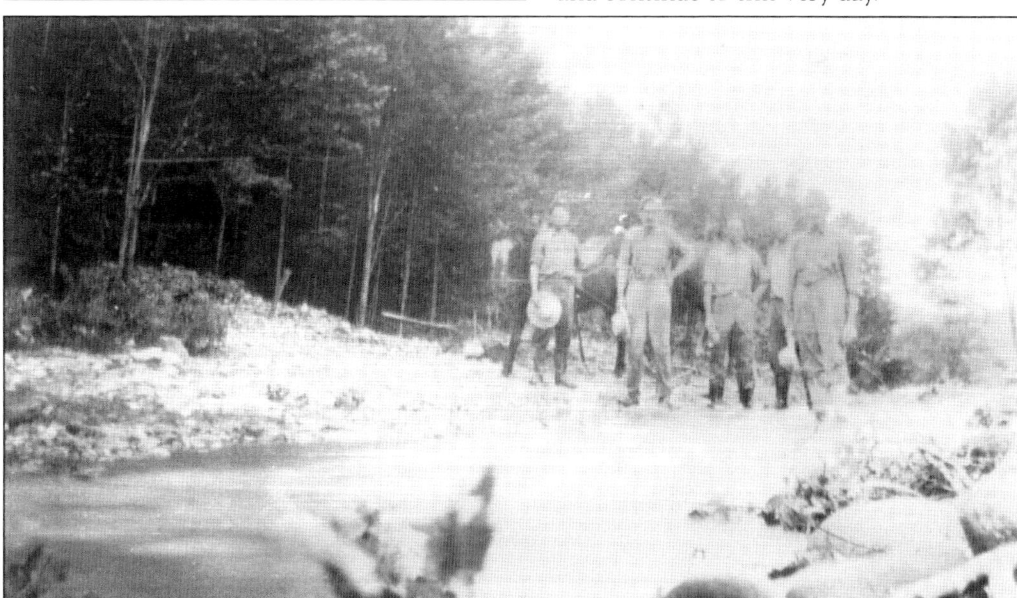

Four

HAMLETS, HOUSES, AND STORES

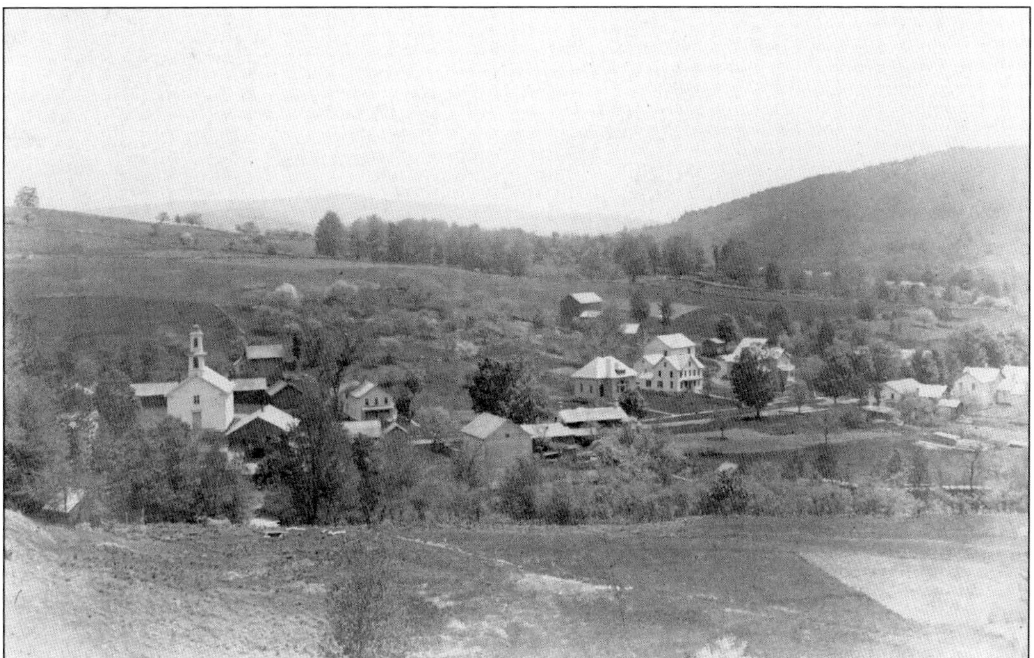

This is a view of the upper part of Grahamsville, or Chestnut Valley, as it was sometimes known. The carriage house extending on either side of the Methodist church (at left) is there to house carriages of those who were worshipping or attending other church events. The Daniel Pierce Library (boxy, one-story building) shows up clearly just a ways down from the church. The original library building was erected in 1902, and the photograph appears to have been taken shortly after that. The photographer waited for a clear day to get this shot.

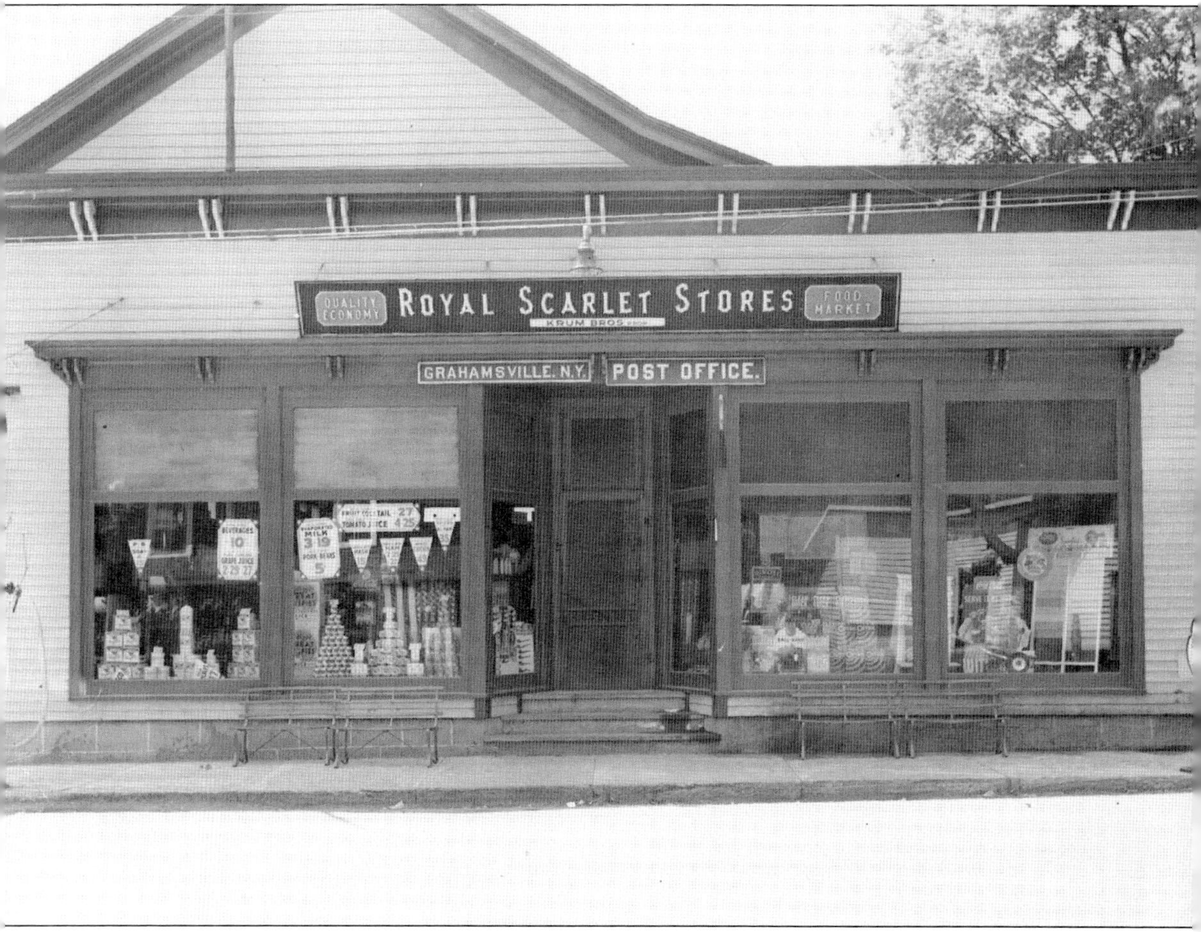

It is hard to believe that, in 1905, the little community of Grahamsville had four stores where food, clothing, and an array of items were sold. Brothers Clarence and Sumner Krum left their imprint on the area with their store. This photograph shows the Krum Bros. business when it was designated a Royal Scarlet Store. They had the post office and a gas pump and also sold paint and generally provided a whole range of products for their customers. (Scott and Robin Mahnken collection.)

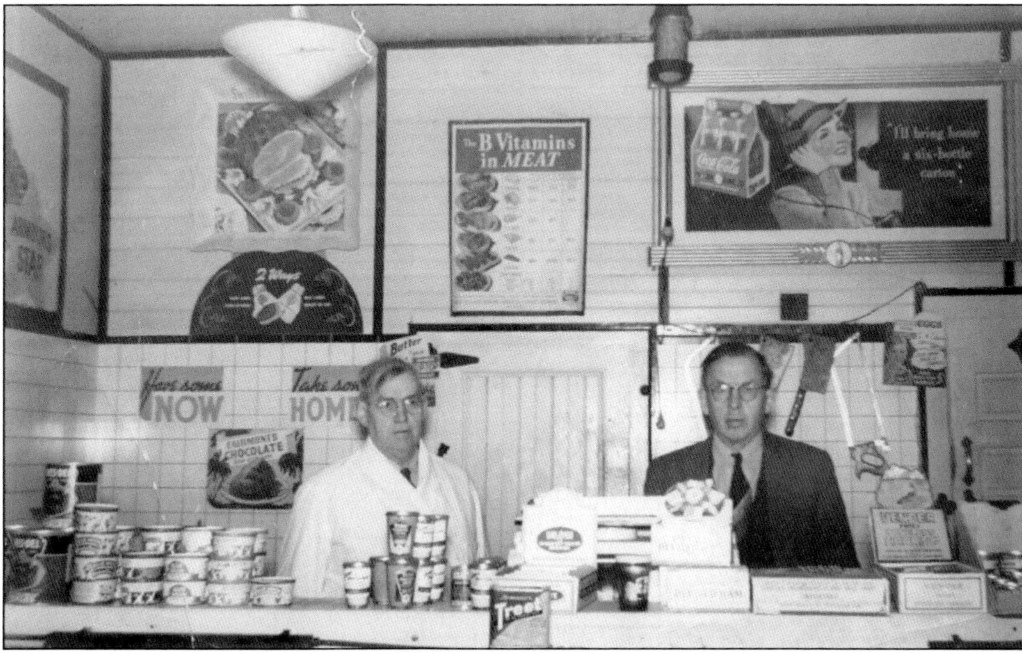

Here are Clarence and Sumner Krum standing behind the meat counter. This photograph was taken by the Forst Packing Company, Inc., and depicts some of the flavor of yesterday's country store. Note the poster reading "The B Vitamins in MEAT" and the wonderful Coca-Cola advertisement, "I'll bring home a six-bottle carton." (Scott and Robin Mahnken collection.)

Grahamsville Meat Market

Grahamsville, New York

We are carrying a full line of Choice Meats and Sea Food as follows.

Beef			Pork			Smoked Meat
Round Steak	lb.	$ .25	Pork Chops	lb.	$ .26	Bolognas
Sirloin		.28	Fresh Ham		.28	Frankfurters
Porterhouse		.28	Fresh Bacon		.15	Liverwurst
Chuch		.15	Side Pork		.25	Hams
Brisket		.12	Shoulders		.20	Bacon
Rib Roast		.15	Pork Sausage		.25	Veal Loaf
Rolled Roast		.16	Loin Chops		.28	Shoulders
Hamburger		.15	Liver		.16	Oysters
Beef Liver		.15				Etc.

Call and see us, we will give you our best attention.

The Grahamsville Meat Market's list of prices reflects an earlier time when food costs were much, much lower. In 1905, E. Carney described the local meat market in rhyme, saying, "And up in town a market neat, / Where G. Hornbeck supplies the meat / To feed the city folks who come / To make with us their summer home. / In summer when the weather's hot / Or if it's cool it matters not, / You'll see a load of meat so nice and fresh and sweet, / 'Tis fit for anyone to eat."

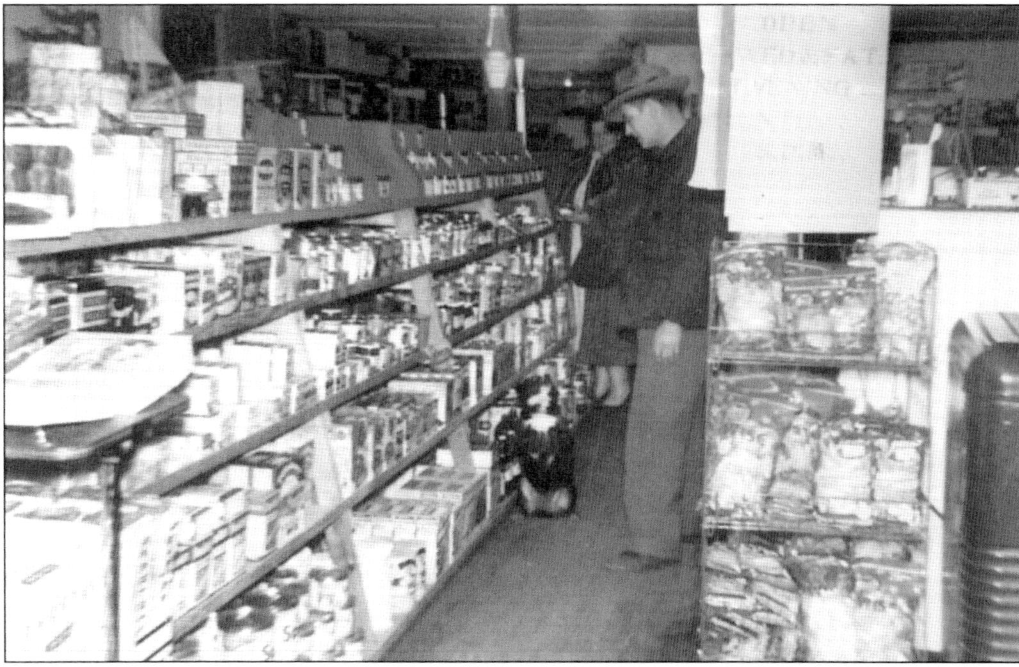

The Old Porter Store in Grahamsville became the DuBois Store in the early 1950s. Pictured here are a Mr. Caldwell, Lassie (the dog), and Marie Mickelson. A posted sign tells customers that the store is "open Wed. and Sat. evenings until 8." (Virginia Caldwell Bishop Collection.)

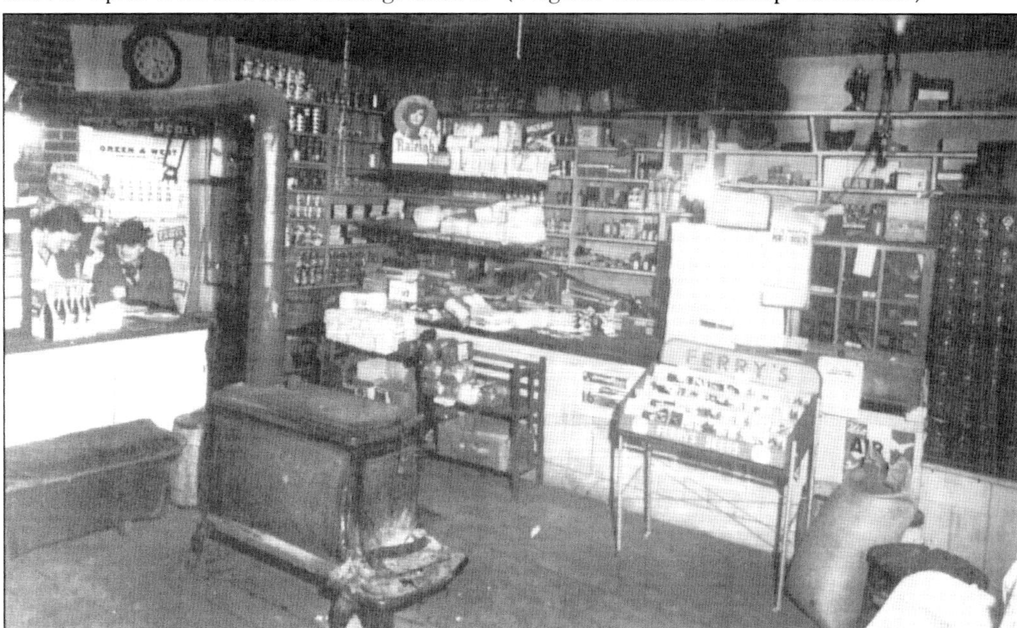

This photograph shows the interior of the Richard Store at the time the business was closed to make way for the Rondout Reservoir. The wood-burning stove took center stage in the store. A visitor would have been able to get their mail, choose Ferry Seeds for a garden, and buy buckwheat flour, bread, a kerosene lamp, Camel cigarettes, and much, much more. The *Kingston Daily Freeman* reports that buckwheat flour sold for $4 per 100 pounds in 1922. (Karl Richard collection.)

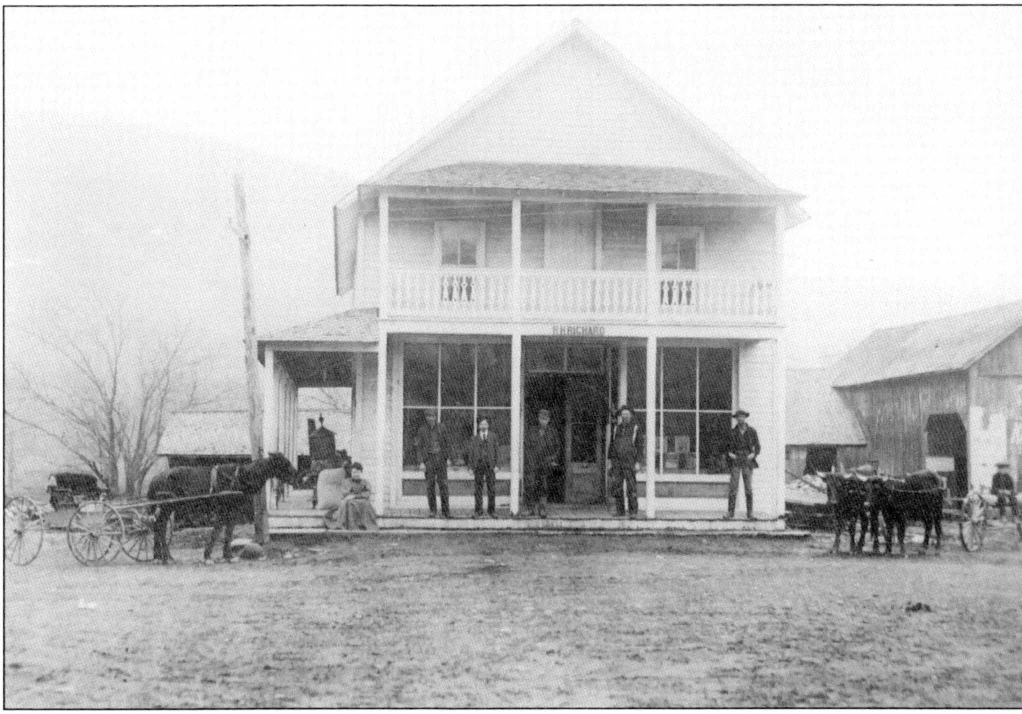

The Montela Post Office was located on the corner of South Hill Road as it met the Rondout Valley road. Though it was once known as the Frank Dixon Store, the store sign said "H.H. Richard" when this photograph was taken around 1905. The photograph's notation labels Byron Sheeley's horse on the left and Charlie Smith's oxen on the right. Montela had its first post office approved in 1886, and Frank Dixon was the first postmaster. The post office closed in 1943 because the Rondout Reservoir was being built. (Cynthia Moshier Wagner Collection.)

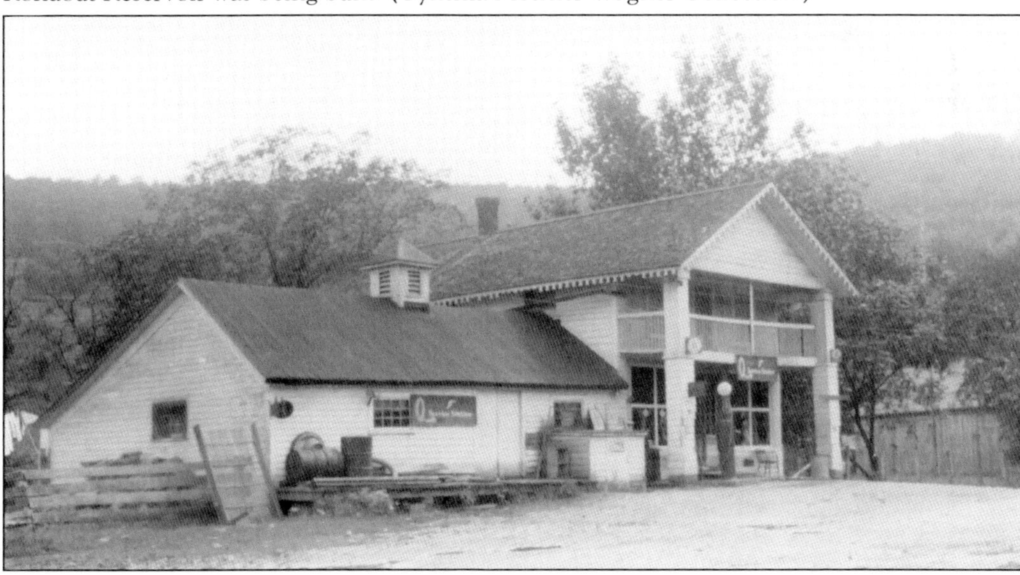

Pictured here is the Claryville Store before it expanded. One gas pump and a sign denoting a telephone mark a new era, but the captain's chair evokes a memory of days past. (Helen Erts DuBois Collection.)

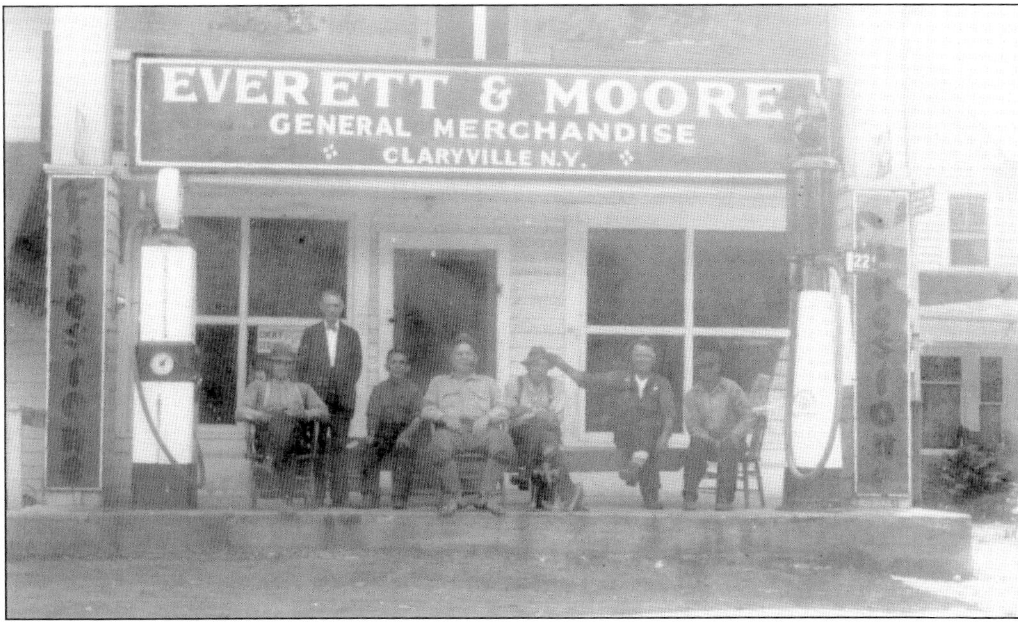

Here called Everett & Moore General Merchandise, this is the same Claryville store under different ownership. Firestone signs and two pumps frame the front of the store as seven old-timers gather to talk and get their pictures taken.

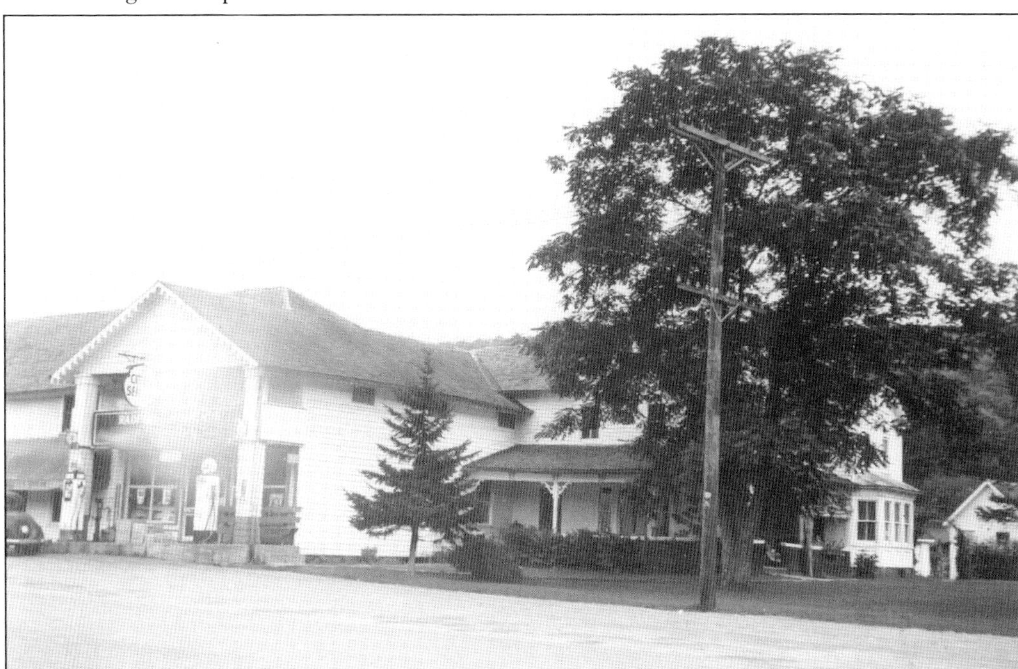

The Claryville Store grew bigger. Known as the Rad Moore store for many years, in this photograph it still has two gas pumps. Helen Erts DuBois described it as a "store with addition of 2nd story to storage area and addition of home attached. 2nd story was bedrooms for my aunt's boarding house. I worked there summers from about age of 10 for $1 a day. Hours 7 am to 6 pm, longer if necessary." (Helen Erts DuBois Collection.)

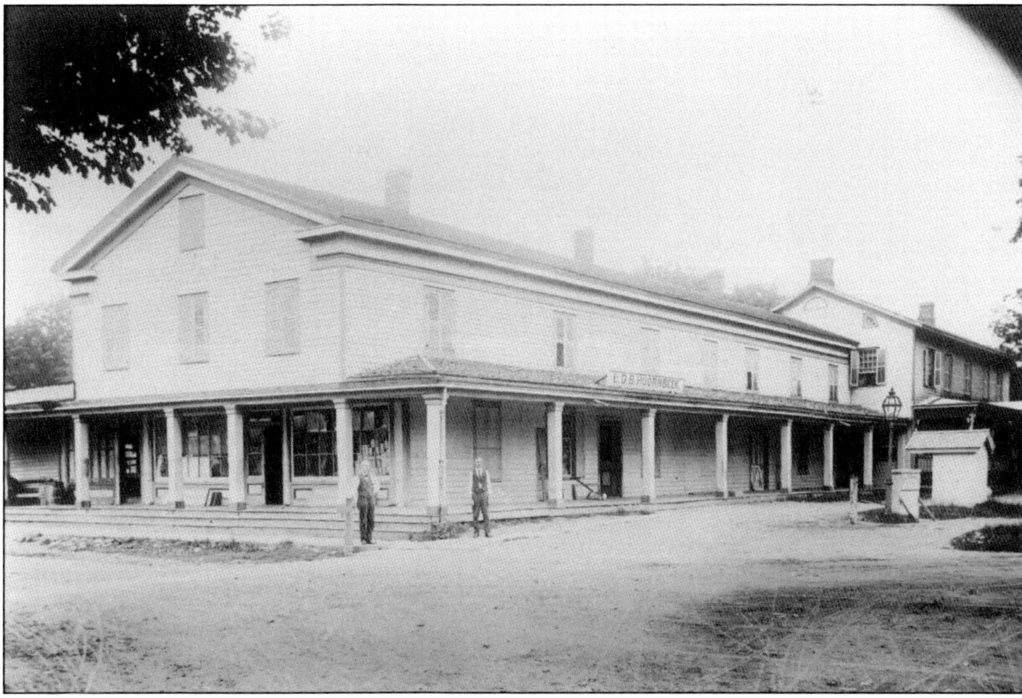

The sign reads "L.D.B. Hoornbeek." The store was located across from the Grahamsville Hotel on the right side of what is present-day Route 42 just before it reaches the blinking light. Here is how the building was described in a 1905 verse: "While L.T. Hornbeck at the Hall, / Dispenses groceries to all, / Who call on him, and he'll supply / Notions to all who wish to buy. / And if a shave or hair cut / You need, why you can get it there."

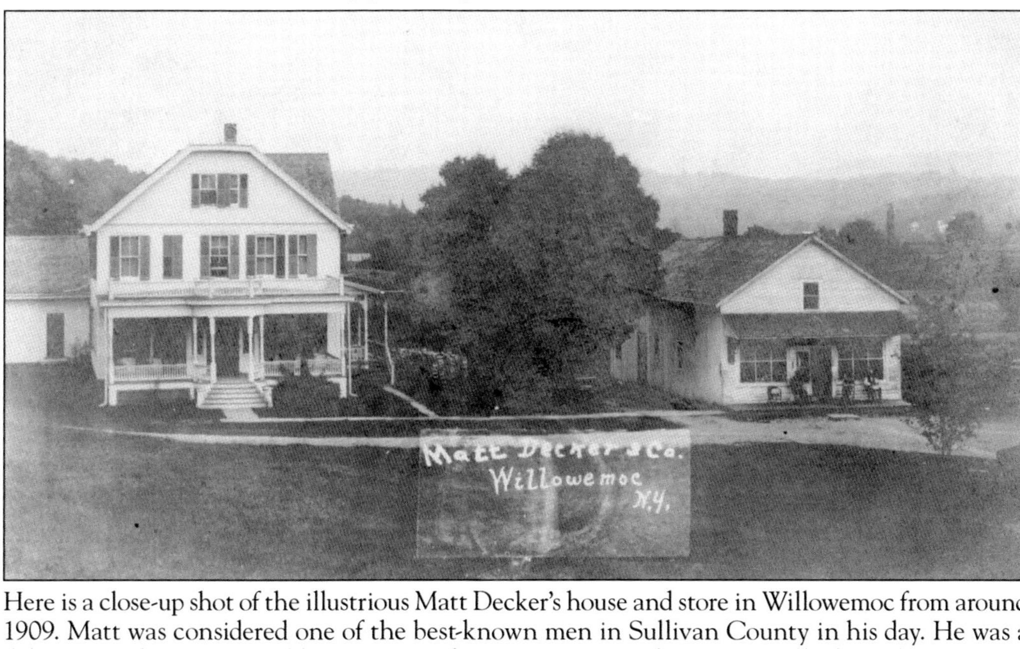

Here is a close-up shot of the illustrious Matt Decker's house and store in Willowemoc from around 1909. Matt was considered one of the best-known men in Sullivan County in his day. He was a delegate to the 1912 Republican National Convention in Chicago. Locally, his other interests included a one-third interest in the Grahamsville Knife Factory, which started up in 1903.

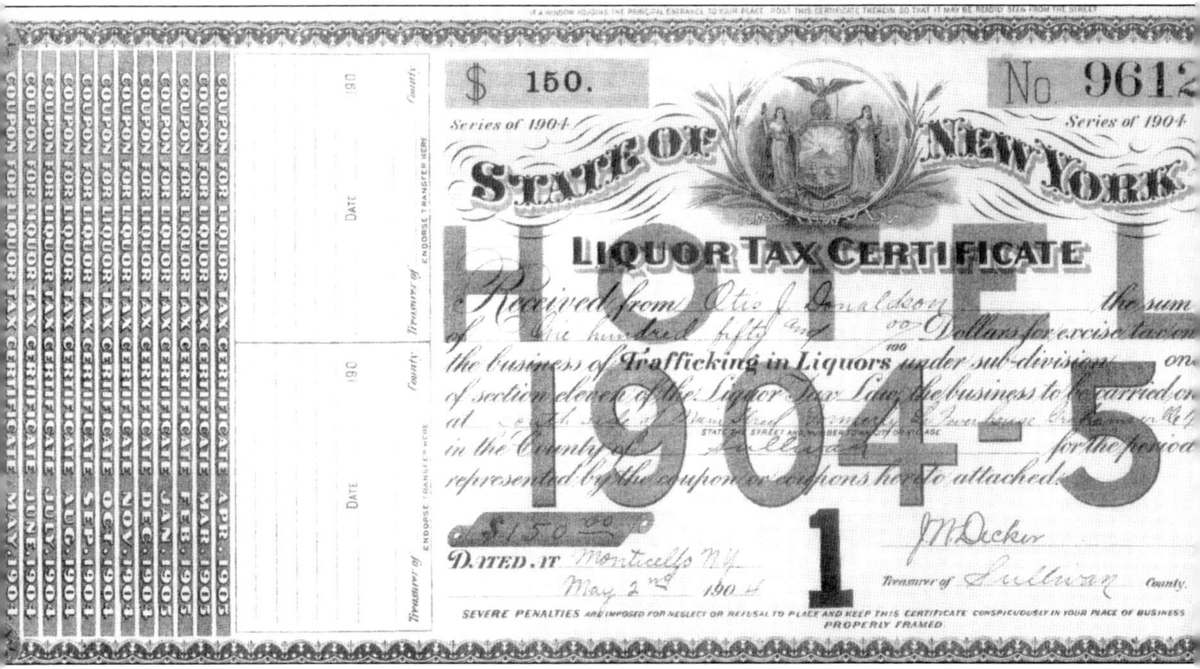
$ 150.

No 9612

Series of 1904 Series of 1904

STATE OF NEW YORK

HOTEL

LIQUOR TAX CERTIFICATE

Received from Otis J. Donaldson the sum of One hundred fifty and 00/100 Dollars for excise tax on the business of Trafficking in Liquors under sub-division one of section eleven of the Liquor Tax Law, the business to be carried on at ... in the County of Sullivan for the period represented by the coupon or coupons hereto attached.

1904-5

$150.00

1

Dated at Monticello N.Y. May 2nd 1904

Treasurer of Sullivan County.

SEVERE PENALTIES ARE IMPOSED FOR NEGLECT OR REFUSAL TO PLACE AND KEEP THIS CERTIFICATE CONSPICUOUSLY IN YOUR PLACE OF BUSINESS PROPERLY FRAMED

COUPON FOR LIQUOR TAX CERTIFICATE APR. 1905
COUPON FOR LIQUOR TAX CERTIFICATE MAR. 1905
COUPON FOR LIQUOR TAX CERTIFICATE FEB. 1905
COUPON FOR LIQUOR TAX CERTIFICATE JAN. 1905
COUPON FOR LIQUOR TAX CERTIFICATE DEC. 1904
COUPON FOR LIQUOR TAX CERTIFICATE NOV. 1904
COUPON FOR LIQUOR TAX CERTIFICATE OCT. 1904
COUPON FOR LIQUOR TAX CERTIFICATE SEP. 1904
COUPON FOR LIQUOR TAX CERTIFICATE AUG. 1904
COUPON FOR LIQUOR TAX CERTIFICATE JULY. 1904
COUPON FOR LIQUOR TAX CERTIFICATE JUNE. 1904
COUPON FOR LIQUOR TAX CERTIFICATE MAY. 1904

Otis Donaldson was the proprietor of the Grahamsville Hotel in 1904 when this Liquor Tax Certificate was issued. The Grahamsville Hotel, formerly the LaFever House, was also known as the Grahamsville House. Town folk and travelers then had the opportunity to have a drink where they were staying or eating. This opportunity does not exist today, as Neversink, Sullivan County, is one of the few towns in New York State to be dry. This means no alcoholic beverage can be purchased anywhere in the township—not a six-pack of beer in a convenience store or a glass of wine in the several eateries in the town. (Virginia Caldwell Bishop Collection.)

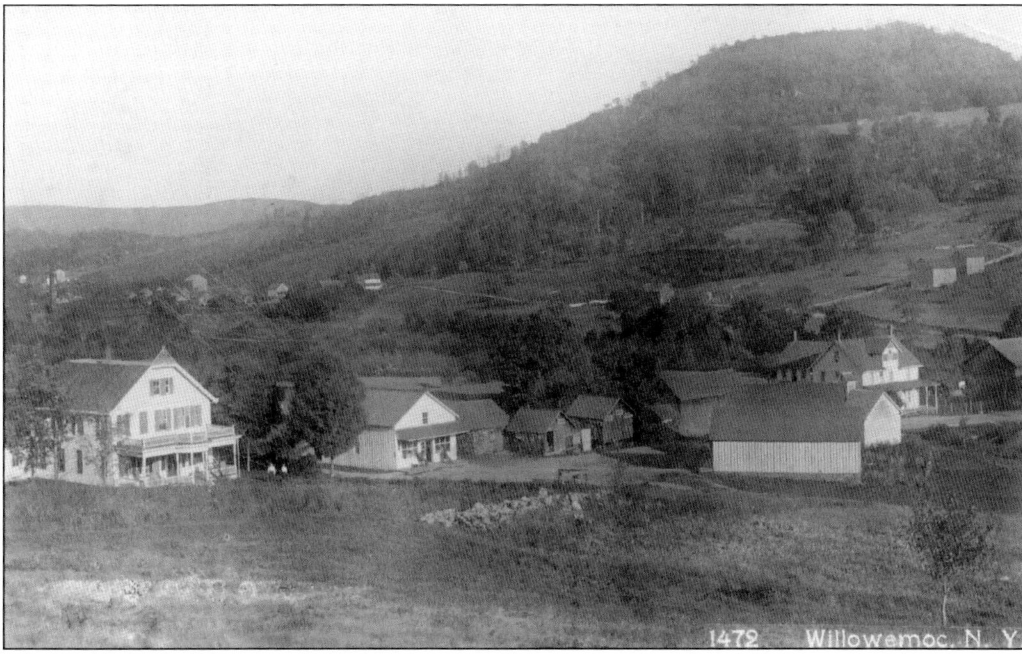

The hamlet of Willowemoc, nestled cozily by the Willowemoc Creek, is pictured here around 1913. Willowemoc's post office opened in 1871 with Matthew Decker as the first postmaster. By 1913, many residents were leaving the area to follow the work elsewhere. The Willowemoc stream is sometimes known for its fly-fishing.

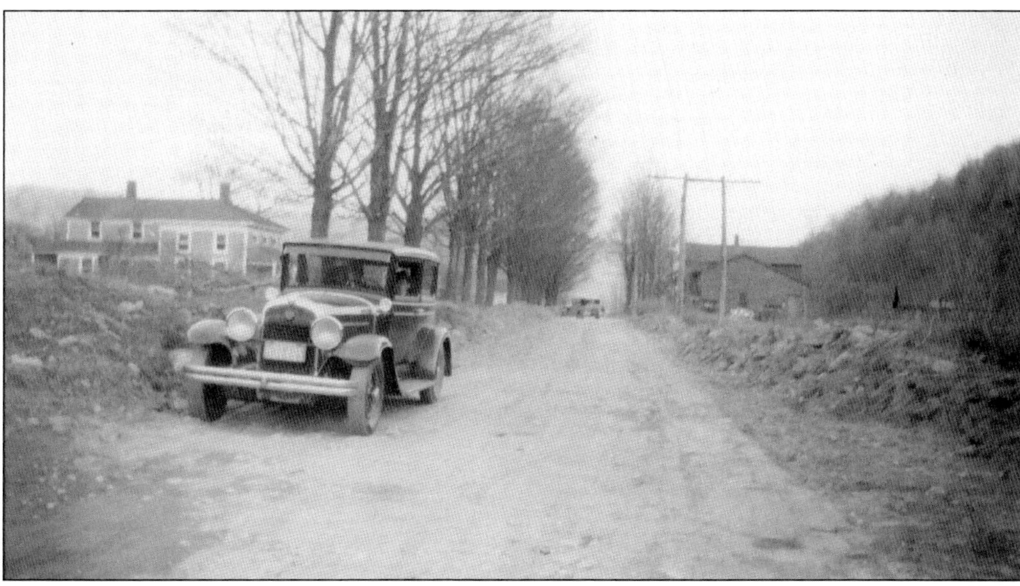

The Unionville of yesterday sports a dirt road. This same road became New York State Route 55. Unionville had a one-room school, a church and a cemetery. Those are all gone now. Newly erected signs tell the driver that Unionville, past and present, is part of Catskill Forest Preserve. (Scott and Robin Mahnken Collection.)

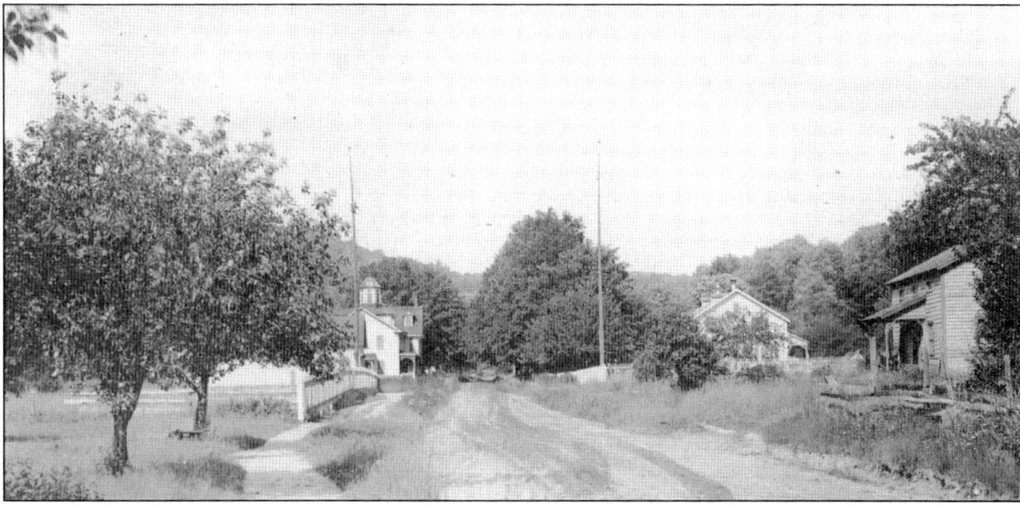

The road to Claryville, New York, is pictured in its early days when the road was all dirt—muddy in the spring and dusty in the dry summer. The sidewalks in evidence here were no doubt created so that the ladies' long dresses would not drag in the mud. This small community rose to prominence during the tannery days. By 1910, many tannery workers had moved elsewhere, and others stayed to find new work and make their home in the area. The Upper Neversink River runs parallel to the Claryville area.

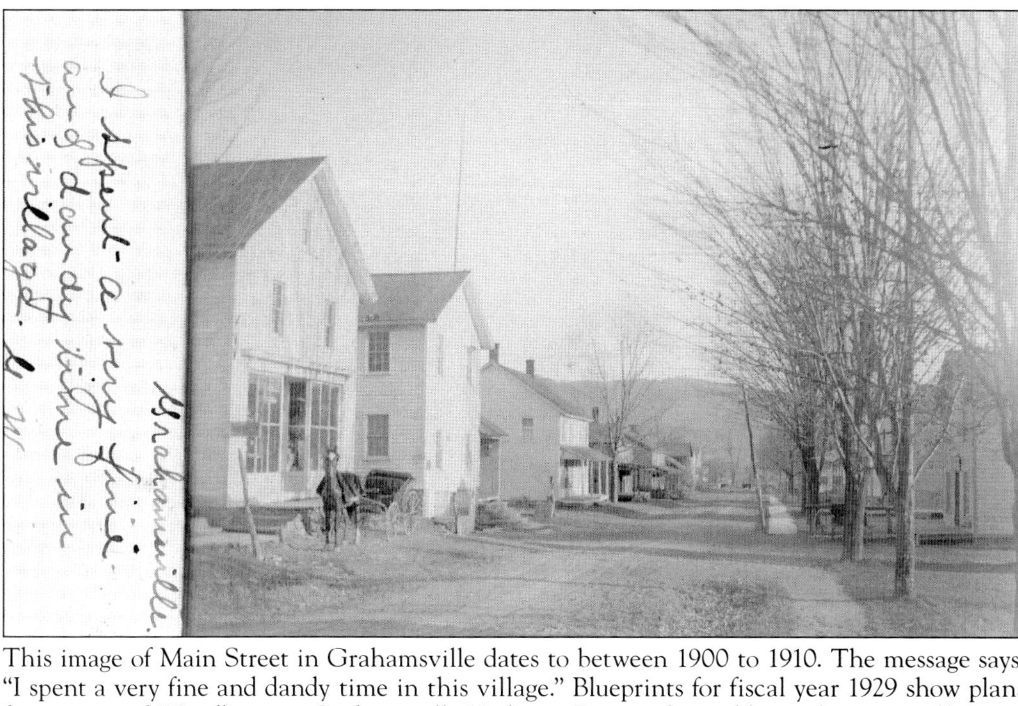

This image of Main Street in Grahamsville dates to between 1900 to 1910. The message says, "I spent a very fine and dandy time in this village." Blueprints for fiscal year 1929 show plans for a proposed Woodbourne–Grahamsville Highway. Dirt roads would soon be a part of history. (Virginia Caldwell Bishop Collection.)

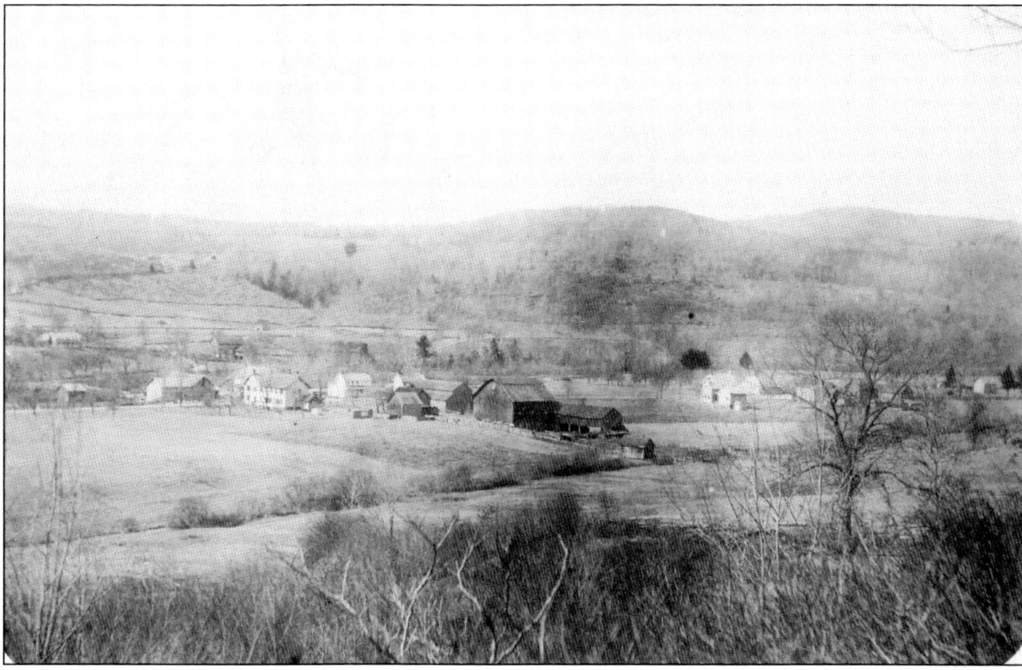

This is an image of Montela, New York, looking toward South Hill. A somber note on the back says, "Now bottom of Merriman Dam," meaning the Rondout Reservoir. (Cynthia Moshier Wagner Collection.)

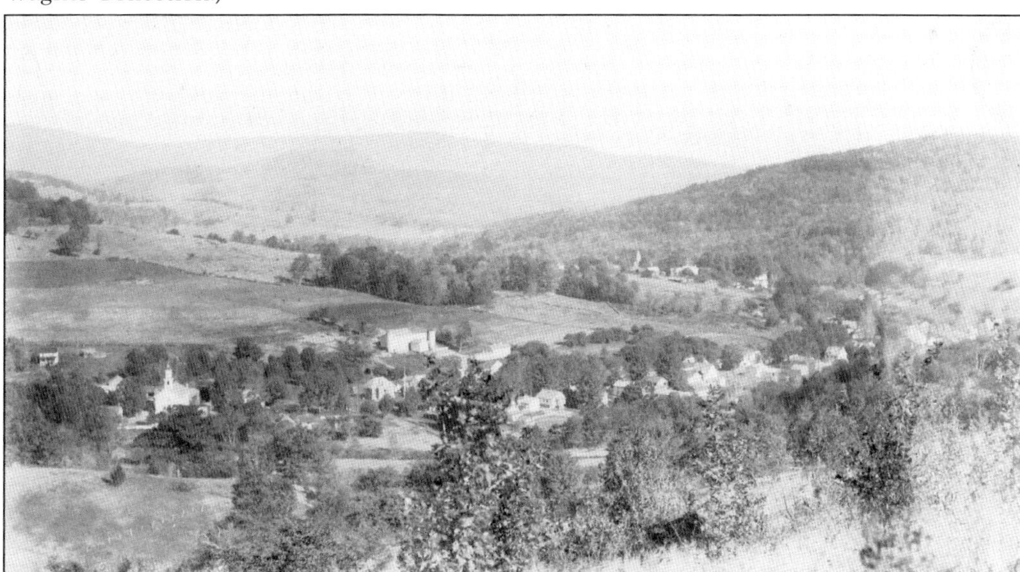

The small community of Neversink, New York, also known as Neversink Flats, is clearly shown with this Otto Hillig photograph. The first Neversink Post Office was established in 1828. The original community was taken by eminent domain, and the area is now under the Neversink Reservoir. When driving on New York State Route 55 from Grahamsville to Liberty across the Neversink Dam, travelers can see where the original community was by looking look down to the right, close to the dam itself. A smaller Neversink sprang up on New York State Route 55 between that spot and Grahamsville and exists to this very day. (Addy Collection.)

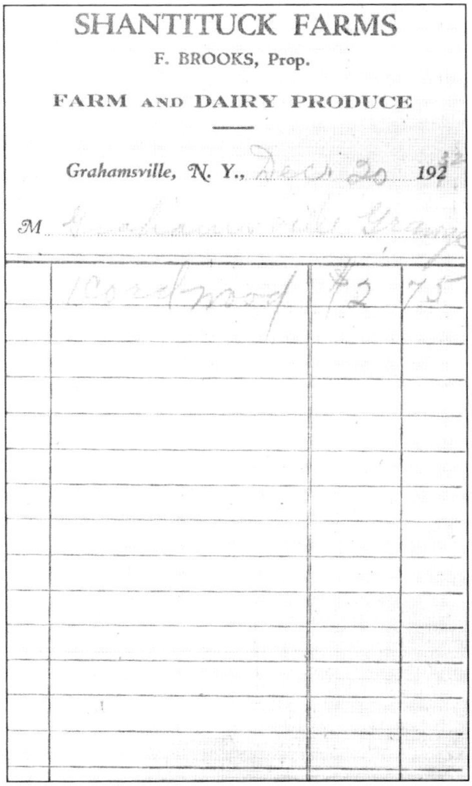

SHANTITUCK FARMS

F. BROOKS, Prop.

FARM AND DAIRY PRODUCE

Grahamsville, N. Y., Dec 20 192

M Grahamsville Grange

1 cord wood	$2	75

This bill to the Grahamsville Grange for a cord of wood is another reminder of how little things cost in the 1930s. Wood has often been the fuel of choice in the Northeast and remains so even today. A price of $2.75 for a cord of wood would certainly help today's budgets.

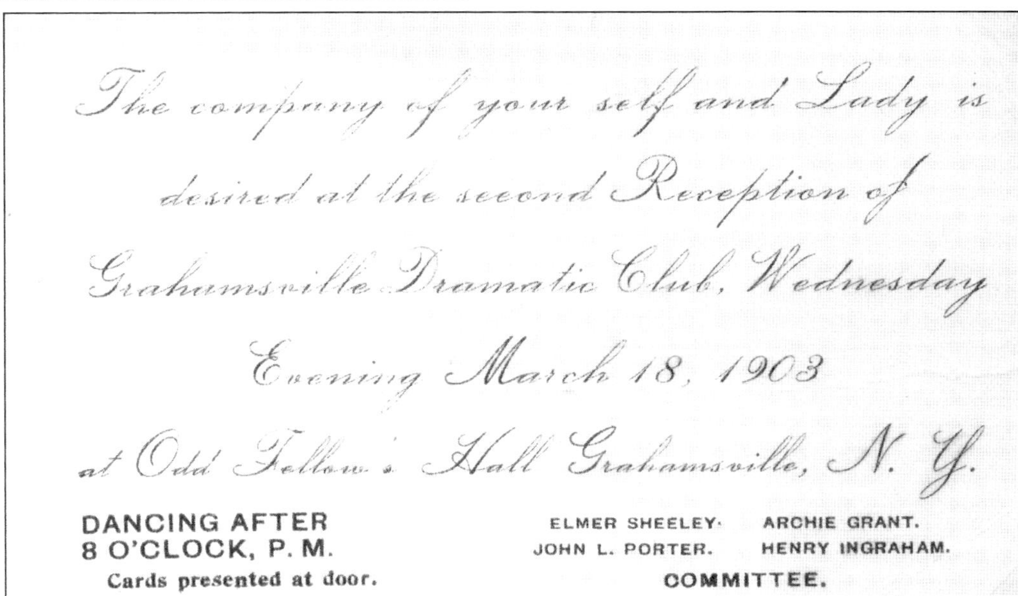

The company of your self and Lady is desired at the second Reception of Grahamsville Dramatic Club, Wednesday Evening March 18, 1903 at Odd Fellow's Hall Grahamsville, N. Y.

DANCING AFTER
8 O'CLOCK, P. M.
Cards presented at door.

ELMER SHEELEY. ARCHIE GRANT.
JOHN L. PORTER. HENRY INGRAHAM.
COMMITTEE.

Grahamsville in 1903 had dirty, dusty roads, but the hamlet was booming. One can just imagine horse-drawn carriages pulling up to the door for this event, with ladies in their normal garb of long dresses being assisted by attentive gentlemen. The names Elmer Sheeley, John L. Porter, Archie Grant, and Henry Ingraham are part of local history, and the Odd Fellows Hall still stands. (Virginia Caldwell Bishop Collection.)

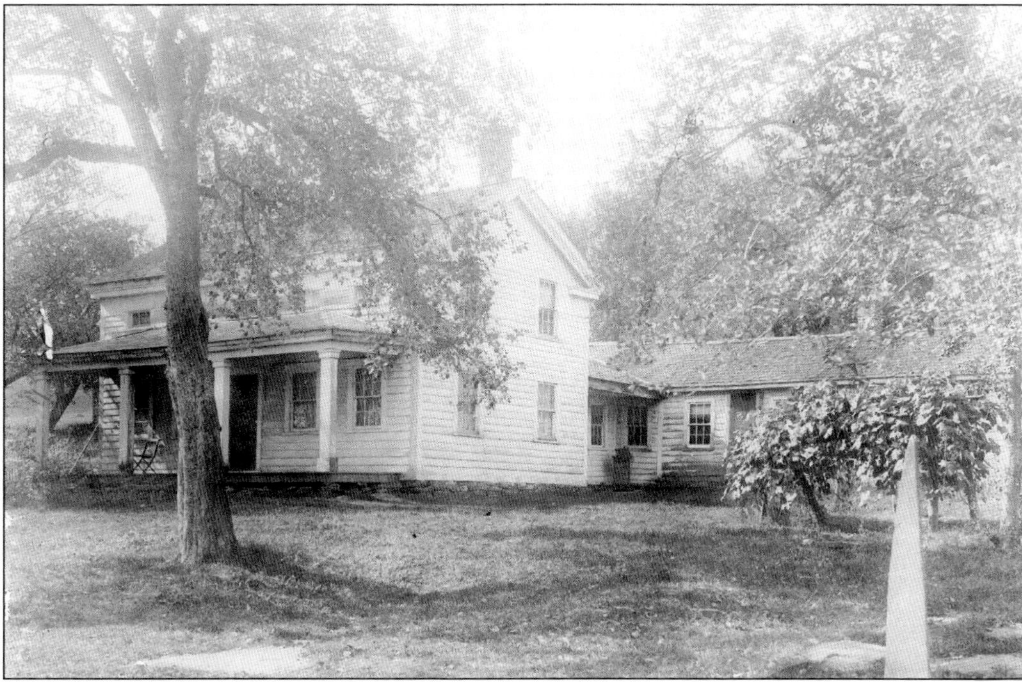

Melvin (father) and Charles (son) Porter's old farmhouse on the Sundown Road is identified in the caption on the back of the photograph. Rev. J. Milton Harris reported that "it was a fine farm with good buildings." The photograph is signed by "Enos."

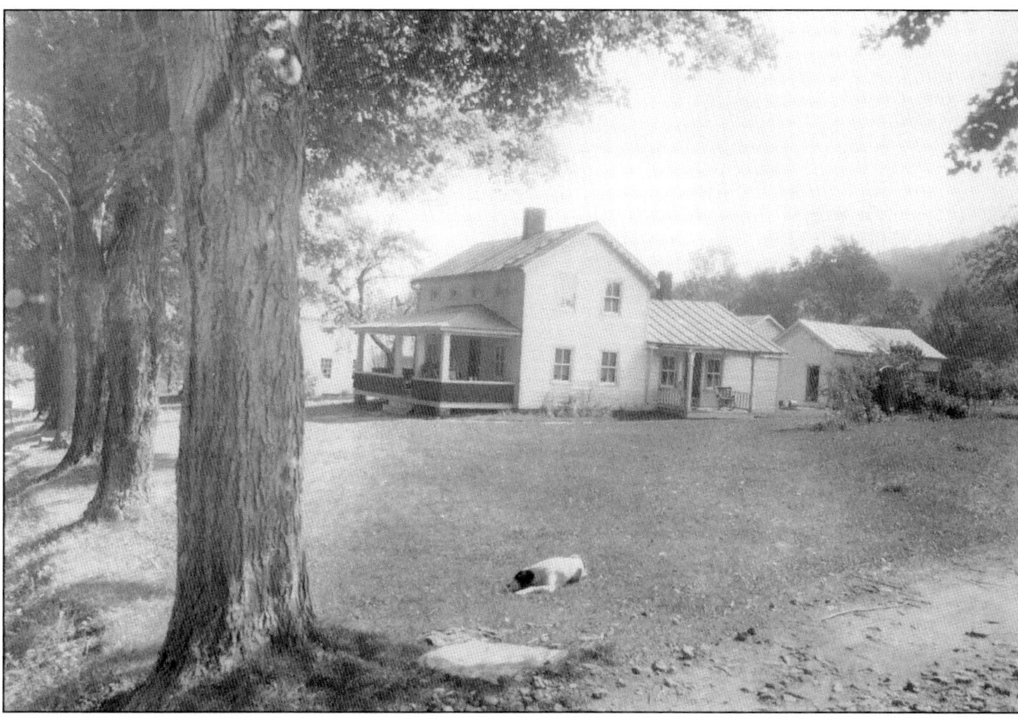

The Ben Hill house in Eureka was taken for the flooding of the Rondout Valley. Note the ladder on the roof, probably kept there for chimney cleaning and in case of a chimney fire.

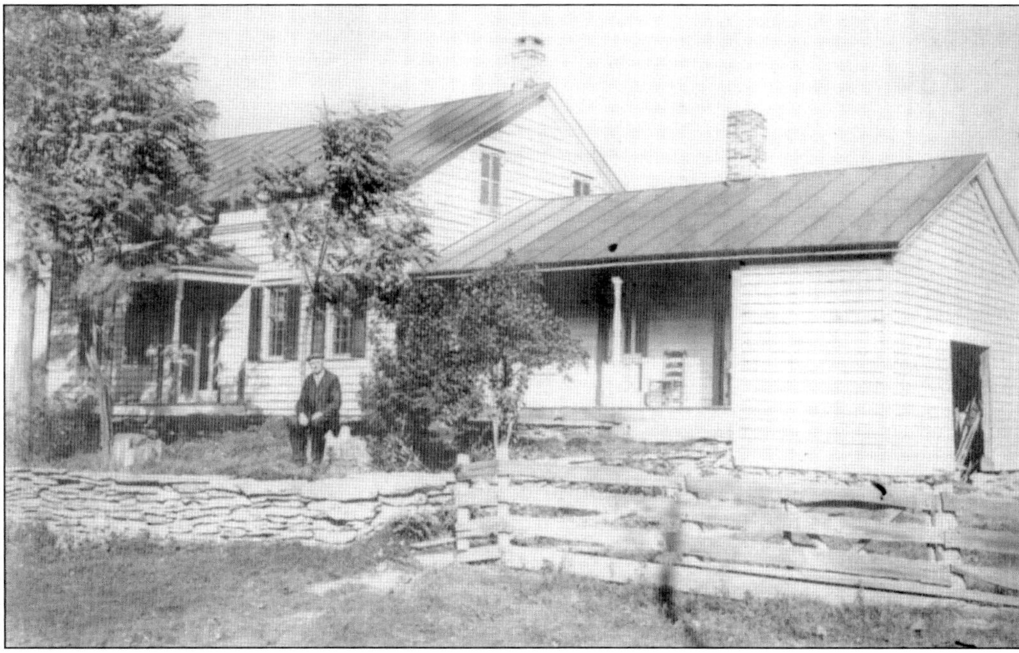

Hull Rosencrans is pictured at his home on Route 42. The house was located across from present-day Big Hollow Road. This farm was owned in the 1940s by Robert Many, who had a poultry business. The location was once a toll stop where money was collected for passage on the road. (Virginia Caldwell Bishop Collection.)

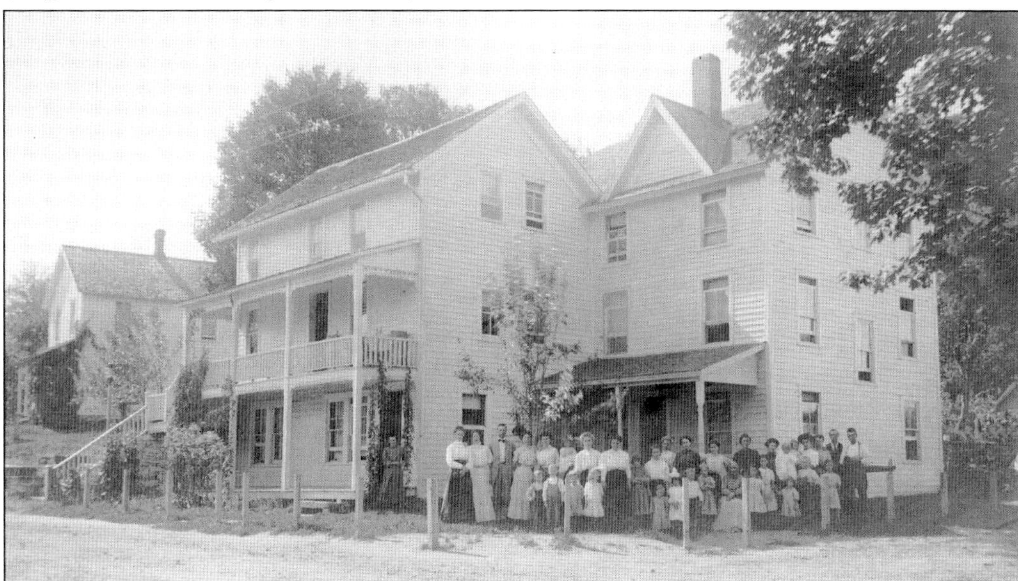

The original Neversink community became a respite for summer vacationers. The cool waters of the Neversink River were a big draw for New York City residents who lived in hot tenement buildings with no air-conditioning. Once the New York, Ontario & Western Railway ran trains to the country, it soon followed that city dwellers would discover how cool and wonderful it was to spend time in the country. This boardinghouse or hotel was called the Edgemere, and its proprietor was Charles E. Freer. The photograph was taken around 1910. (Langton-Raffa Collection.)

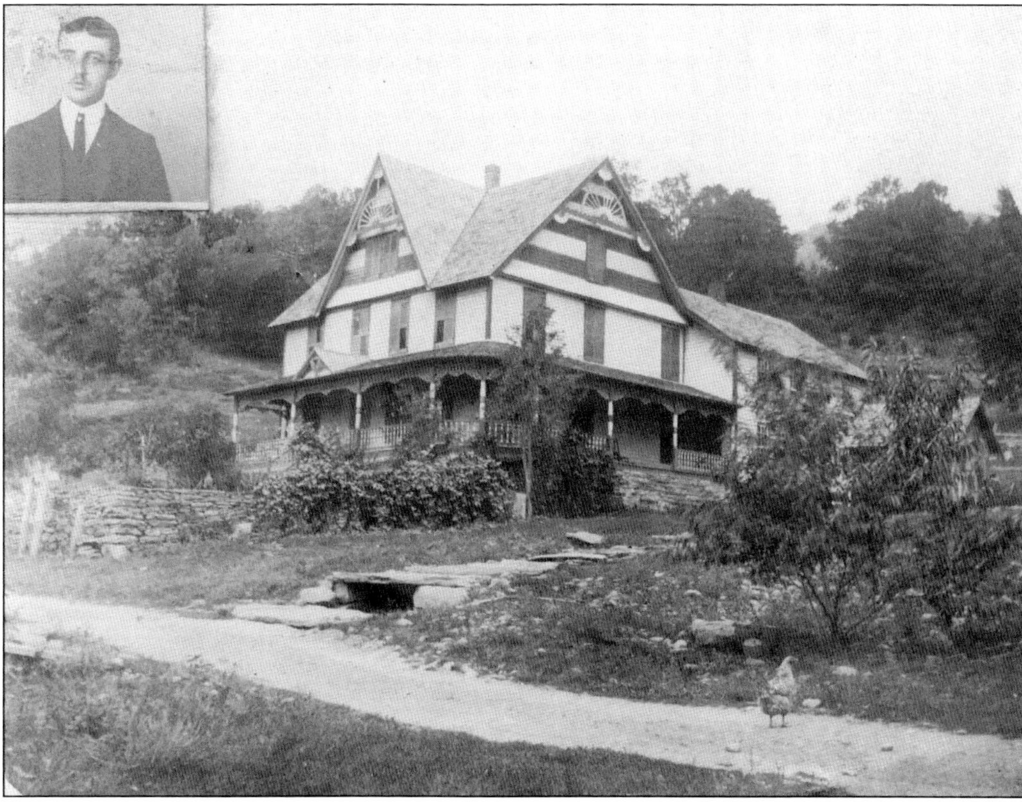

Here is the John Cross house located just up from the Lows Corners Baptist Church. The one-lane dirt road hardly looks big enough for one vehicle, let alone two.

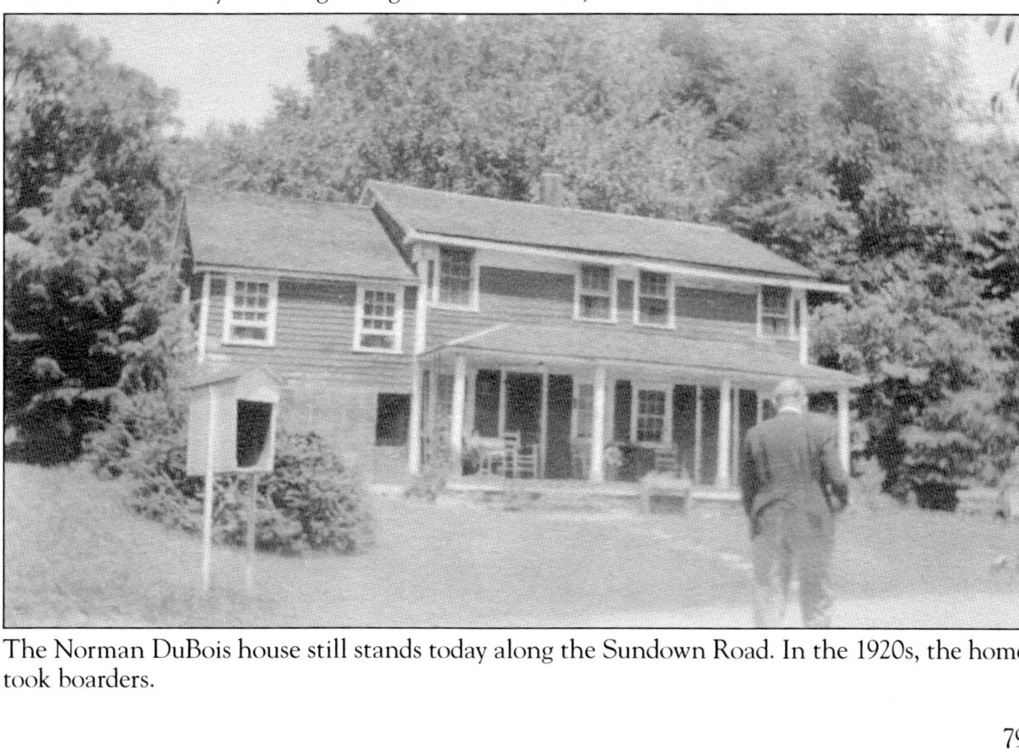

The Norman DuBois house still stands today along the Sundown Road. In the 1920s, the home took boarders.

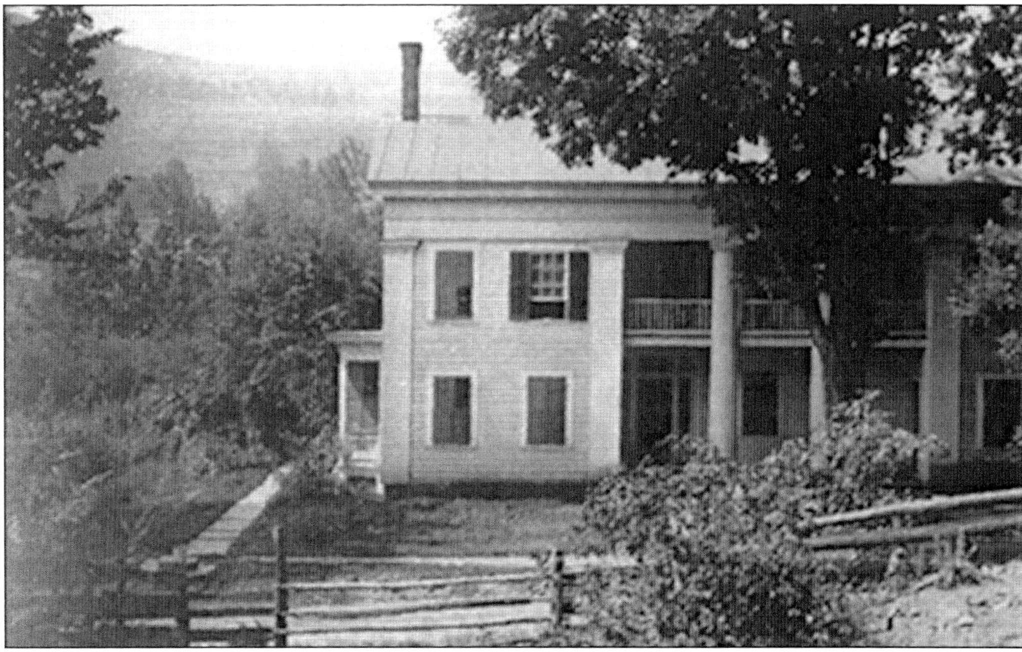

This house is full of history. Research shows that the original building was a tavern owned by C. Burton. It was located on the Napanoch-Denning Turnpike. There are undocumented rumors that a speakeasy was located in the rear of the building in the 1920s. It was known as the Sycamore House and the Hawthorne House during different periods, and it became a private home that at one time was owned by the LaMoree family. This photograph is from around 1910. In 2005, the C. Burton Hotel was placed in the National Register of Historic Places. (Don Erath Collection.)

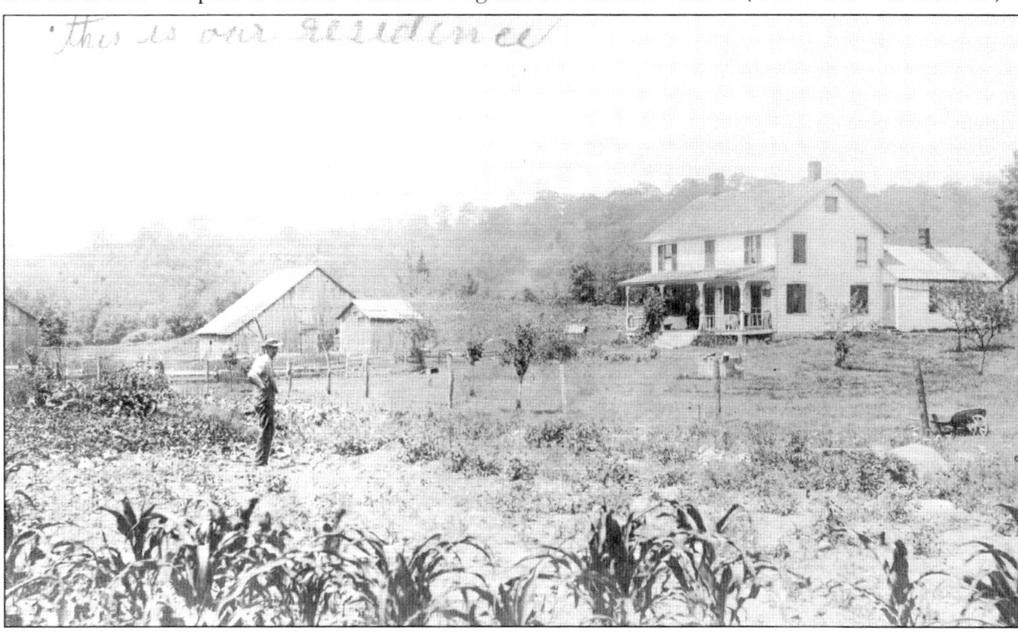

Mrs. Josiah Decker of Willowemoc writes "This is our residence" on a real-photo postcard mailed in August 1903. The card was sent from Willowemoc and to Decker's dear friend Jennie Hoag at Lew Beach. (Carol Smythe Collection.)

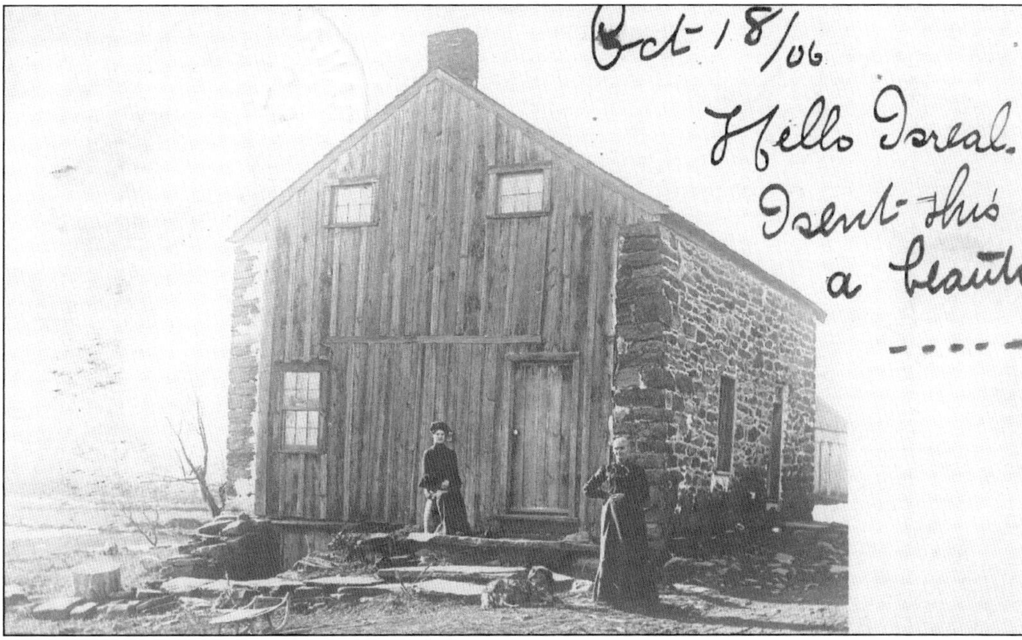

This image is the only known photograph of this area home. The real-photo postcard was mailed from Grahamsville in 1906 to Israel Slater of Grahamsville. Historians find it interesting because of the detail of the stone front and back of the house. Stone was rarely used for homes in this area.

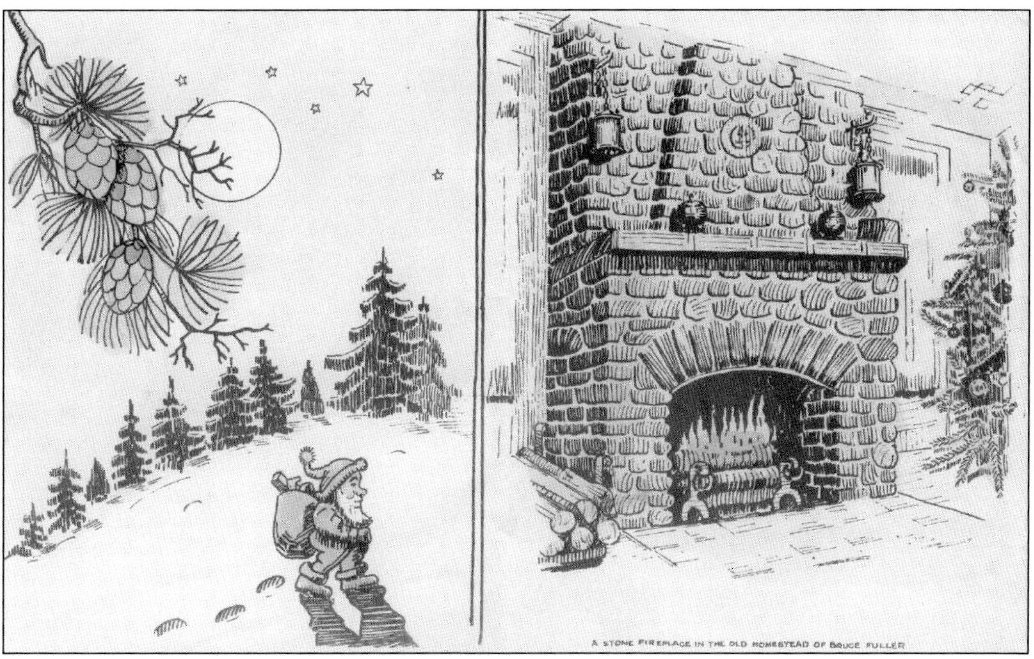

This drawing of the stone fireplace in a Eureka home gives one an idea of the immense loss that residents faced when the Rondout Reservoir was built. Whether they lived in Eureka, Montela, or Lackawack and whether they lived in a family home with much history or in a cabin, their lives were changed forever.

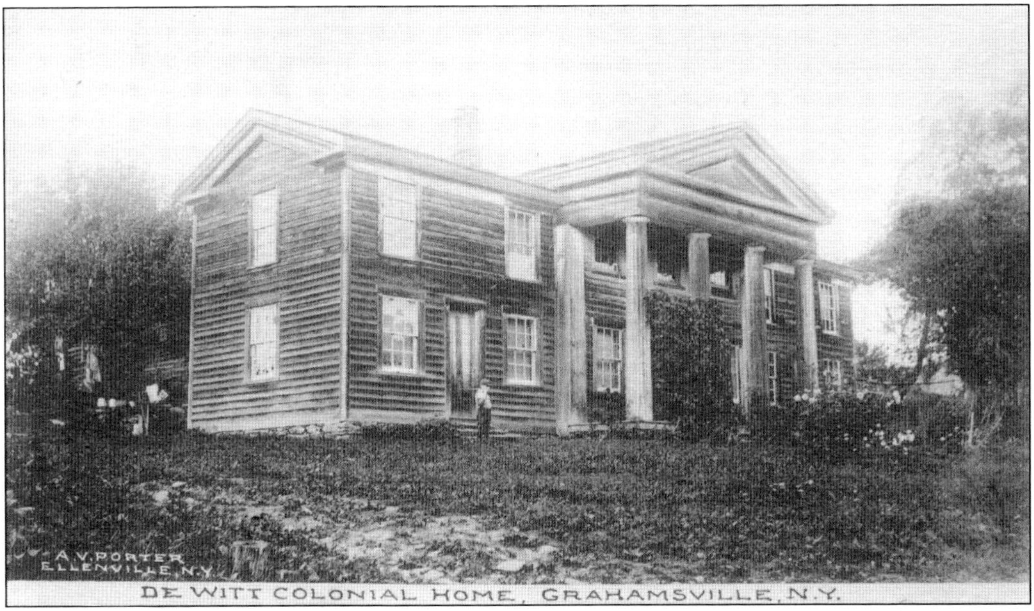

The DeWitt Colonial House is recognized in the Grahamsville Historic District as the Marenius Dayton House. It was probably built in the 1820s and is considered "the finest example of Greek revival architecture in northern Sullivan County." The house served as an inn and an official stagecoach stop for travelers according to *The Grahamsville Historic District* by Marylin Barr.

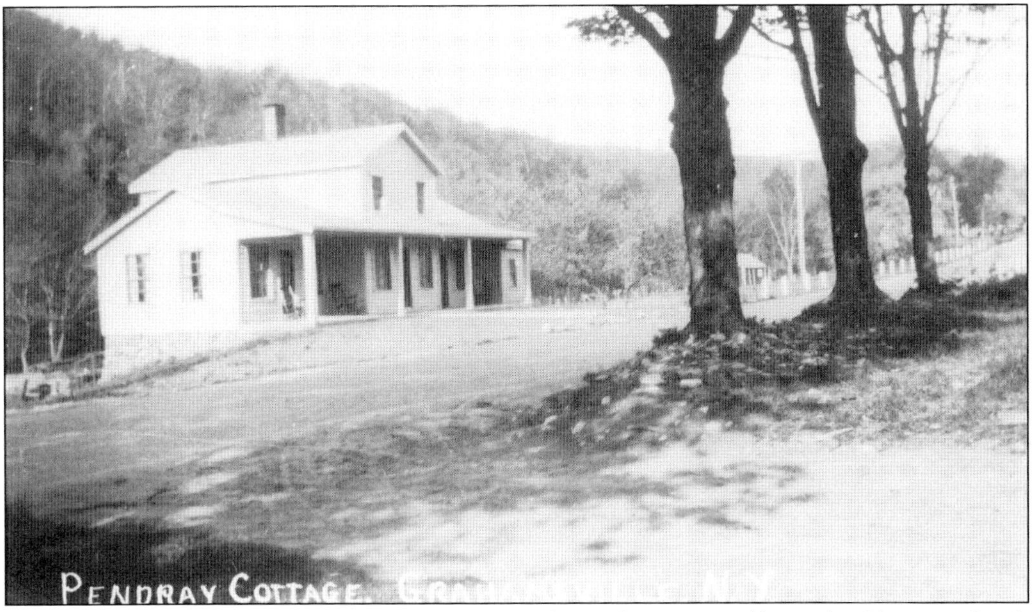

The Pendray Cottage on New York State Route 55, located in Unionville on the Chestnut Creek side, took summer boarders. This c. 1900 card was sent home to Brooklyn and shows a contented visitor with the message: "This is a great life in the wide open spaces (mountains)."

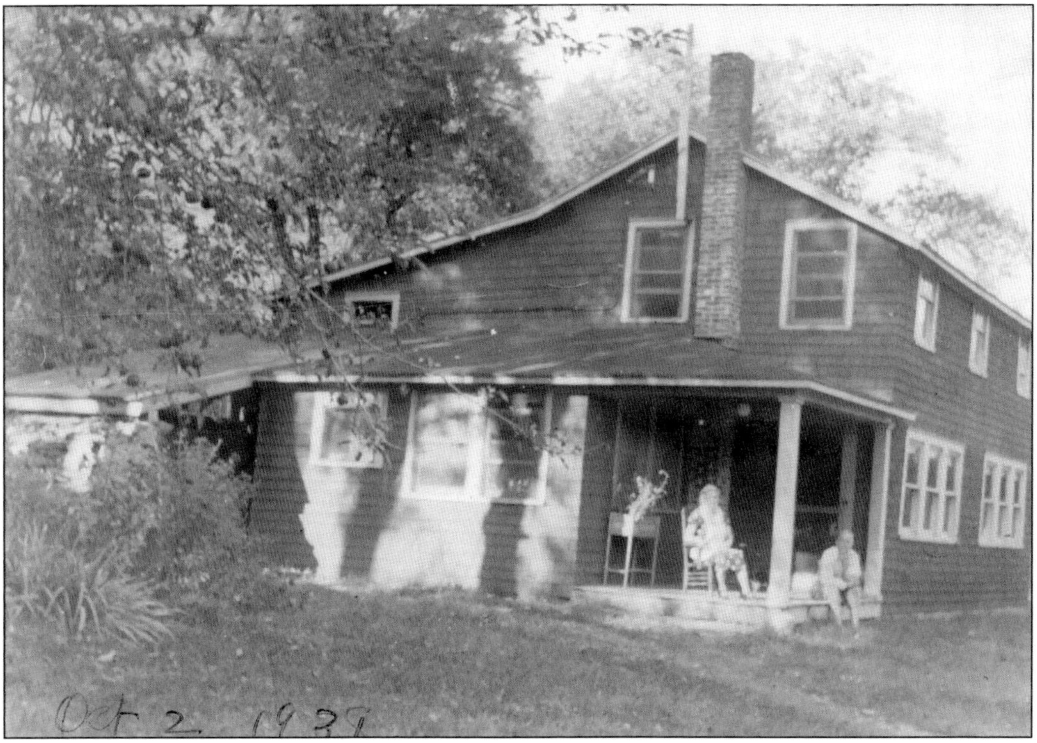

Ora Cross sold this house and property in 1921 to a family from Red Hill. The house sat on the Sundown Road overlooking the Upper Rondout Creek. Scott and Diana Grey presently live in the same location, although in a different dwelling.

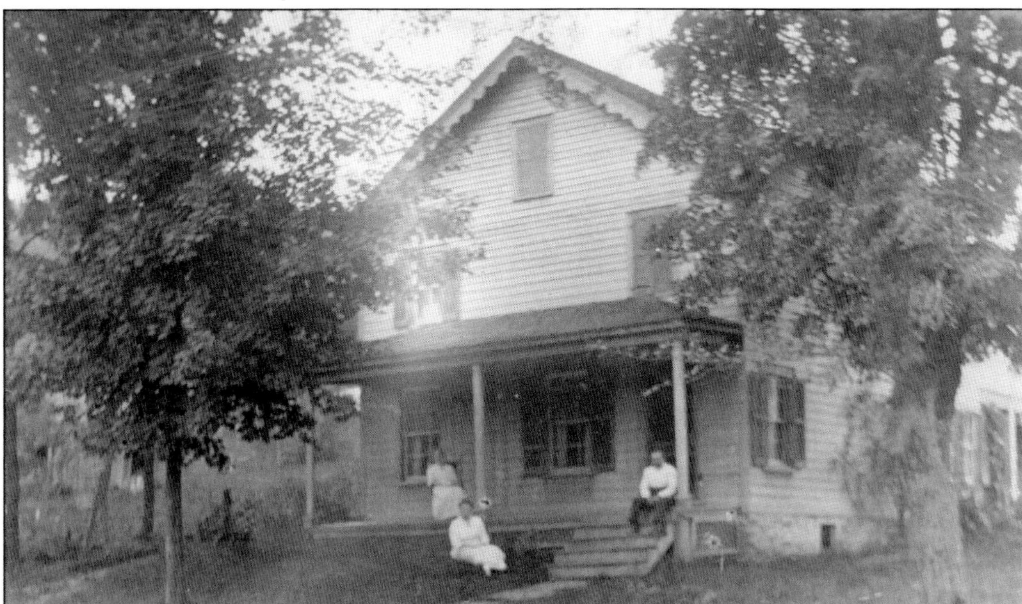

This is A.B. Sheeley's house on Moore Hill in Grahamsville. Eastman Kodak made the folding pocket camera in 1906. This allowed black-and-white photographs such as this one to be printed directly onto postcard backs. (Barbara Purcell Collection.)

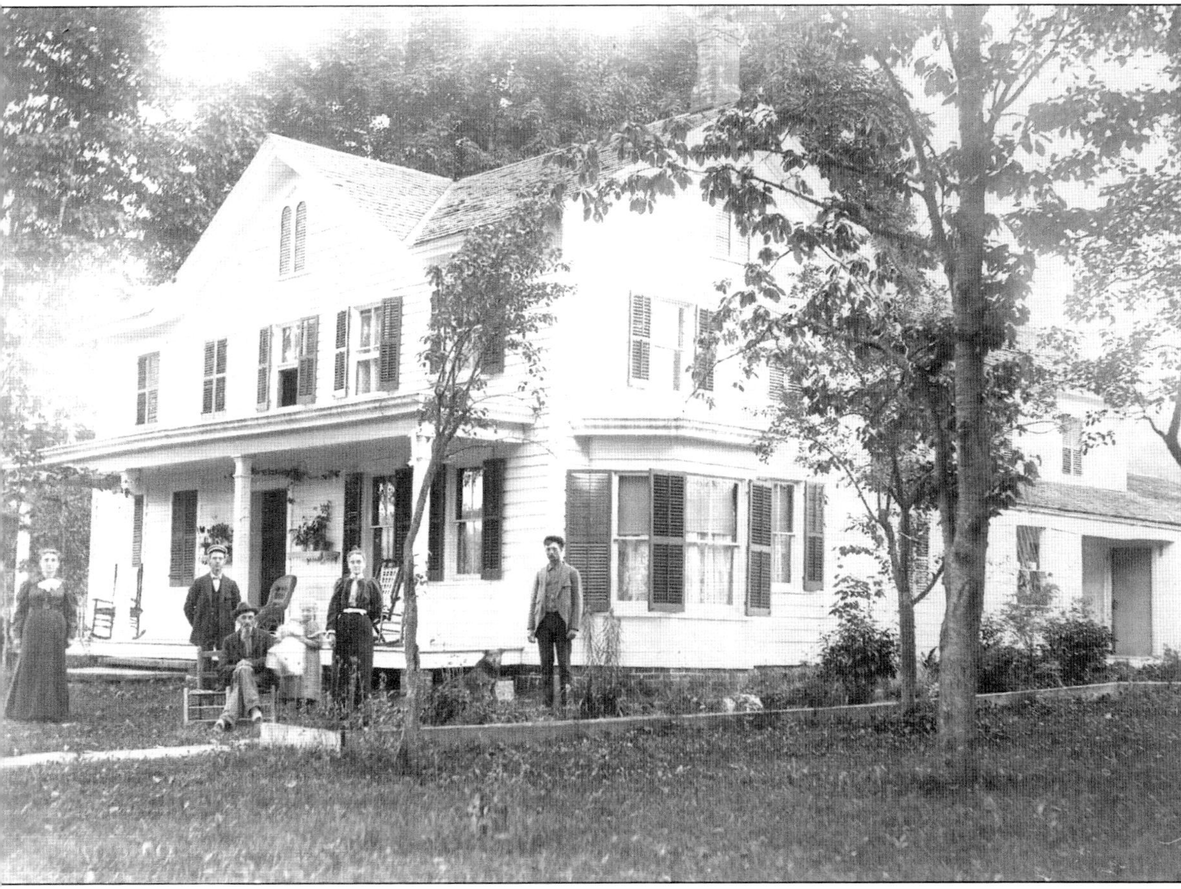

Otto Hillig of Liberty took this photograph of the Sheeley homestead in Eureka. Pictured are Wash and Louisa Sheeley, Hattie and Albert Sheeley, Nellie and doll Riva, and George LeRoy. The time period is between around 1905 and 1915. (TVM.)

Five

AGRICULTURE

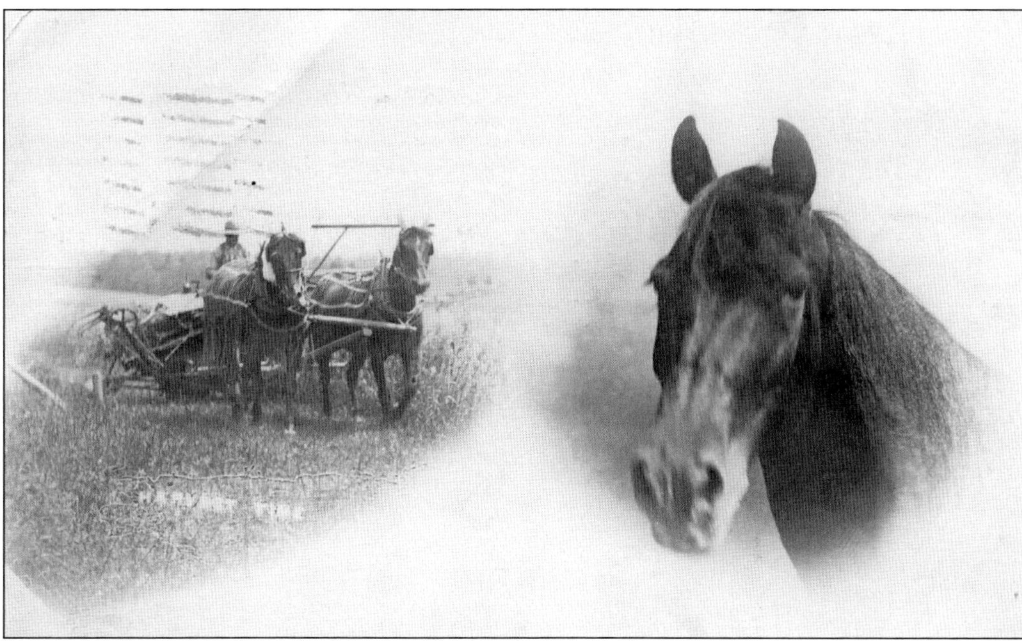

This 1911 real-photo postcard sent to Seymour Cypert of Hasbrouck, New York, indicates how much horses were valued in those days. Their photographs were put on postcards such as this one, which shows three horses. The animals were almost always known by their first names. To someone not in the know, a reference to Dan might mean either a family member or a treasured horse. (LaVerne Cypert Black collection.)

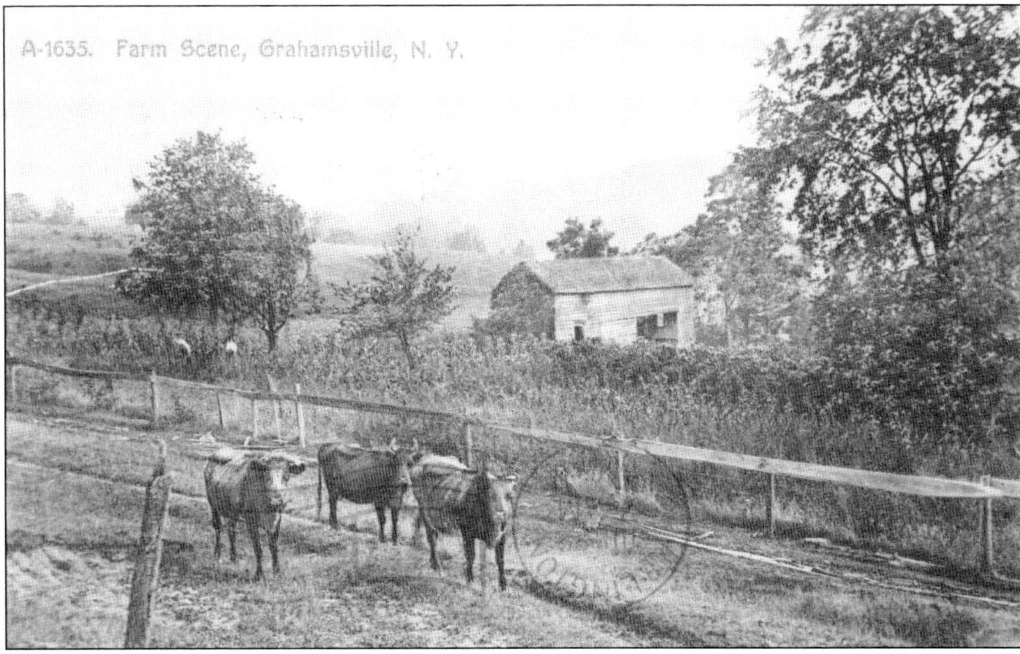

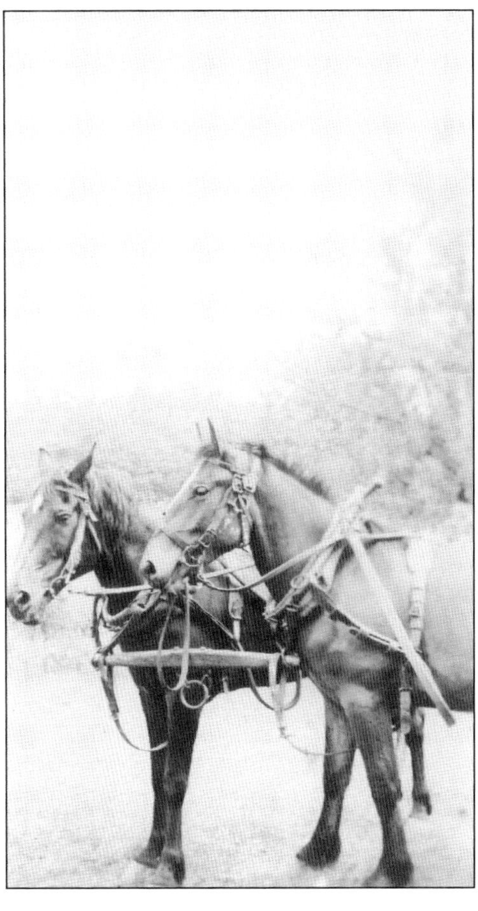

A 1911 bucolic postcard is representational of the farm scene in the Catskills at that time. The photograph was published by the Krum Bros. store in Grahamsville and was printed in Germany. The message on the back says in part, "This country is so beauteous," and the card was mailed to Rev. William Coombe, a well-known minister who was serving in a different city.

A good team of horses was worth a lot to a farmer in those days. That is why family photo albums would often include an image of their prized team. The back of this photograph says simply, "Dad's horses Sundown." It probably dates to around the 1920s.

It was no wonder the farmers of the Neversink area, who had formed an organization known as the Farmer's Club of Neversink, decided to hold an agricultural fair. The first one was known as the Grahamsville Farmers' Club Annual Exhibition of 1879. The ticket shows space for "class" and "entered by." The ticket shown was used to denote "First Premium" (first prize). Early records show that 425 tickets were sold that day. In 1898, the Neversink Agricultural Society was created, and that group has managed the fair right up to this very day. The fair is known as the Grahamsville Fair or the "Little World's Fair" and is the last independent fair in New York State. The fair missed operating only one year, 1928, when a terrible flood hit the Chestnut Valley.

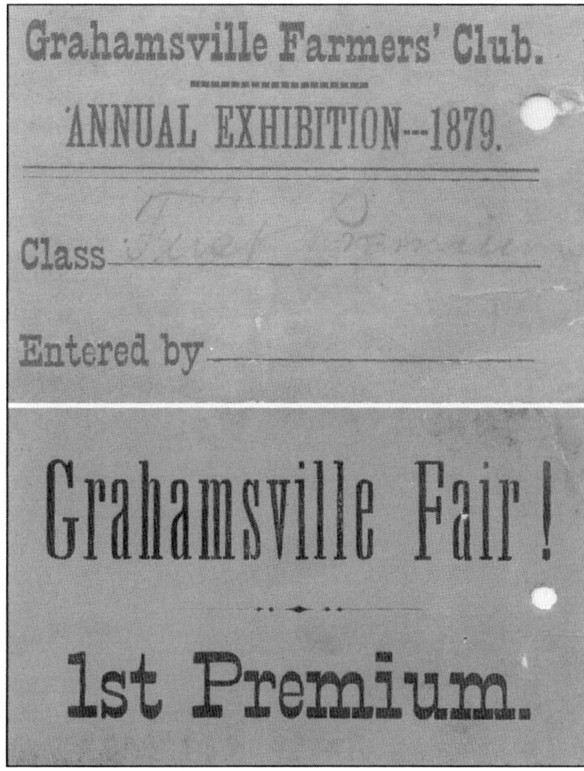

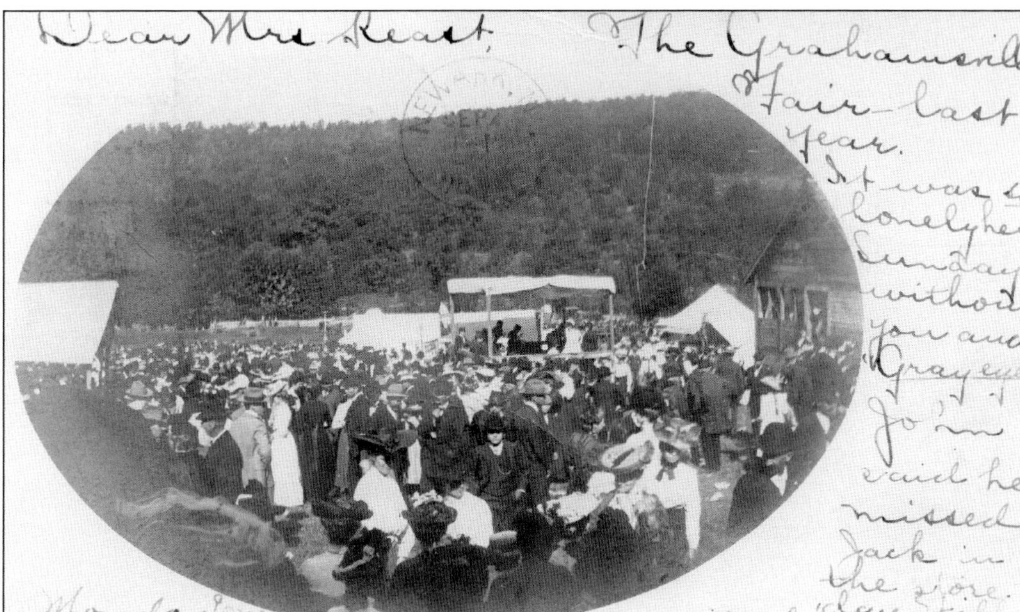

This early postcard was mailed in 1905 but references that the photograph was of the fair in 1904. This fair pictured is being held in the same spot where it takes place today. In 2013, the 134th fair was held. Teams of oxen would have been shown during early fairs because they were in primary use at that time. Gradually, teams of horses would have replaced them. Today, there are no small farms, and current farmers use tractors. (Carol Smythe Collection.)

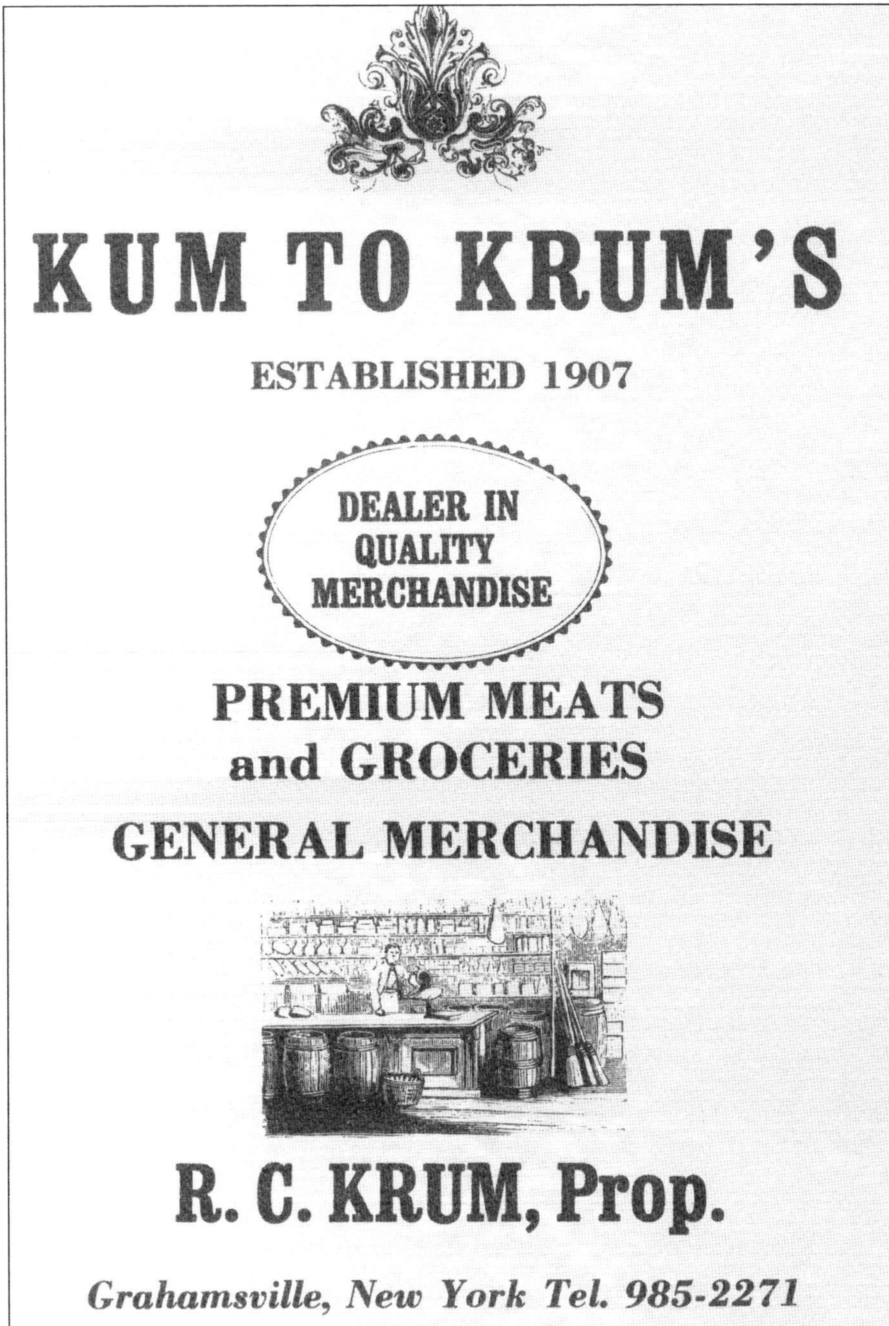

The imagery of a country fair just as cars were being phased in and carriages had become obsolete is a distant memory today. Women were still wearing long dresses, which they would soon leave behind in favor of shorter skirts. The illustration shows a time period around 1915. This was the cover of the 1979 Grahamsville Little World's Fair booklet, which celebrated 100 years of the fair. Krum's General Store, sponsor of the cover, no longer exists, but the fair survives.

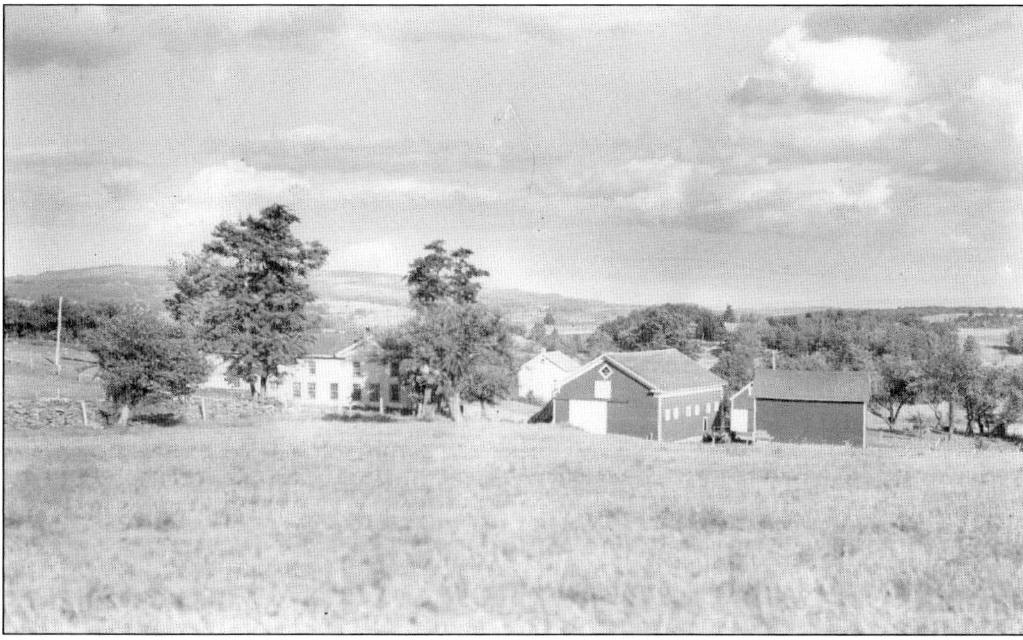

Photographer Otto Hillig of Liberty took this picture of the Oscar Grant farm in Bradley, just a few miles away from the original village of Neversink. In the 1800s, this was a well-known stagecoach stop. No buildings remain on the property today; they were torn down the last time the property changed hands. (Virginia Caldwell Bishop Collection.)

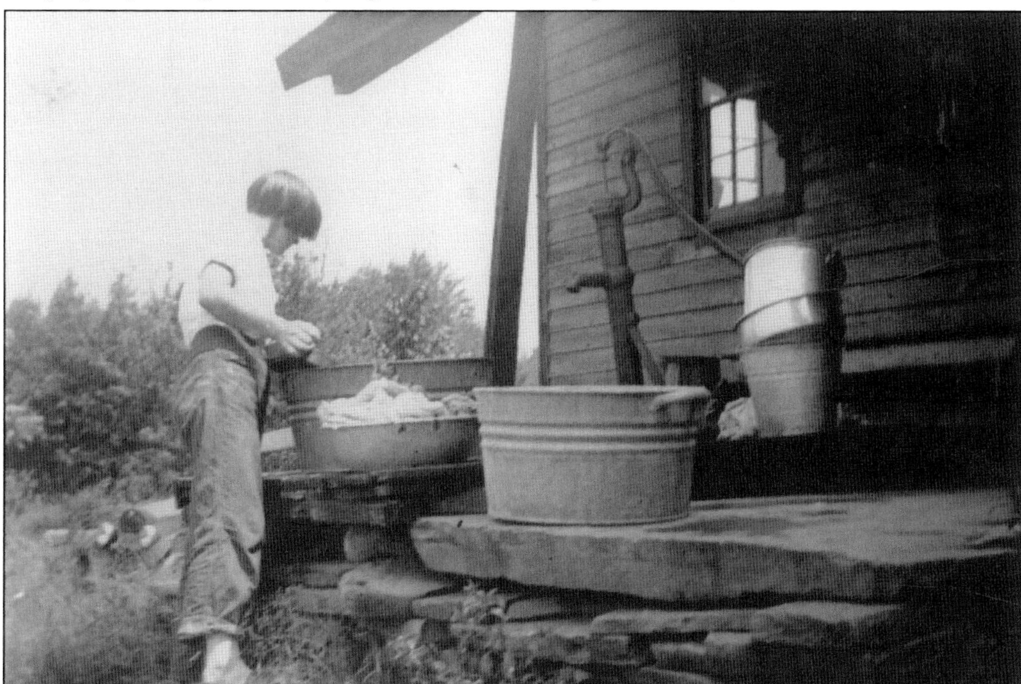

In this 1931 image, a South Hill farmwife is doing the family laundry by hand. One washtub is resting on the well stone that covers the family well. Note the hand pump. Doing laundry in those days was extremely labor-intensive, and it is no wonder wash day was once a week.

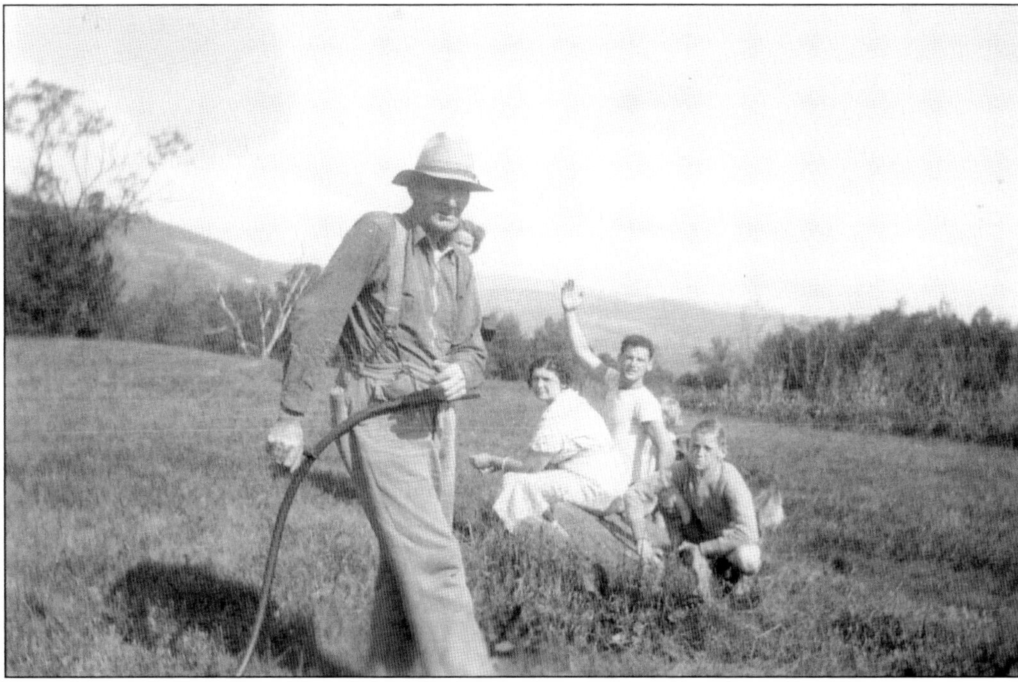

Preston Palmer leans on his scythe as summer boarders sit watching as farm chores are done. Palmer often hired out to help different farmers in the Neversink area and in the late 1930s and early 1940s might have been referred to a "hired man."

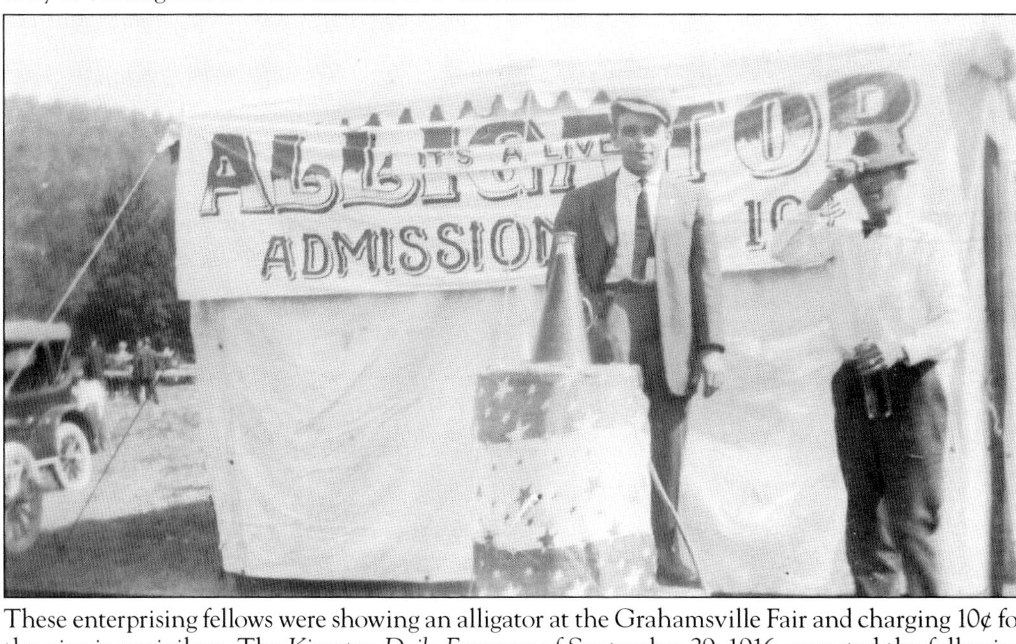

These enterprising fellows were showing an alligator at the Grahamsville Fair and charging 10¢ for the viewing privilege. The *Kingston Daily Freeman* of September 29, 1916, reported the following in the Ellenville news column: "George Van Wyck and A.J.L. Wolt were among the exhibitors at the Grahamsville Fair, having a tent in which they exhibited a live alligator. They acquired Rosenberger's closed candy wagon and megaphone and started early in the day and they certainly did their part making the 'World's Fair' a big success."

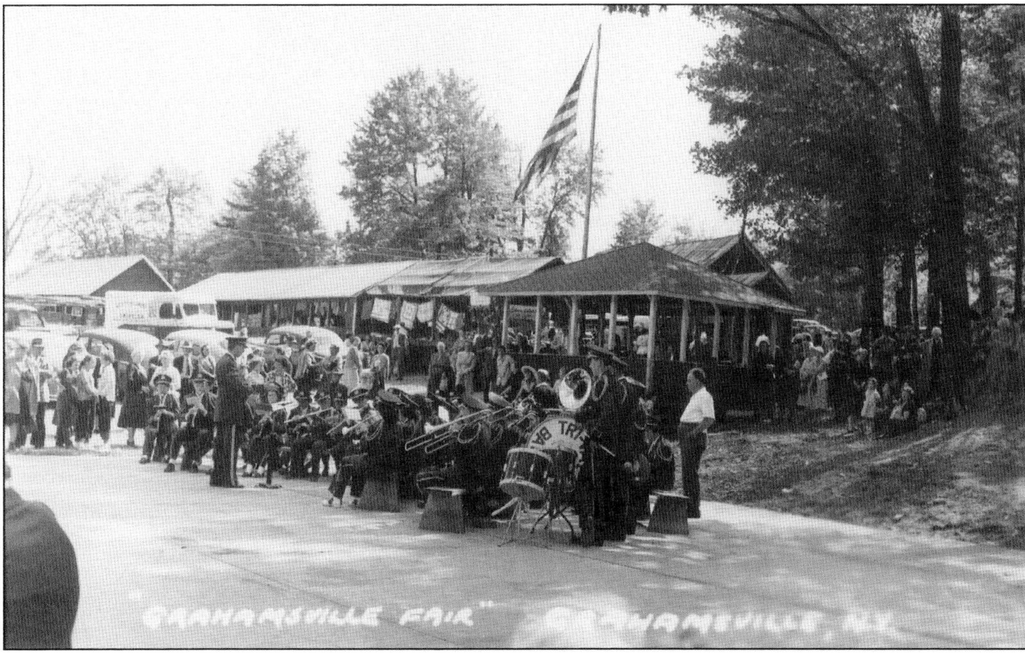

This snapshot of the Grahamsville Fair was taken around 1936. The hems on ladies' dresses have risen, and the car styles have changed, but it is still an agricultural fair at the time of this photograph. A certain formality of dress remains. Note the uniforms of the brass band members. Men are wearing suits and ties, and many women are still wearing dresses.

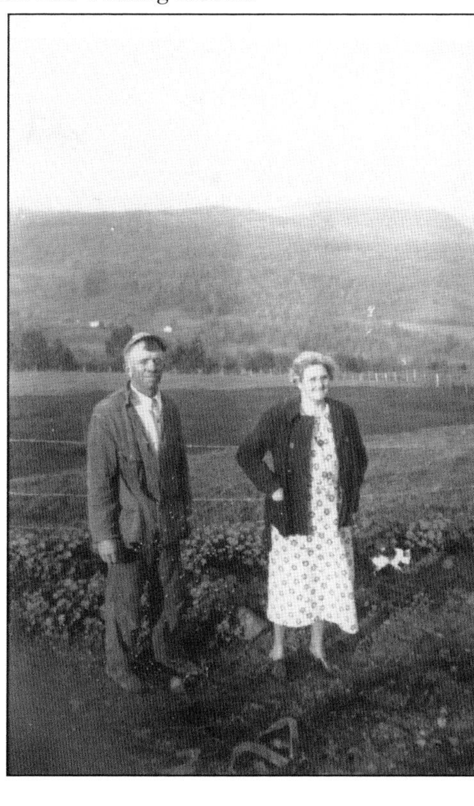

John and Ann George owned a 300-acre farm on the side of South Hill facing the Rondout Reservoir. Their address was Eureka. This photograph was taken in 1938. The farm was bought in 1868 by John George's father-in-law. According to some earlier records, the house was located at an elevation of 500 feet above the reservoir. The view included Peekamoose, Slide, Table, VanWyck, and Denman Mountains; Red Hill; and the Shawangunks. The road going up to the property is called John George Road to this very day. (Cathy Keator collection.)

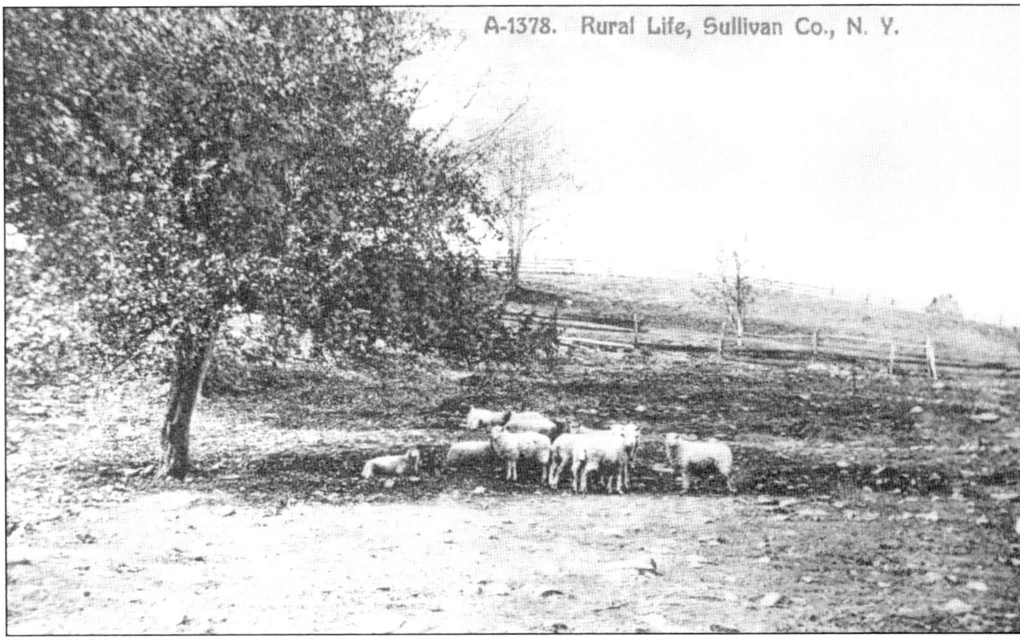

Sheep were an early agricultural staple in the area, and researchers say that sheep are documented on first farms throughout the area. Mutton Hill near the Neversink Reservoir is an example where farm usage translated to an area name. A weekly newspaper in nearby Liberty, New York, reported on June 3, 1892, that Neversink raised more sheep than any other town in Sullivan County.

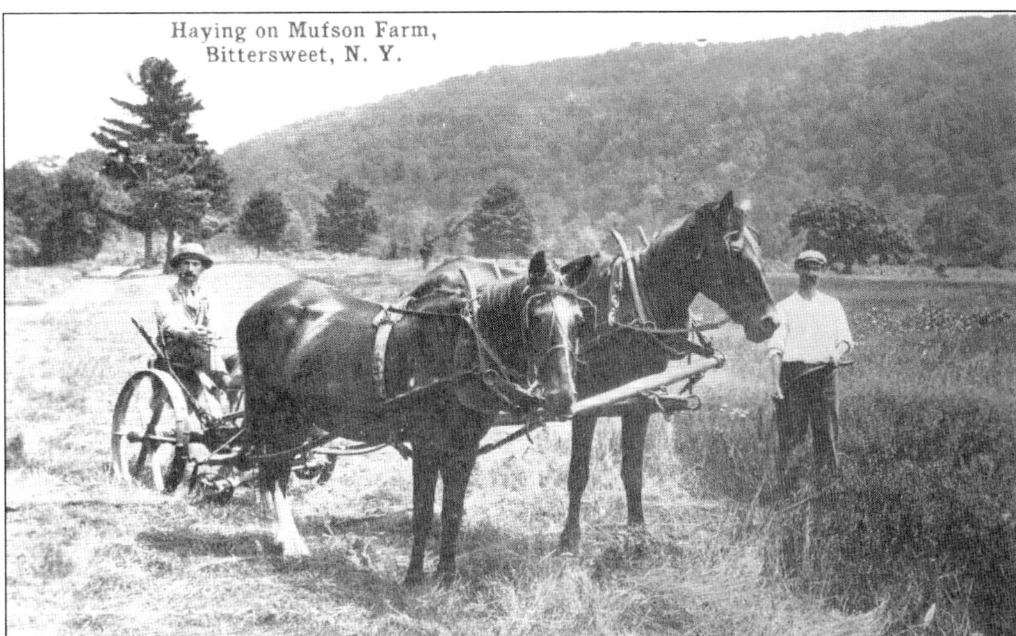

An old-fashioned mowing machine pulled by a team of horses brought relief to many a farmer who had cut hay by hand. Henry Sackett is standing to the right of the team holding a scythe, which some farmers used up to the 1950s. Mufson Farm in Bittersweet joined other properties that were taken for the building of the Neversink Reservoir.

Pictured here around 1960, the Edna Rudolph farm on Red Hill has been owned by the Bob Richards family for a number of years. They are full-time residents but do not farm. (Helen Erts DuBois Collection.)

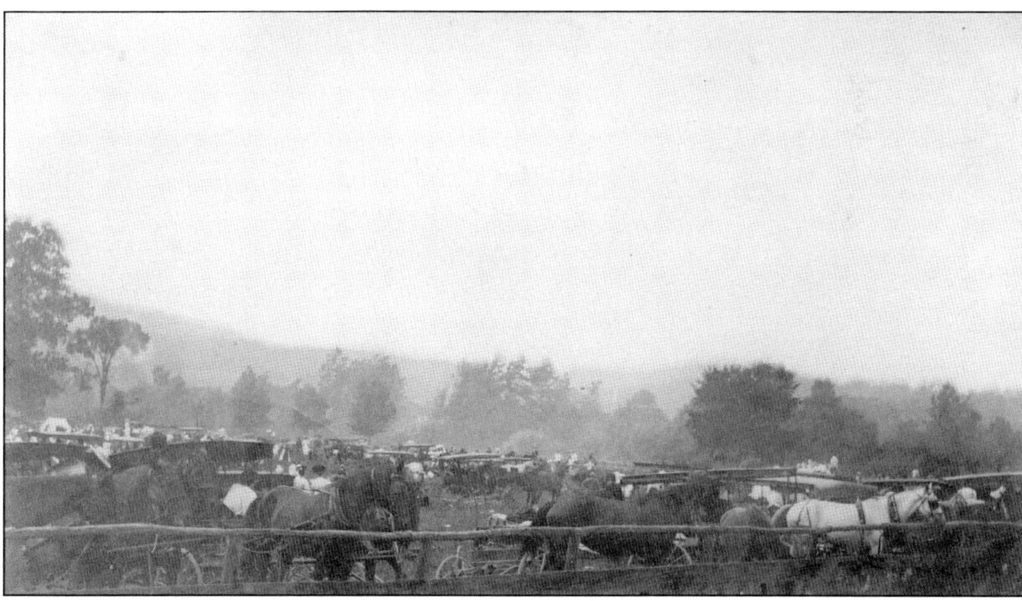

Note the hot-air balloon drifting over the parking field full of horses and carriages. This is the Grahamsville Fair around 1905. (Virginia Caldwell Bishop Collection.)

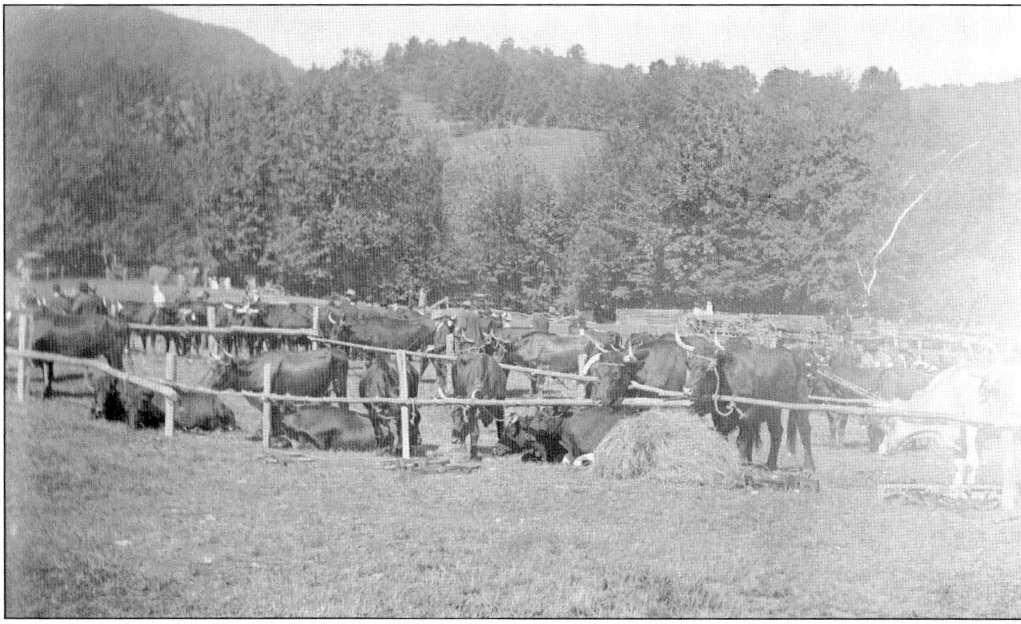

Photographer A.V. Porter of nearby Ellenville, New York, took this photograph titled "The Cattle at the Fair." Cattle brought for judging would have to be given food and water, and these animals can be seen munching on a pile of hay. It often took people a whole day to bring their livestock to the fair for judging. There were no trucks or roads suitable to transport livestock, and their owners walked them all the way to the fair. (Richard George Murray Collection.)

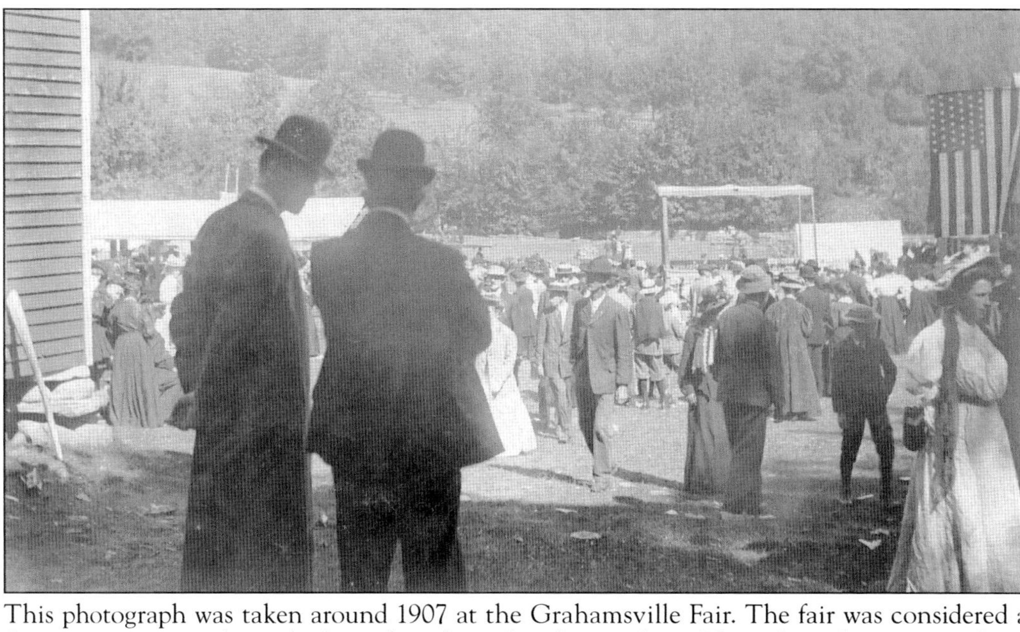

This photograph was taken around 1907 at the Grahamsville Fair. The fair was considered a festive occasion, and people dressed in their churchgoing best. Those long dresses must have stirred up a lot of dust when it was dry and a lot of mud when it was wet. This originally sepia-toned photograph was taken by A.V. Porter of Ellenville. Photographs like this were preserved with pigment from the sepia cuttlefish, which was believed to help preserve the image. (Richard George Murray Collection.)

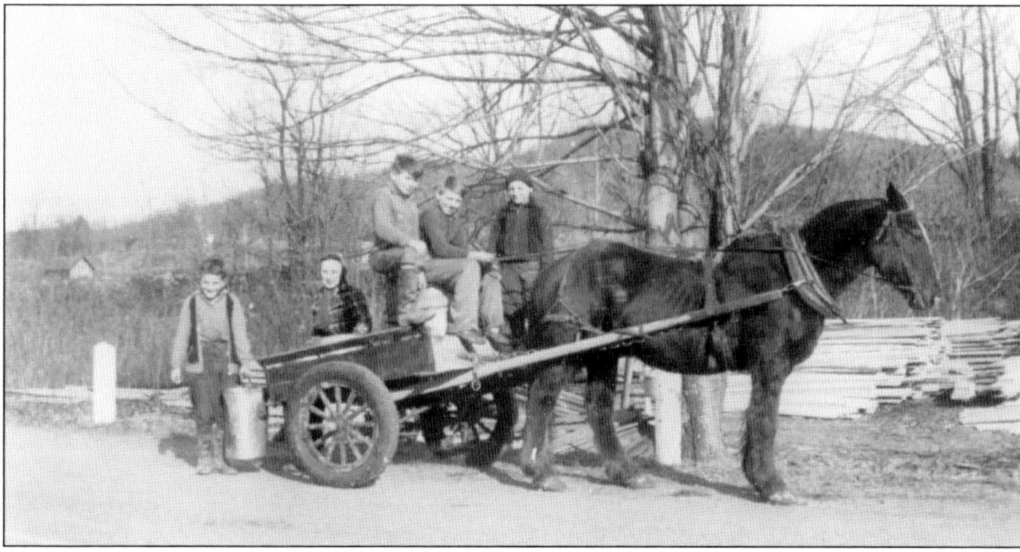

These youngsters were collecting sap from the maple trees in the springtime and are pictured on the Clarence Slater property at the intersection of New York State Route 55 and Pepacton Hollow Road. From left to right are Clinton Hamilton; Helen Tweedy; and Lee, Bruce, and Jack Denman. Somewhere nearby, a big pan of sap is boiling down over a wood fire to make maple syrup. (Denman Family Collection.)

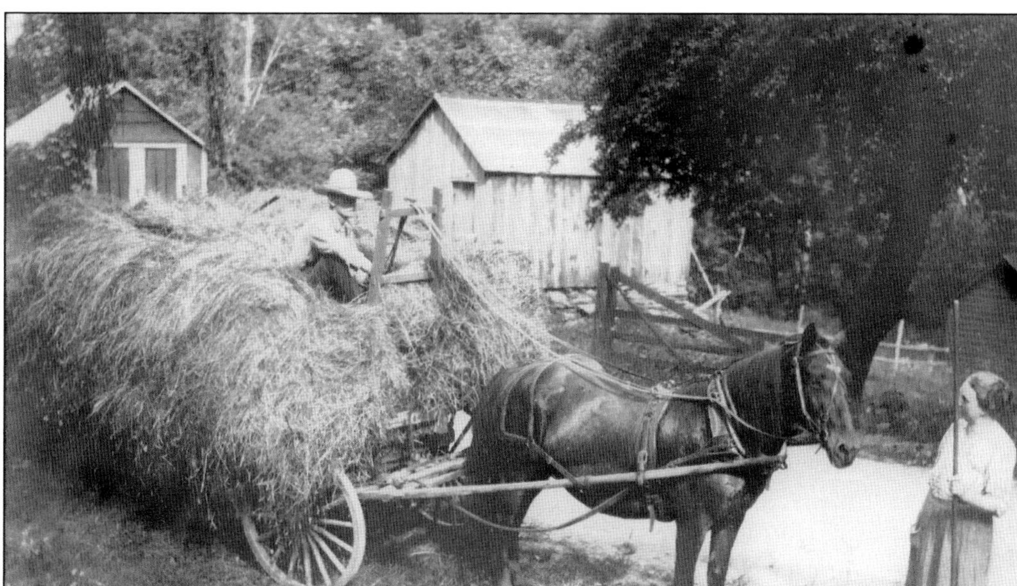

These people are haying in Sundown, New York, with a wagon pulled by a single horse. The pair is identified as William Weil and Mary Sheeley Weil, pictured on September 24, 1927.

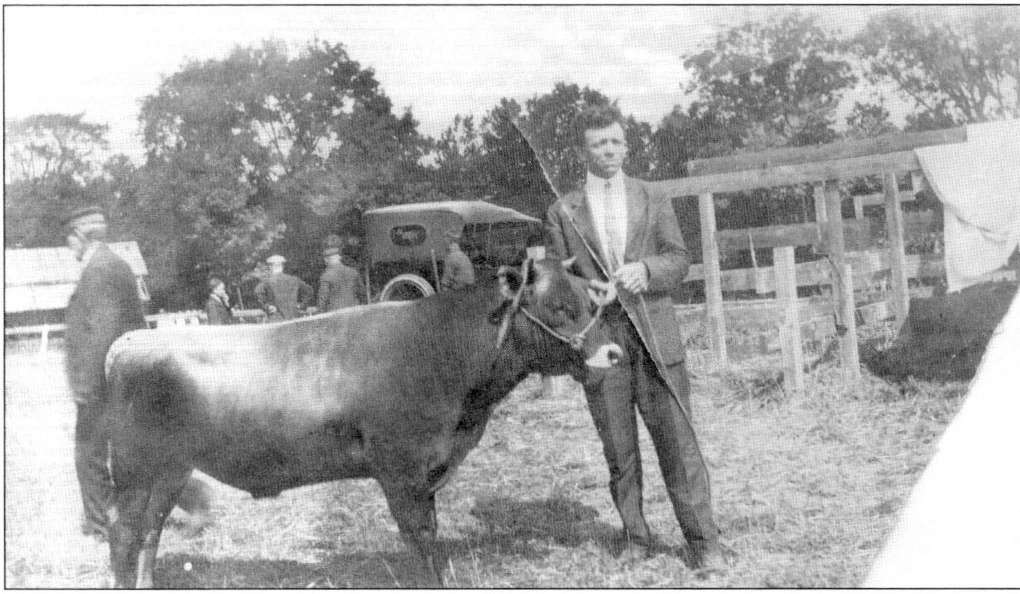

John George is seen showing off a prized livestock, possibly at the Grahamsville Fair. John and his two brothers, William and Herbert, all grew up on nearby Red Hill. (Cathy Keator collection.)

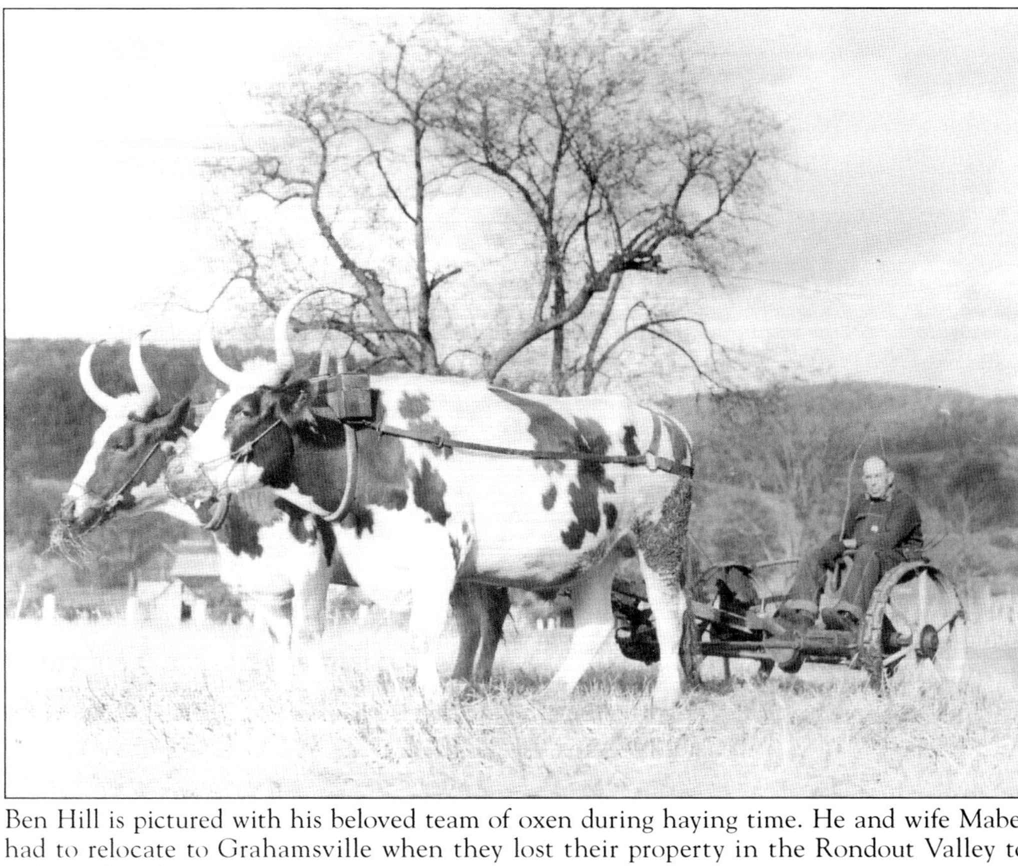

Ben Hill is pictured with his beloved team of oxen during haying time. He and wife Mabel had to relocate to Grahamsville when they lost their property in the Rondout Valley to eminent domain.

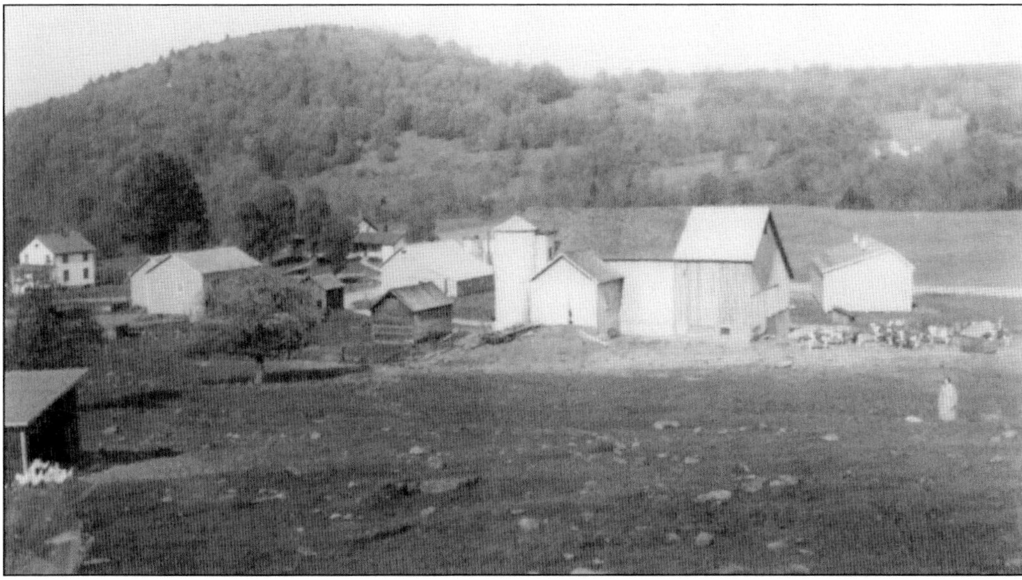

The Robert Many farm of Grahamsville was part of the Montela Local of the Dairymen's League Cooperative Association that was formed April 28, 1923. The Many farm eventually became known as a poultry farm, and it changed hands several times. In 2013, the Town of Neversink was able to acquire the use of enough land from the Many farm to reestablish the Little League field that was flooded out in Lows Corners.

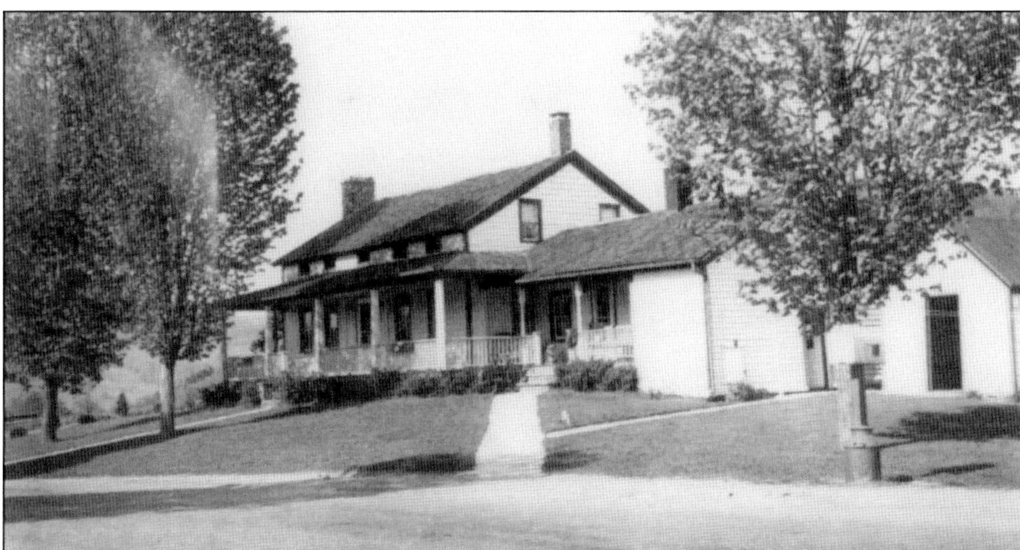

The entire farm totaled 140 acres. Robert Many's father had purchased it around 1900. In the 1920s, Many was supervisor of the Town of Neversink and was active in many farm-related groups. His wife, Elthea, was the local 4-H Club leader. When these photographs were taken, he had a herd of 50 grade and registered Guernsey cattle, a flock of 2,500 white leghorn hens, and 5,000 chicks.

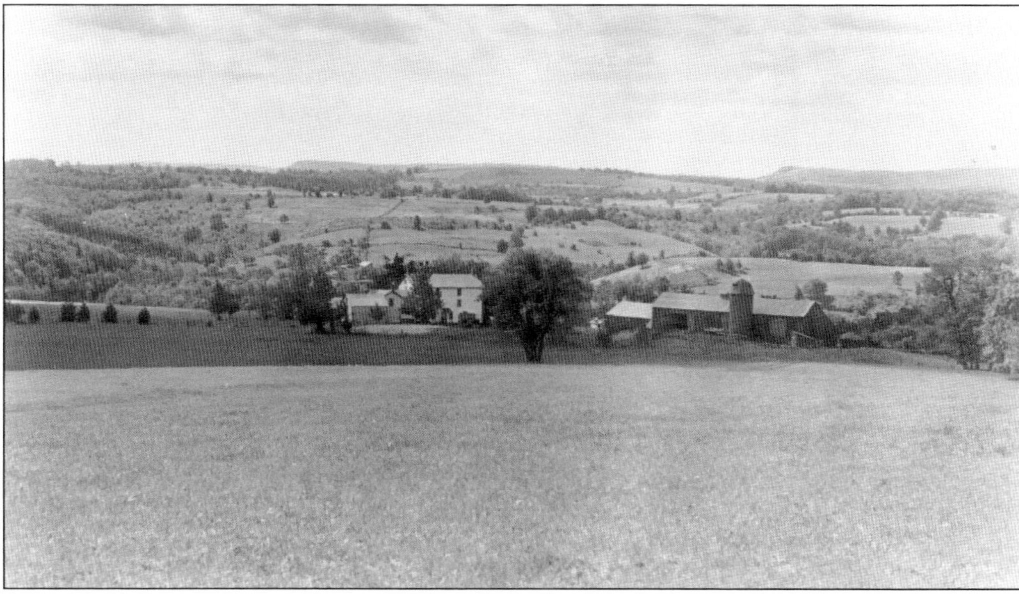

The William and Sarah Grant Denman farm overlooked what is now the Neversink Reservoir. This photograph faces the direction of Liberty, New York. When the land was taken for the building of the reservoir, the house was divided from the barns by the newly located New York State Route 55. The Denman home was known as Mount Pleasant to summer boarders who came to the country to escape city heat. (Denman Family Collection.)

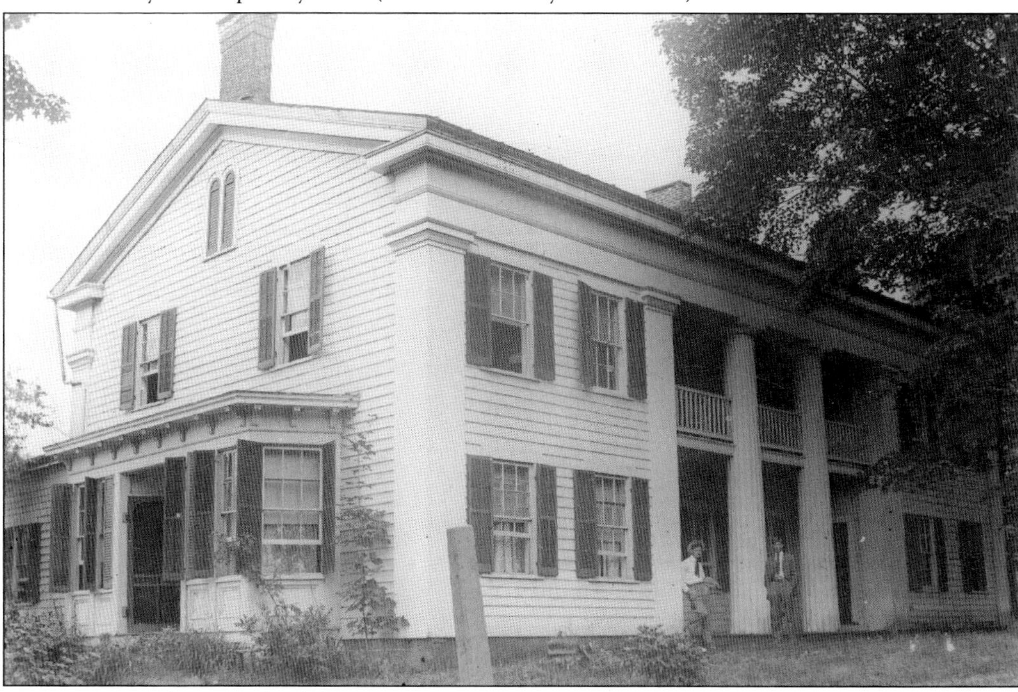

Here is a 1900 photograph of the LaMoree House when it was owned by the Erath family. Several of the Erath sons are standing in the front. The house was later owned by Dr. Karl Messinger. It sometimes functioned as a hotel, and it is rumored that during Prohibition there was a speakeasy located in its rear section. (TVM.)

Six

People

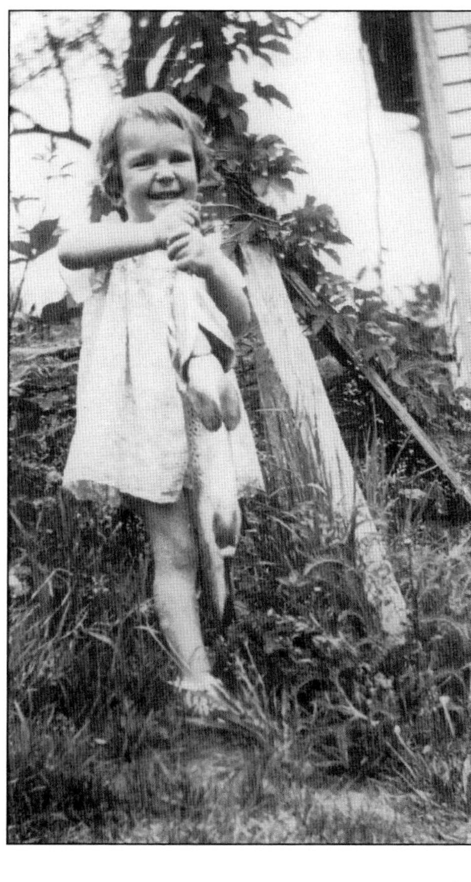

"Alberta with big fish" is the caption on the back of this photograph. Alberta George is shown with a trout almost as big as she was that she caught it in 1935 or 1936. The trout came from the section of the Upper Rondout Creek often known as the Sundown Creek, near her home. Her parents were Herbert and Esther George, and their family home in Sundown, New York, was sold in 2013. (Herbert and Esther George collection.)

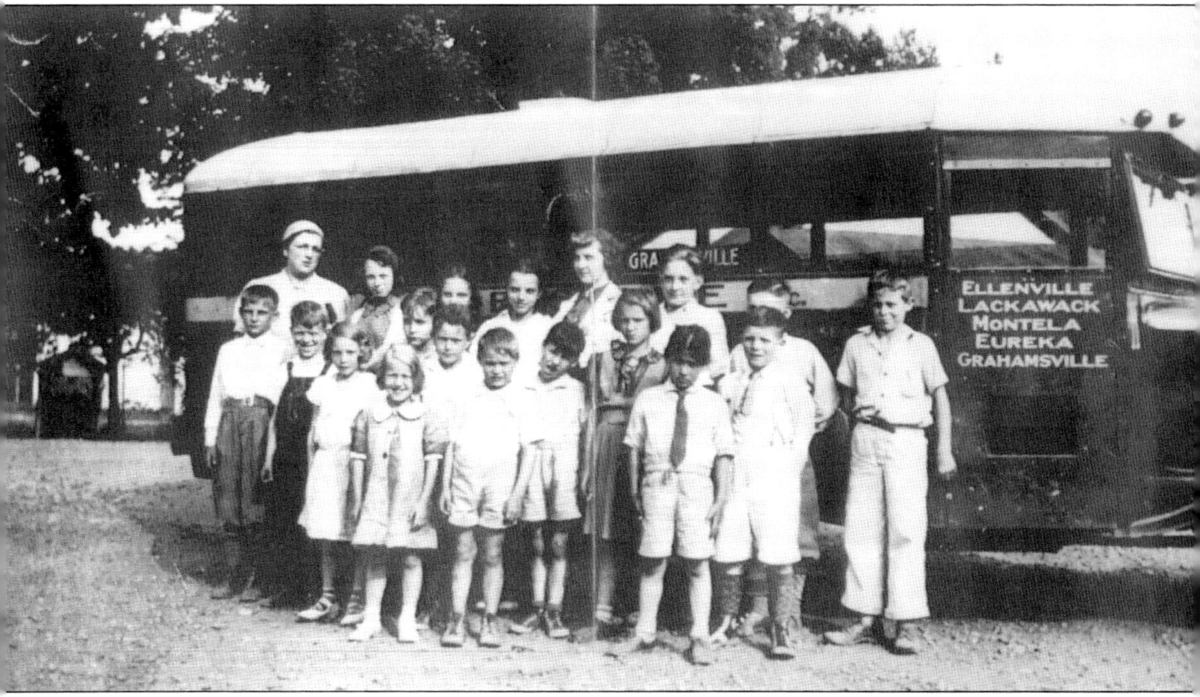

Madelene Hornbeck Adams is seen here with her students from the one-room school at Montela on an outing. This bus ran between Ellenville, Lackawack, Montela, Eureka, and Grahamsville. This photograph dates to shortly before the valley was taken by eminent domain.

Here is Evelyn Hill of Eureka on her first day of school in 1916. The daughter of Ben and Mabel Hill, she was six years old at the time of this photograph. She grew up, married Jack Huntsberger, and became a teacher in area one-room schools. She was dearly loved by all her students.

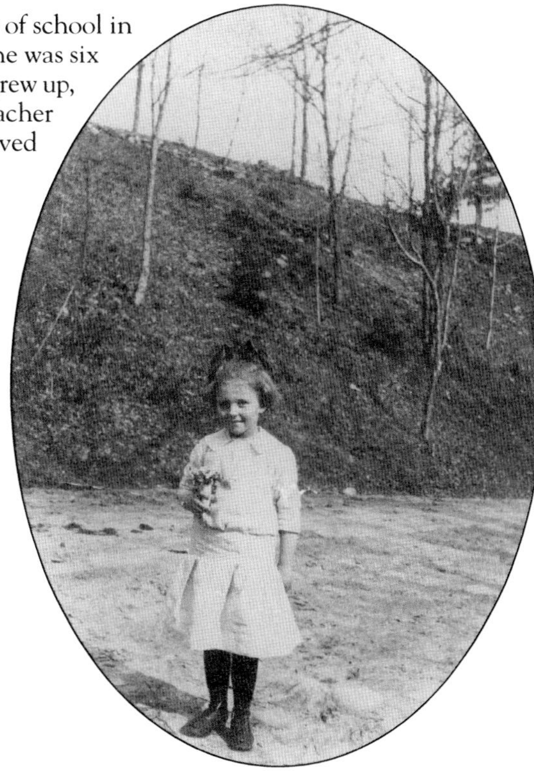

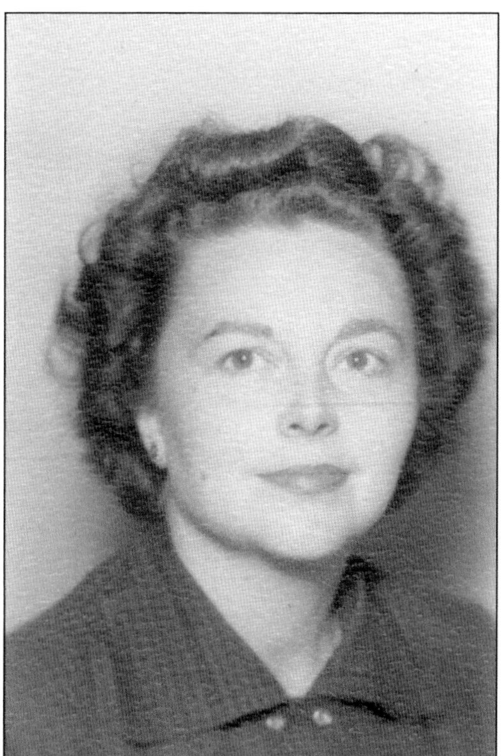

Evelyn Hill Huntsberger went on to work at the new Tri-Valley Central School administrative office. She was secretary to W. Eugene Ross, the first supervising principal. Evelyn was multitalented. She was one of the early members of the Alchemy Club along with her mother, Mabel Hill, and Inez Gridley. Many a young couple asked her play the organ at their wedding. The list of her accomplishments could go on and on.

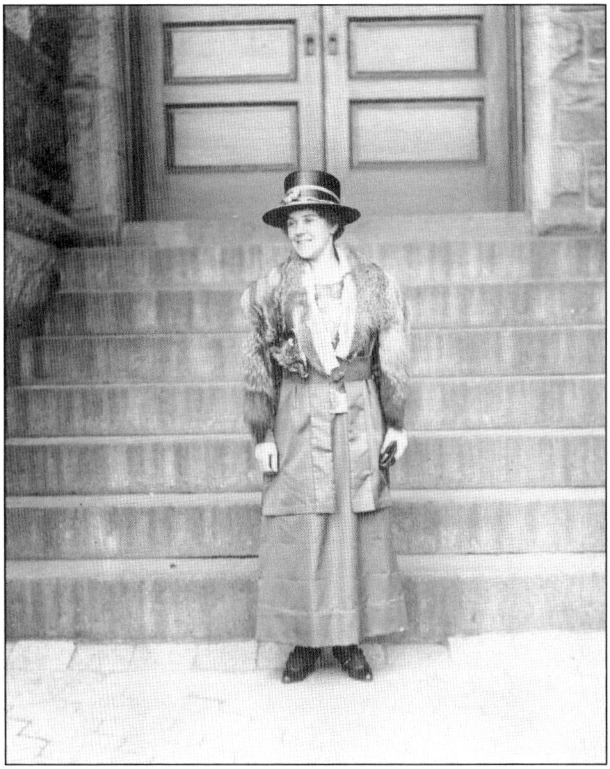

Harriet Reynolds Smith also came from Eureka. She is shown on the steps of Friends School in Baltimore, where she was teaching in 1916, wearing a red fox fur that was given to her by her father.

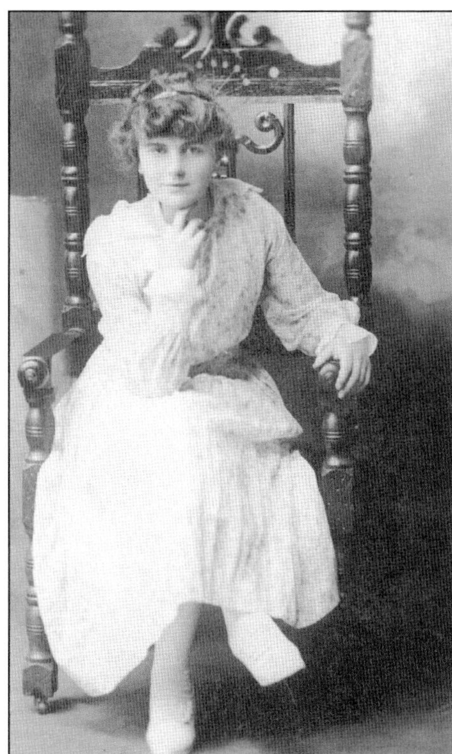

Pictured here is Esther George of Red Hill. The photograph was taken in 1917. Esther was born on July 9, 1897, the daughter of Andrew and Juliana George. She attended a one-room school and then went on to high school at Liberty, where she had to board to attend classes. There was no high school in the towns of Denning or Neversink in those days, and there were also no buses to take Red Hill students to any school.

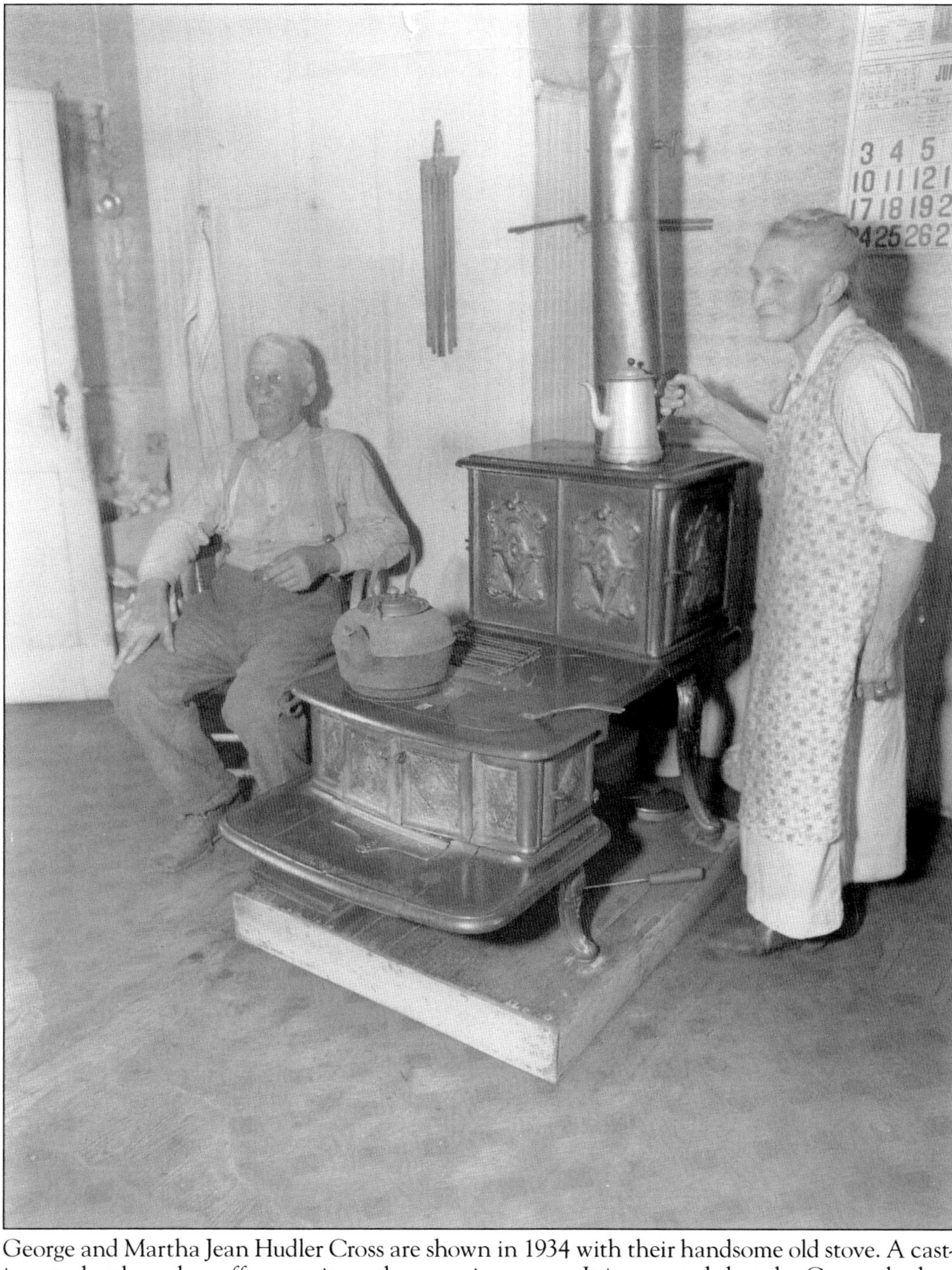

George and Martha Jean Hudler Cross are shown in 1934 with their handsome old stove. A cast-iron teakettle and a coffee pot sit on the warming ovens. It is reported that the Crosses had no children but were generous enough to help several local young people attain a higher education. (Denman family collection.)

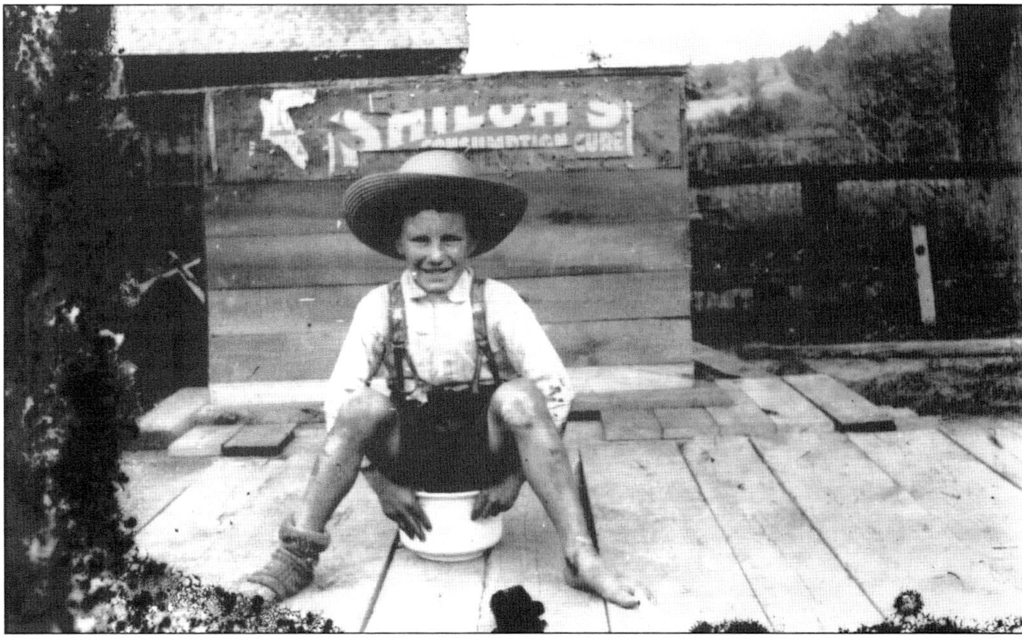

This impish-looking youngster hams it up for the camera as he shows how to use a "thunder mug," as chamber pots were sometimes called, in this Raymond Erath glass plate negative. (Note the faded sign for Shilohs tobacco in the background.) Chamber pots and outhouses have become relics of the past.

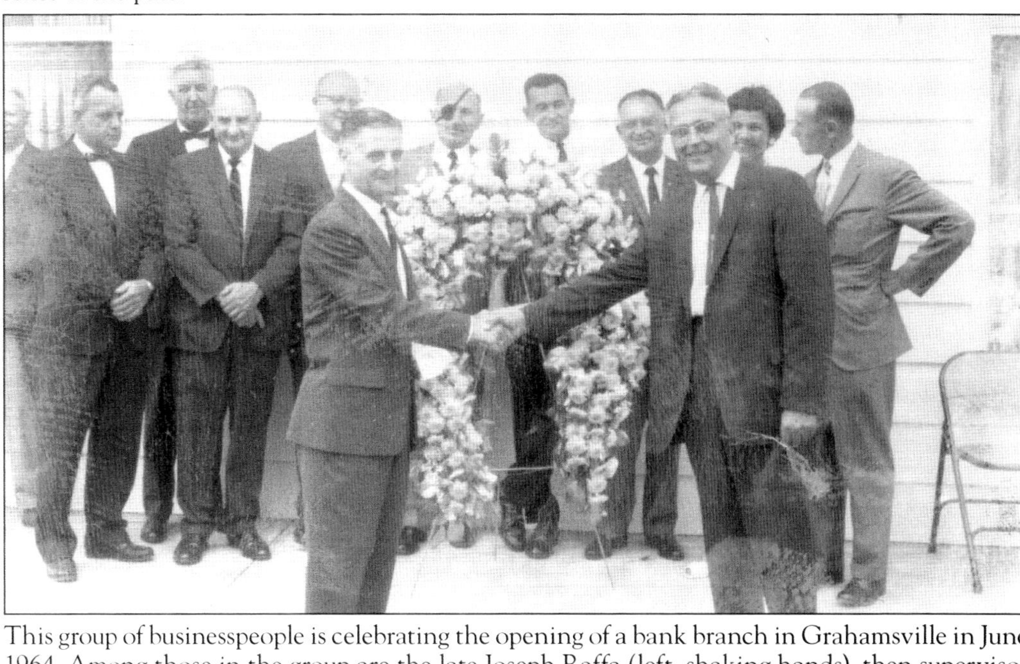

This group of businesspeople is celebrating the opening of a bank branch in Grahamsville in June 1964. Among those in the group are the late Joseph Raffa (left, shaking hands), then supervisor of the Town of Neversink, and Frank Travis (third from left), who was one of the bank's first employees along with Barbara DeWire. The property was originally the William North residence. In August 2013, the bank—then known as Bank of America—closed its branch doors permanently. A new bank, Catskill Hudson, plans to open in 2014.

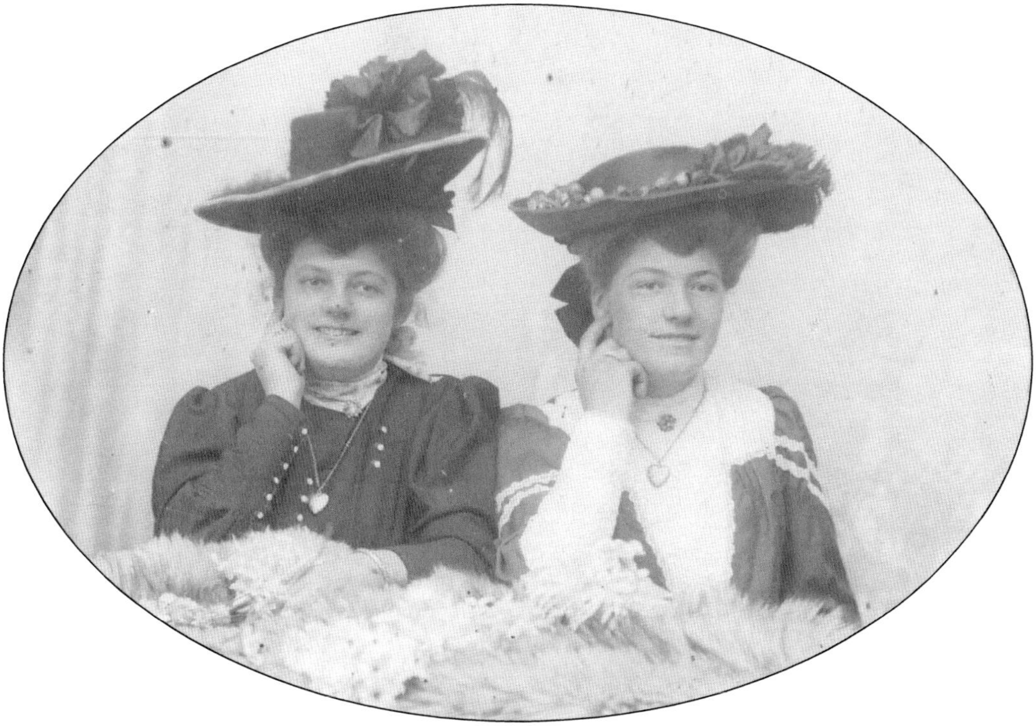
Ellen Yonker and Cora Eck present a delightful picture with their stylish hats.

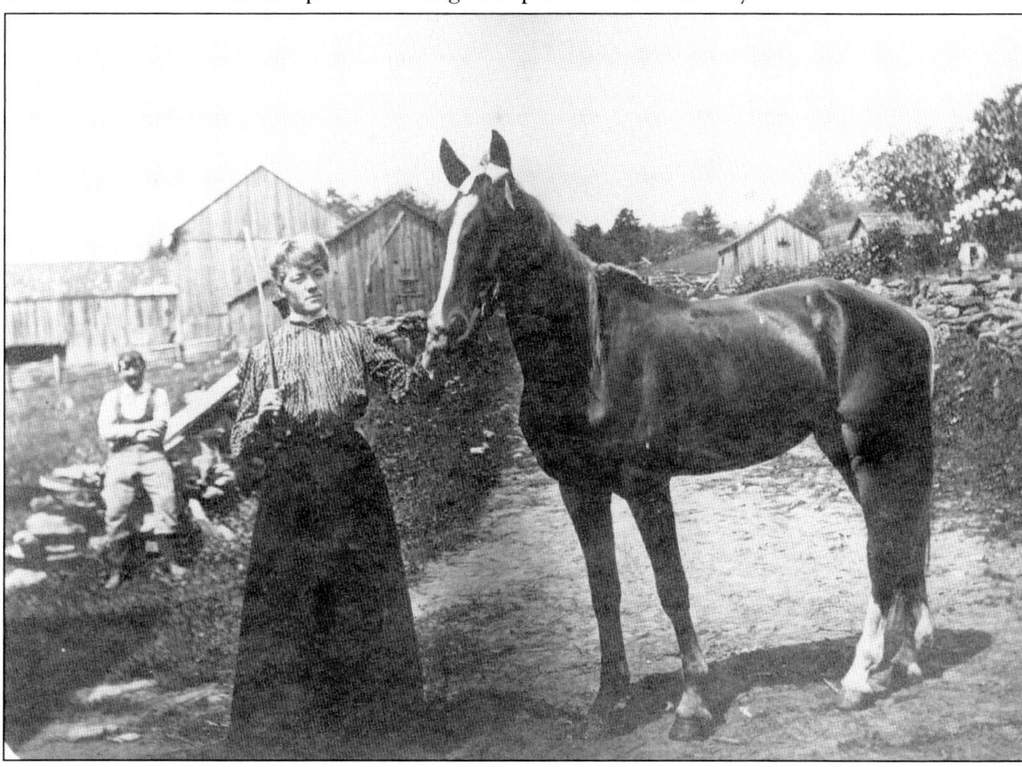
Cora Eck seems quite the horsewoman while "Uncle Lew" Eck looks on.

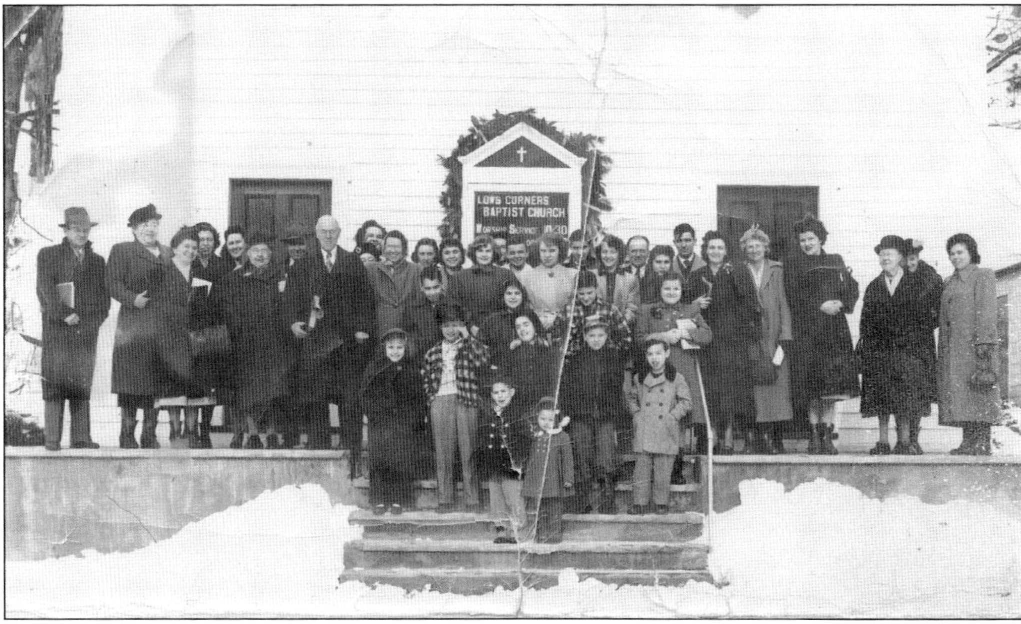

The Lows Corners Baptist Church was well attended in the days when Reverend Harris was the minister. The photograph shows a cheery group of church attendees even with piles of snow on the ground. The case was very different a few years ago when the church disbanded because of a lack of attendance. The church records were turned over to the Time and the Valleys Museum, where they are part of the research room records.

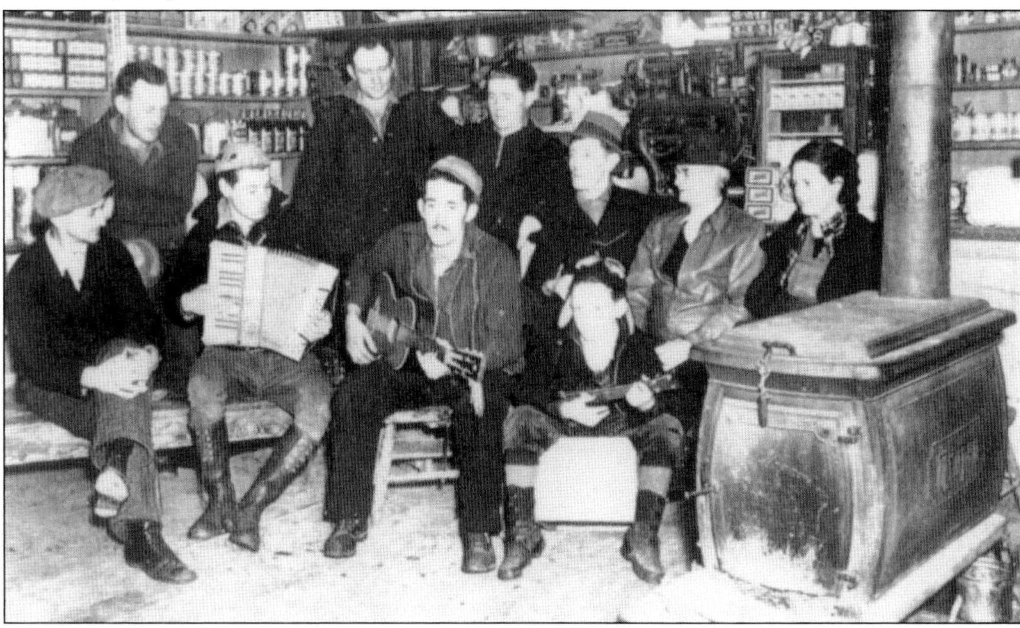

This musical group is gathered around the potbelly stove in the John Richard Store at Montela. John Richard was the last postmaster in Montela before the Rondout Reservoir was built and nothing but memories were left of the community. The group includes John Richard, Earl Terwilliger, Ed Connor, Joe Irwin, Lawrence Smith, Wilson Connor, Charlie Carlile, Esther Richard, and Karl Richard. (Karl Richard Collection.)

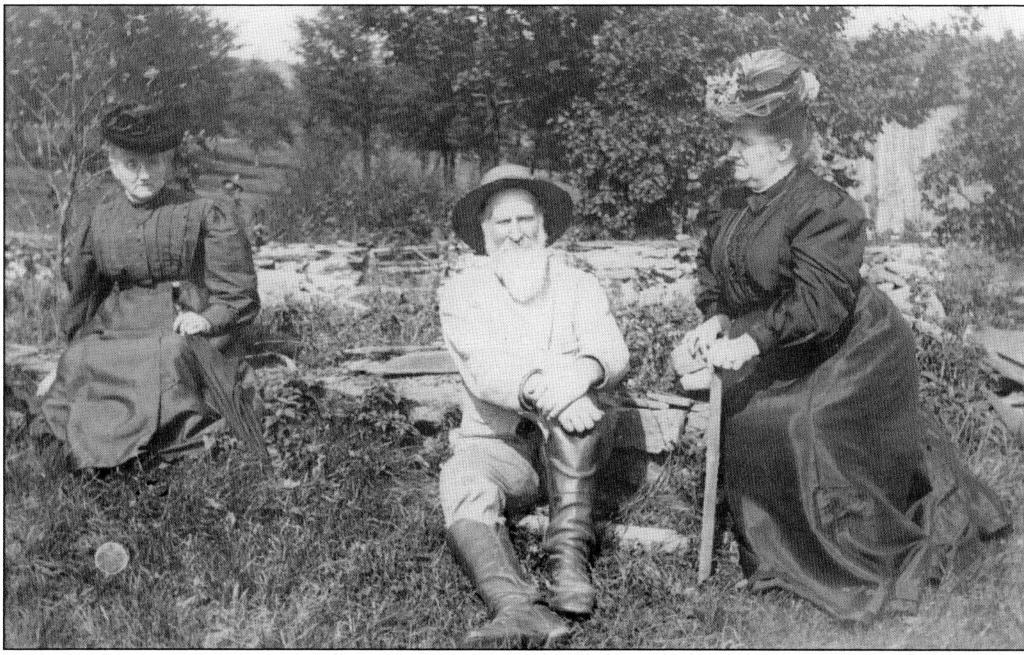

John Curry and perhaps his wife and another unidentified woman are photographed at the Curry Farm on Thunder Hill. Curry's farm would later be known as Prima Farm or the Concord Farm. John and his wife, the former Martha Smith, were the parents of Riley Curry of Grahamsville, who lived to be 105.

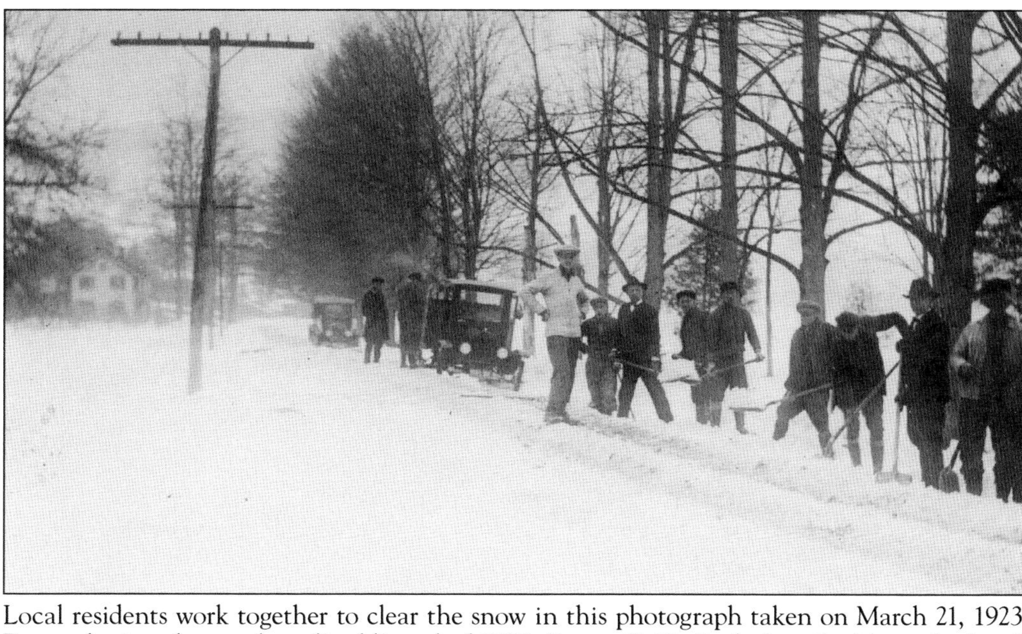

Local residents work together to clear the snow in this photograph taken on March 21, 1923. Remembering the much-earlier blizzard of 1888, Emery B. TerBush described how the locals worked together in that storm. According to him, there was a drift 40 feet deep across the road. "We started tunneling through. When we reached the center we heard someone on the other side tunneling toward us. When the opening was finished, I ran back to our place, got the horse and rode through the tunnel on horseback."

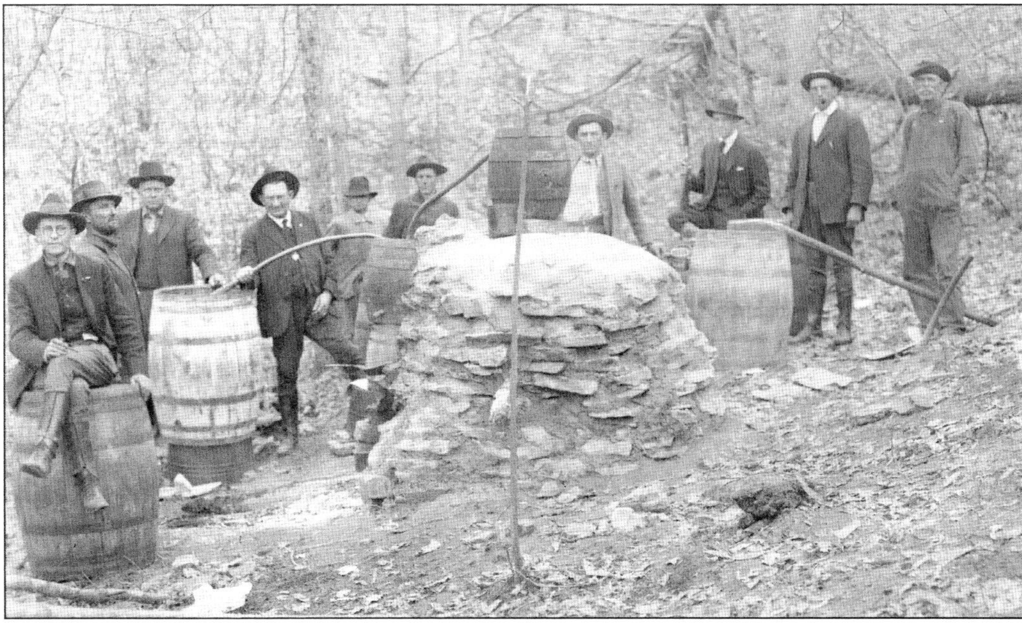

National Prohibition was in effect from January 1920 to April 1933. These dapper Prohibition agents located a still near Grahamsville and were quick to show off their find with photographs. A fascinating new story has recently surfaced that indicates that bottled booze was smuggled into the area from Canada. The banned liquid was buried in barrels of flour that came in from Canada on the train. (Denman Family Collection.)

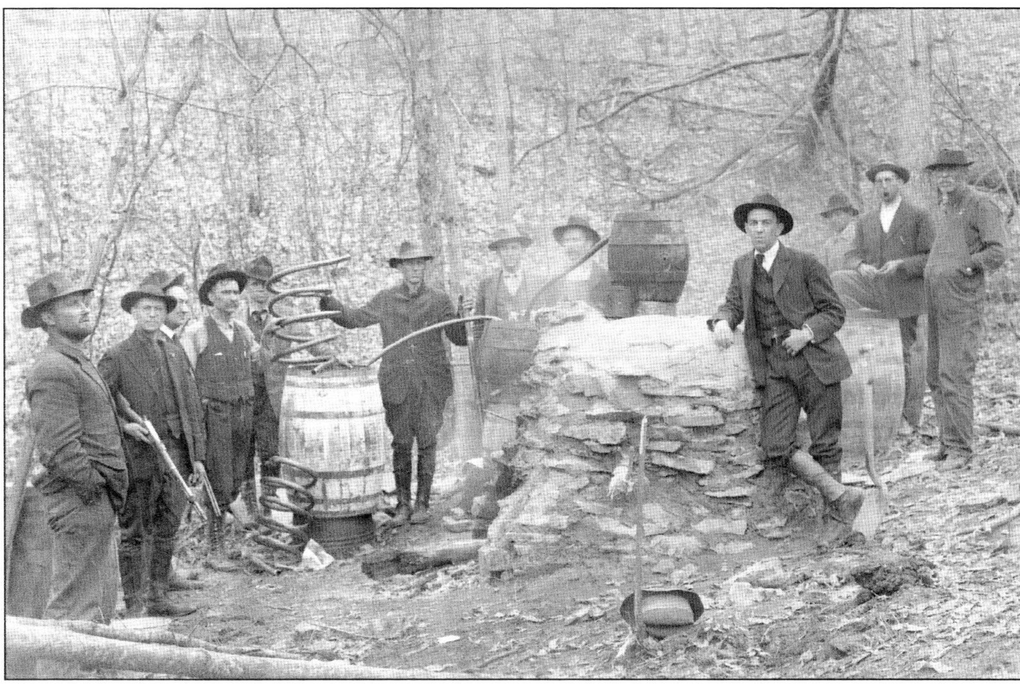

These Prohibition agents look quite satisfied. Only a few years after Prohibition ended, local residents voted to keep the town of Neversink dry, and it remains so to this very day. (Denman Family Collection.)

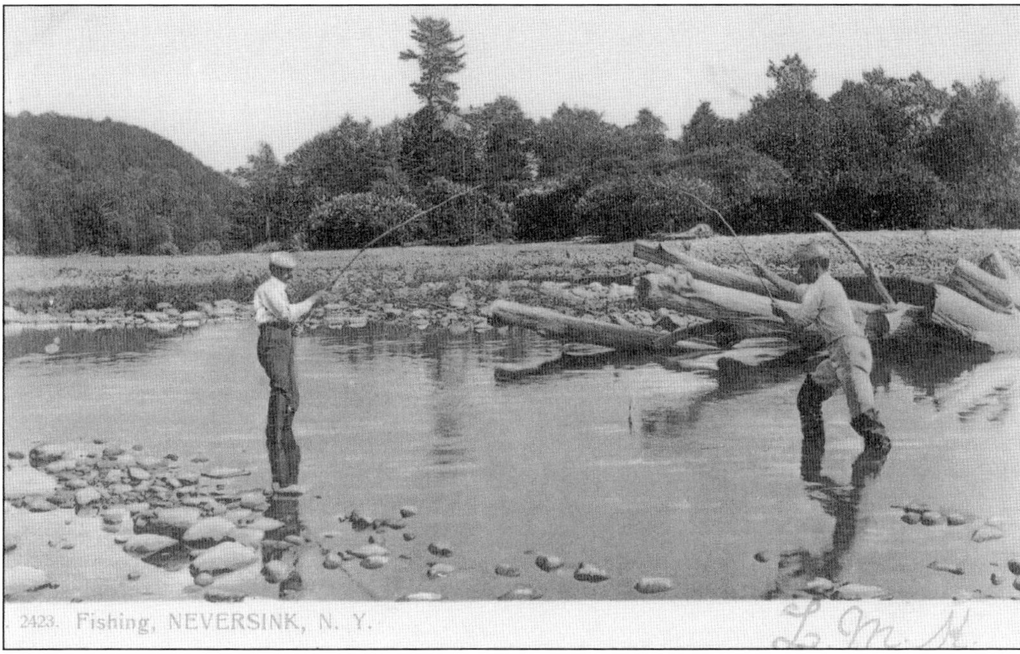

Early fishing was mostly done for food and may have been with a worm or other earth creature on a hook of sorts. Fly-fishing for sport is said to have been at its heyday during the Depression years in this country. It is unusual to see an early postcard image of fishing such as this. This was from an art series by M. Van Keuren for his store between 1907 and 1915. (Carol Smythe Collection.)

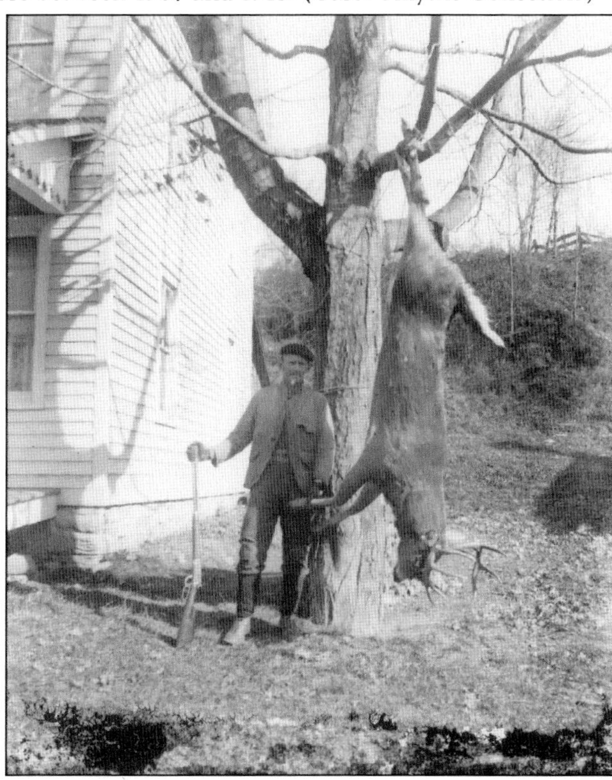

Look at the rack on this buck pictured around 1905. The hunter has done himself proud, bringing home food for the table and a nice set of antlers, too. Hunting was so important to the early residents. Deer were not always plentiful in those days, but as with all game, there were times of plenty. (Raymond Erath Collection.)

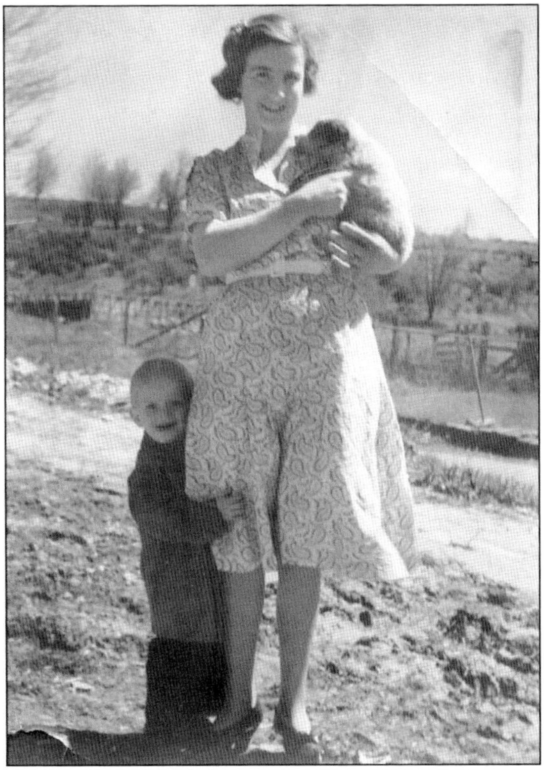

Mary Cypert Mentnech and her son James Mentnech are photographed here around 1941 or 1942. Mary and husband Arthur were displaced from their place in the Neversink Valley because of the building of the reservoir. Mary was interviewed in 2013 about those days; she passed away in August of the same year. (James Mentnech family collection.)

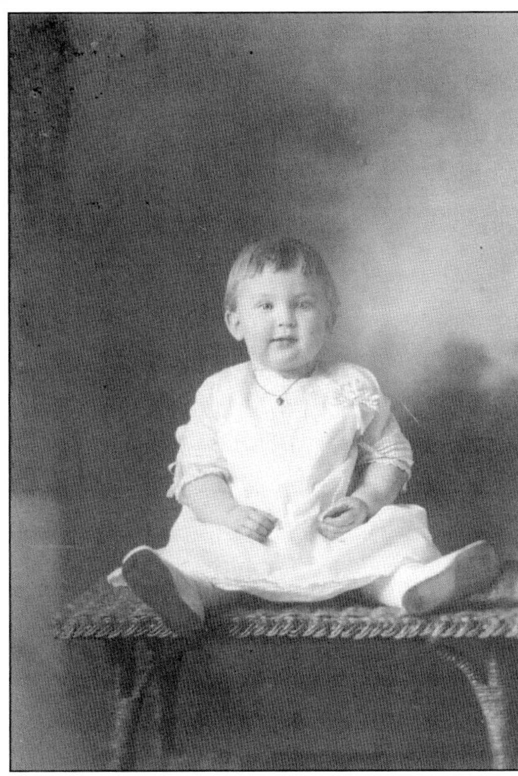

Here is Esther Louise Dierfelter when she was one year old in the early 20th century. She grew up in the Eureka area of the flooded Rondout Valley. (Virginia Caldwell Bishop Collection.)

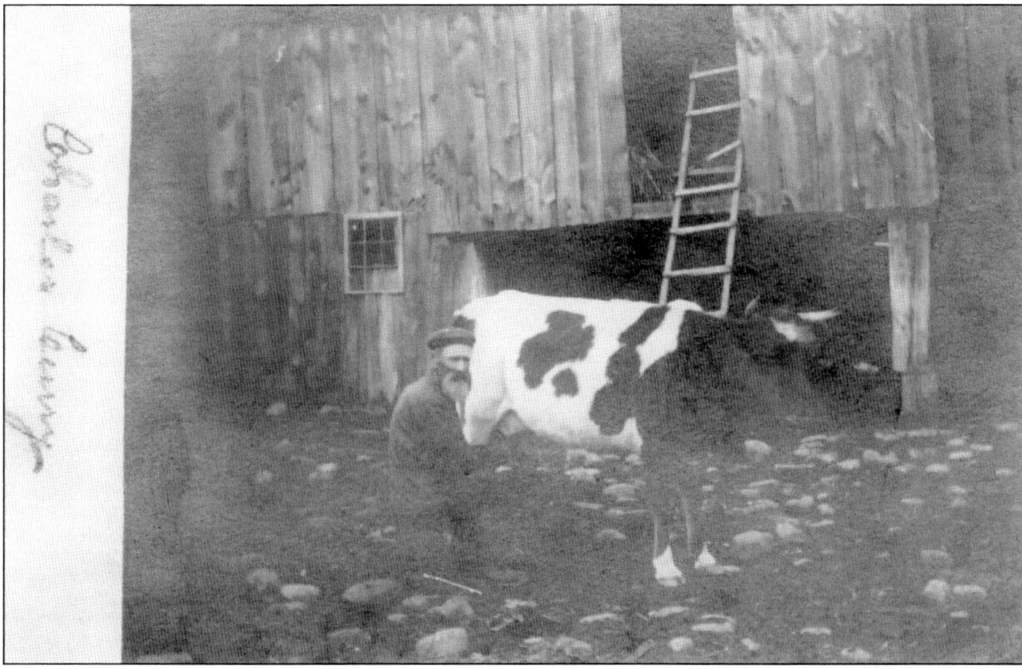

The year is 1908, and the man milking the cow is Charles Curry. It is not too often that one sees an old photograph of someone milking a cow! Charlie was a very important part of the Grahamsville community, and there are many who still remember Curry's Hardware Store. (Richard George-Murray Collection.)

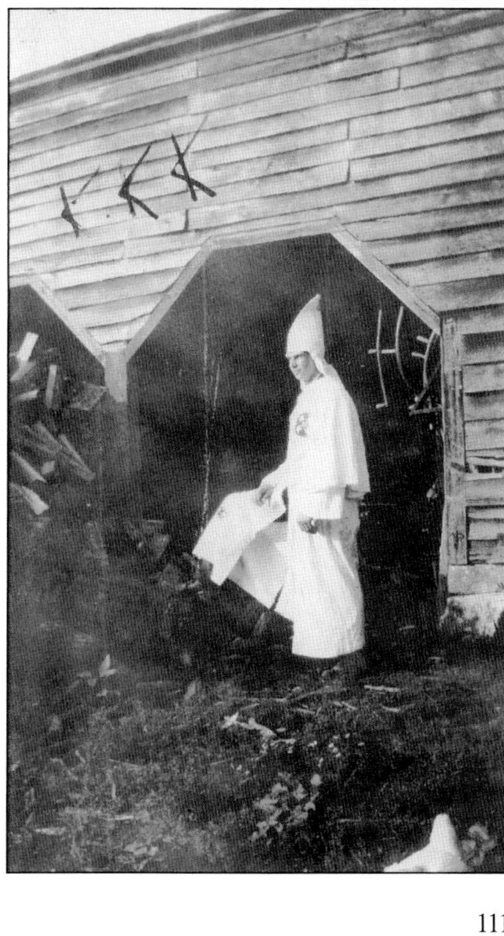

This photograph was taken locally around 1925. The *Grahamsville Weekly* that same year published a little story, "Fiery Cross Burnt Near Neversink." The body of the story said, "It seems that Neversink has not been forgot by the Klan, as on last Friday evening a large cross was burned on the hill back of the schoolhouse. Several shots of dynamite were fired."

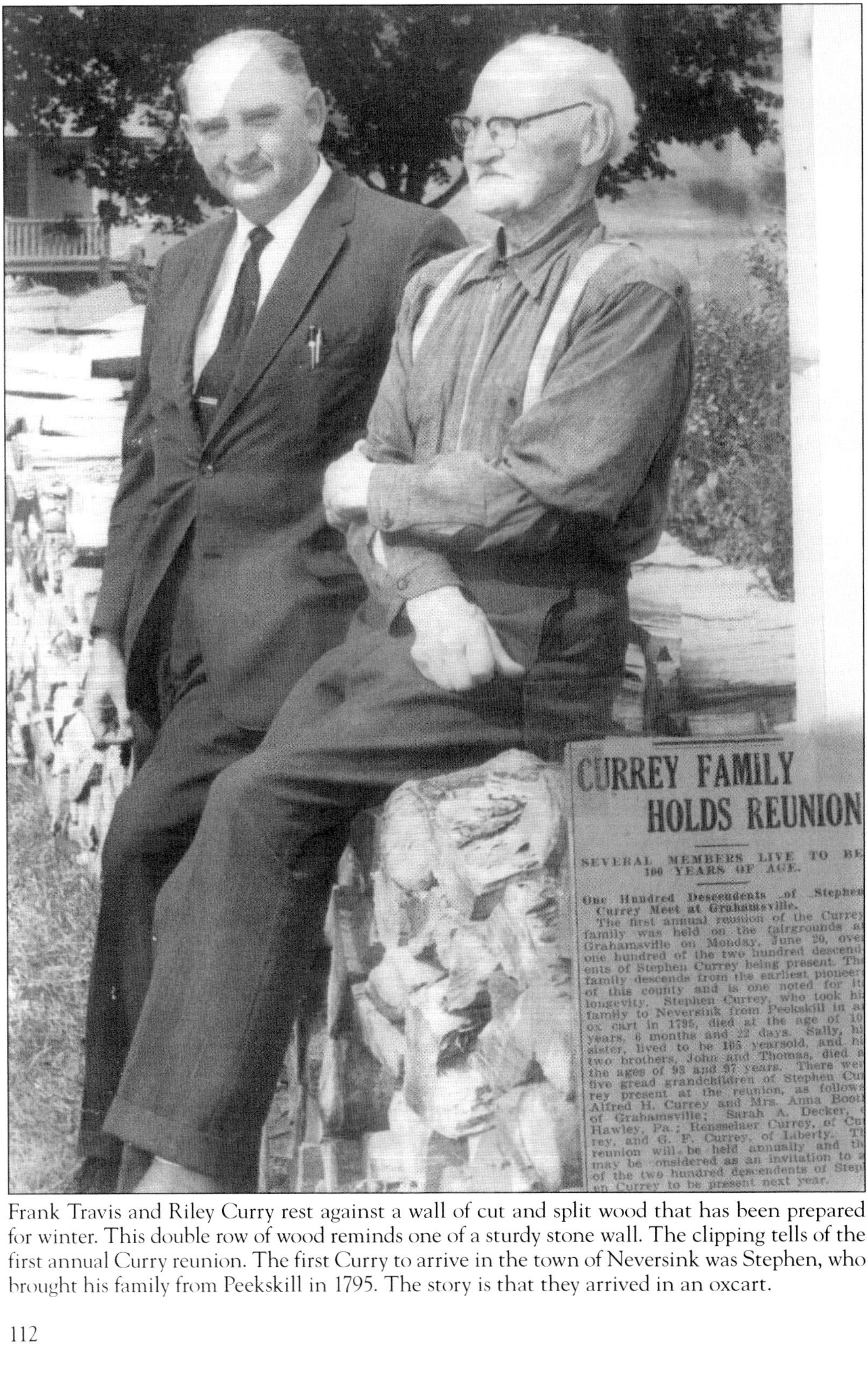

Frank Travis and Riley Curry rest against a wall of cut and split wood that has been prepared for winter. This double row of wood reminds one of a sturdy stone wall. The clipping tells of the first annual Curry reunion. The first Curry to arrive in the town of Neversink was Stephen, who brought his family from Peekskill in 1795. The story is that they arrived in an oxcart.

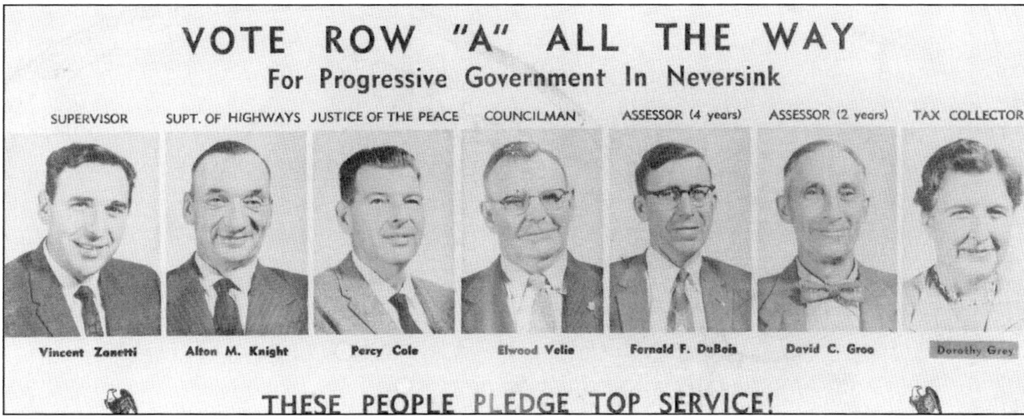

This piece of campaign material is for those running for town government in the Township of Neversink, or the town board, as it is known. Interestingly, it is a blotter, which means it predates the ballpoint pen.

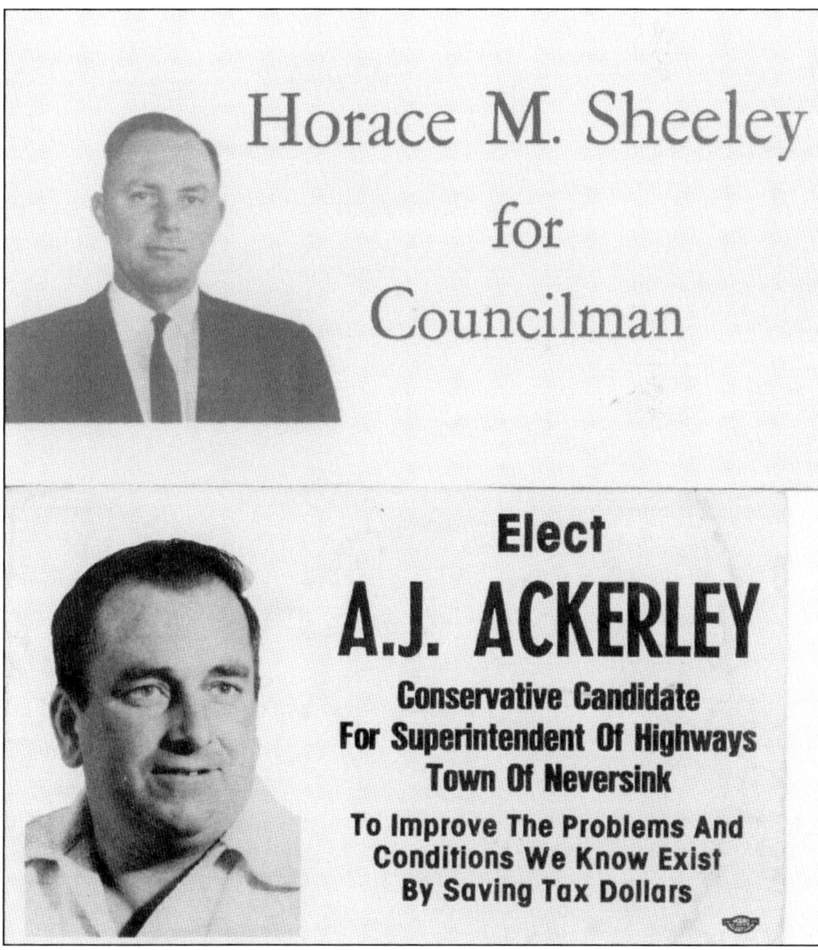

Here are two more candidates for the town board—Horace M. Sheeley is advertising on a card that is blank on the other side and A.J. Ackerley is advertising on the front of a card that features directions for using the Heimlich maneuver on the reverse.

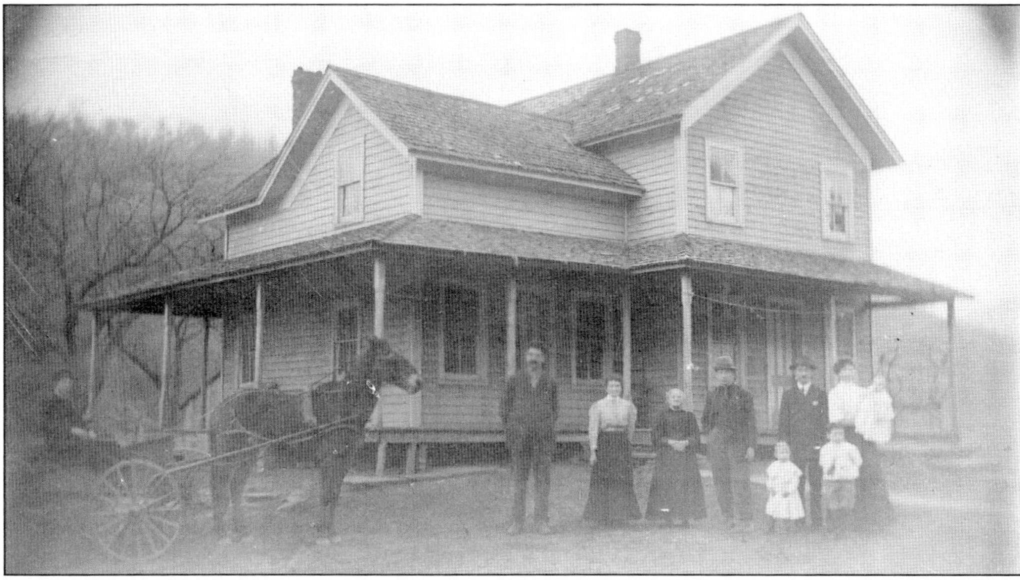

This photograph is well labeled: "My grandmother's home at Ladleton, NY about 1912 (with porch). Harry B. Cole with horse; his father DuBois Cole, my step grandfather; Augusta Ann Cole, my grandmother; her mother, Elmira Crawford; Daniel S. Sagendorf, my uncle; Leslie H. Sagendorf (child), my brother; Frank L. Sagendorf, my father; William C Waizmann, my half-brother; Lizzie H W Sagendorf, my mother; George K Sagendorf (baby), my brother." (Augusta Sagendorf Collection.)

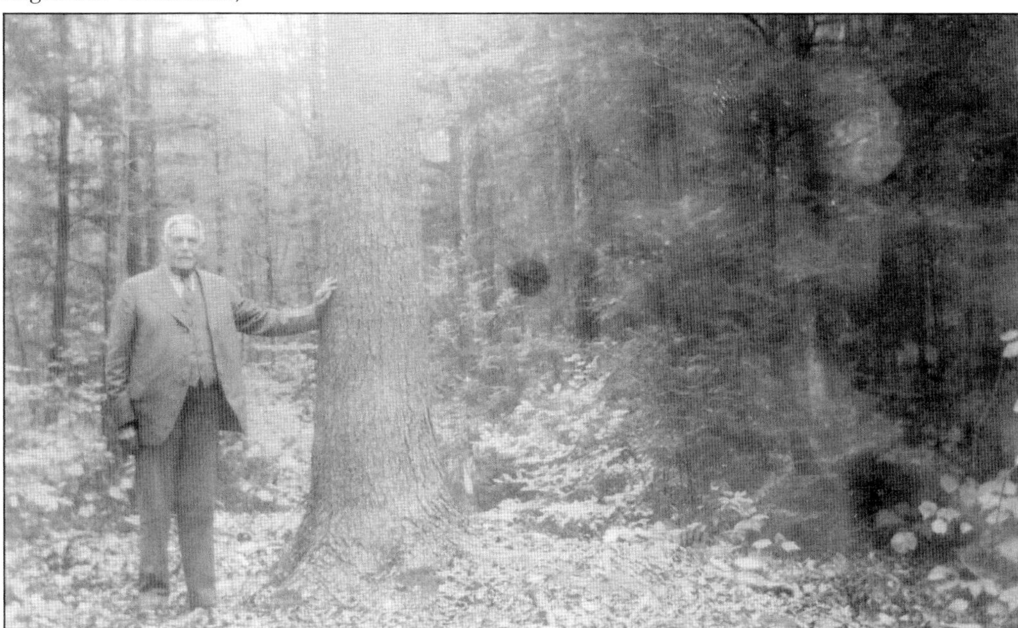

Harrington Putnam Sr. is shown standing by a tree, no doubt on his own property on the East Branch. He had acquired the property in the late 1800s. This was his country home, and he named it Red Lodge. It is reported that he was an avid walker. He thought nothing of hiking from Big Indian, Shokan, or even farther from his home on the East Branch of the Upper Neversink River. Today, only a small group of seasoned hikers would be doing this.

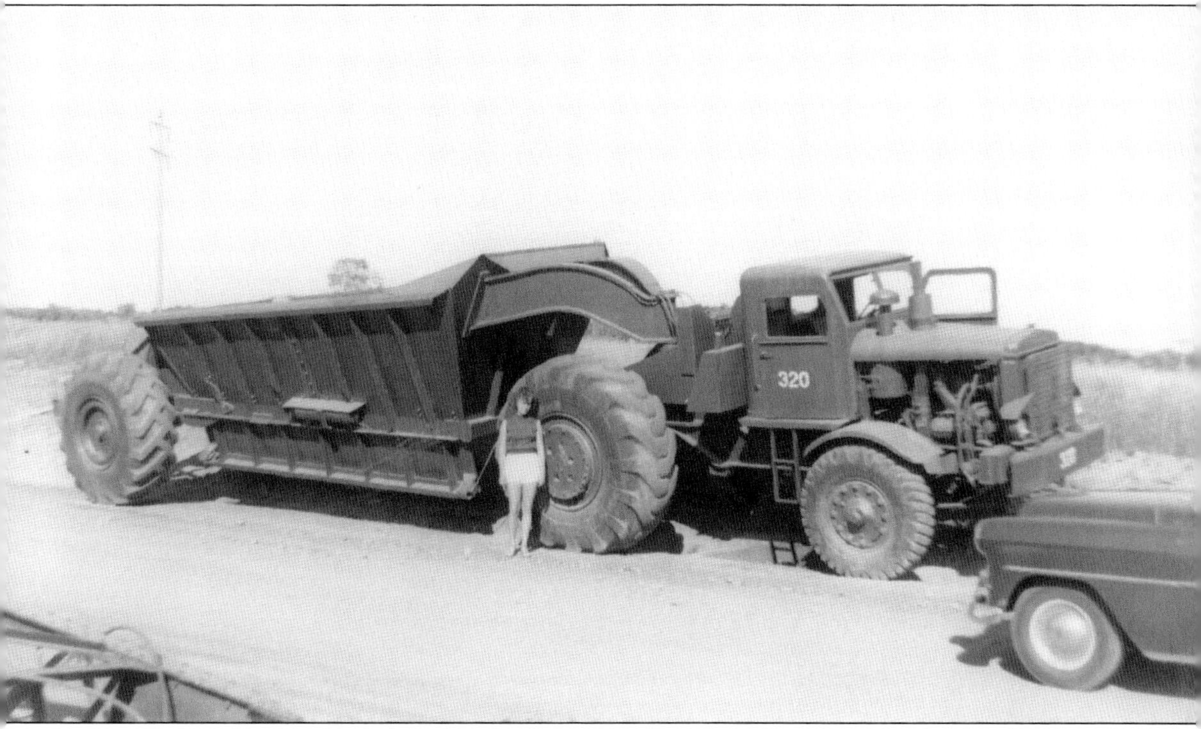

Pictured here is a "Euc" (Euclid truck), which was used to move dirt as contractors needed during the building of the Rondout and Neversink Reservoirs. To give an idea of how huge these dirt movers were, an ironworker took this photograph of his five-foot, six-inch wife standing by a tire. The Eucs were bottom-dumping trucks. During the building of the Ashokan Reservoir, mule-drawn, bottom-dumping wagons were used. (Shader family collection.)

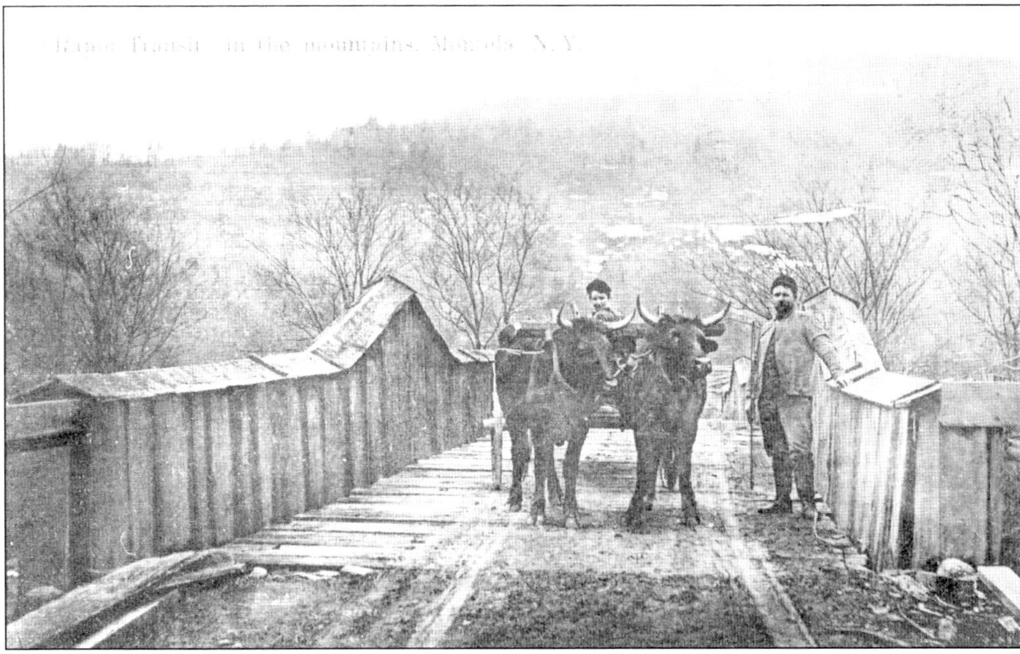

Fannie Richard and Charlie Smith are pictured standing on a bridge crossing the Rondout Creek at Montela. The year is 1913, and the photograph was taken for an Artino series (a commercial postcard series) by Harrison Richards, proprietor of the general store. The bridge itself is an open bridge that was used prior to covered bridges. It is unusual to see a photograph of an open bridge in this area. (Cynthia Moshier Wagner Collection.)

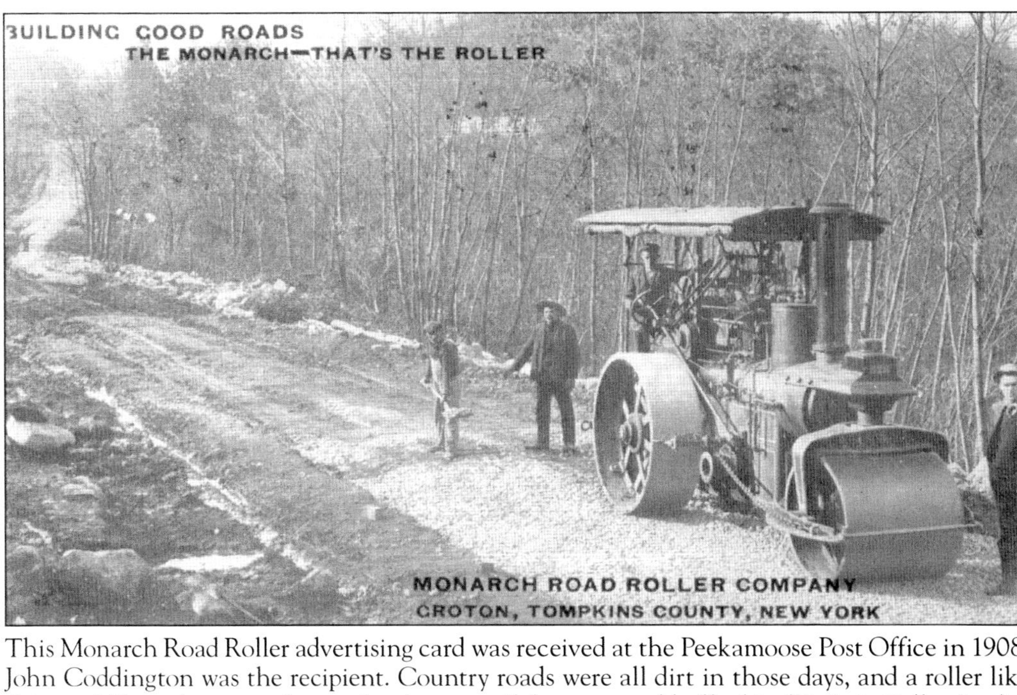

This Monarch Road Roller advertising card was received at the Peekamoose Post Office in 1908. John Coddington was the recipient. Country roads were all dirt in those days, and a roller like this would have been a welcome development if the area could afford it. (DuBois Collection.)

Virginia "Ginny" Caldwell is seen here as a young girl in Grahamsville, probably sometime between 1940 and 1945. She was the daughter of Ralph and Vira Caldwell, and her grandparents were the Otis Donaldsons. Ginny and her husband, Ken Bishop, kept the family place in Grahamsville so they could spend summers in New York. Ken has continued the family tradition since she passed away. (Virginia Caldwell Bishop Collection.)

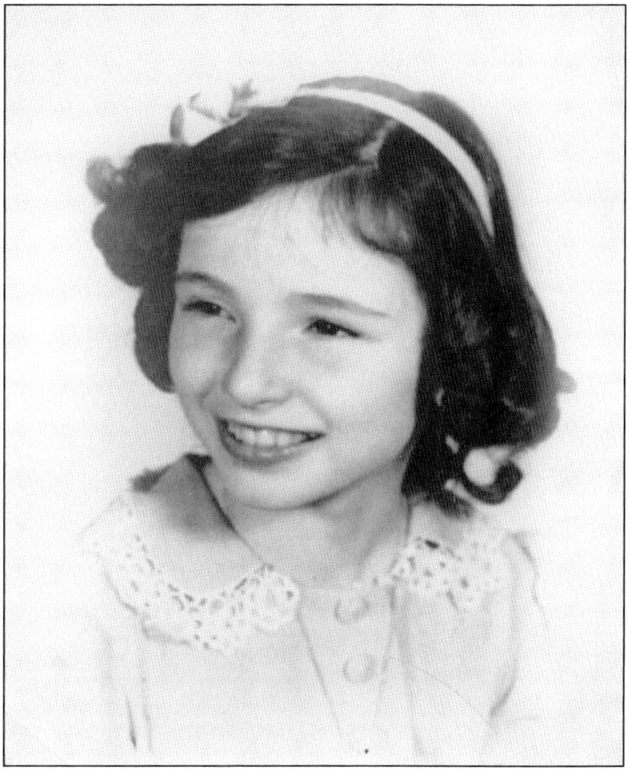

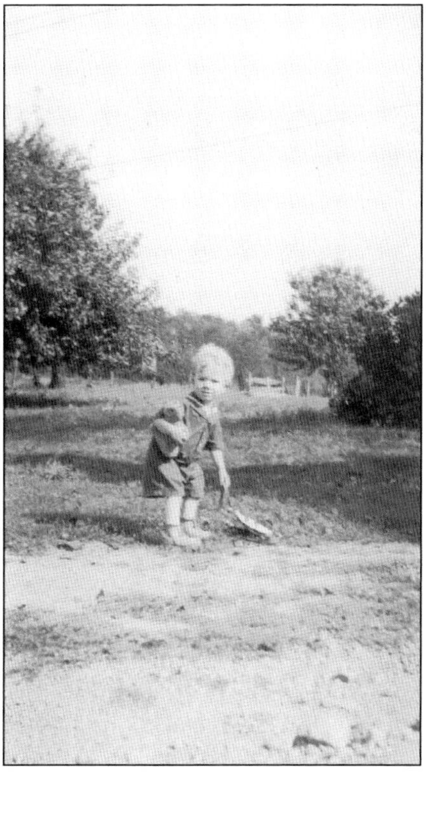

This is Tommy Smith as a young boy in the Grahamsville area, probably around 1938. His grandparents and parents lived on South Hill Road. He was the son of Hank and Linda Smith and, like Virginia Caldwell Bishop, attended and graduated from Tri-Valley Central School. One of his sons now lives on South Hill on a parcel of the original family property.

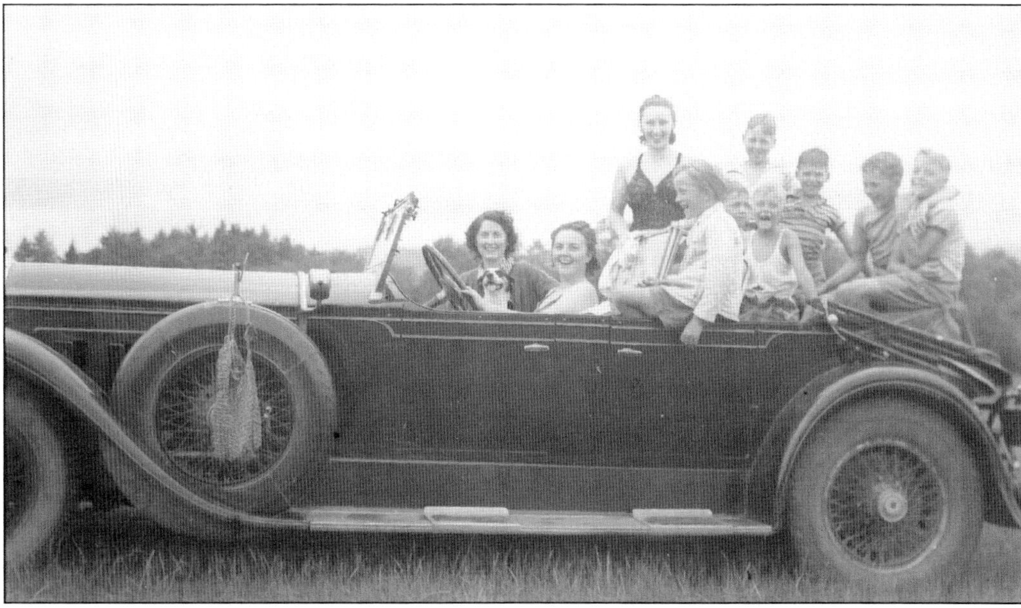

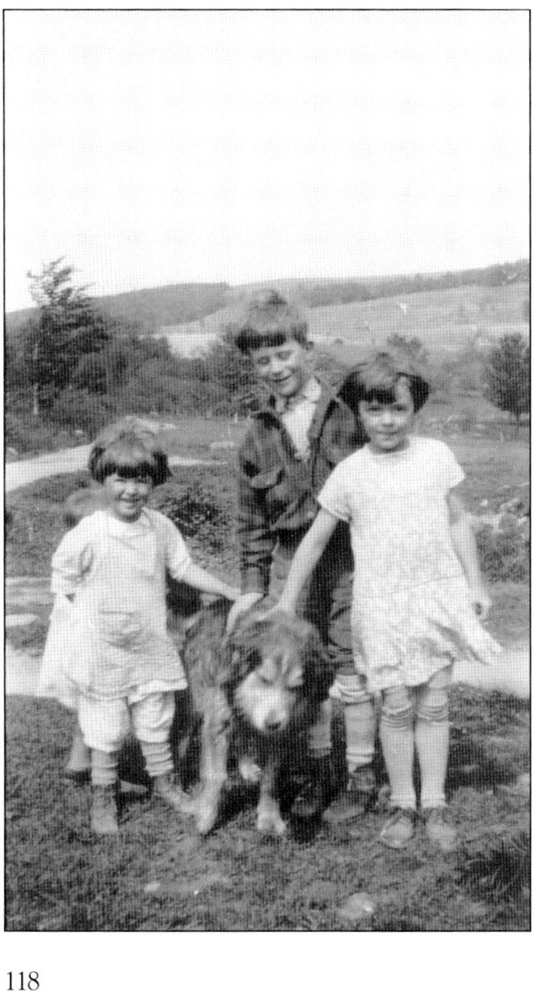

Teacher Evelyn Huntsberger is driving this Packard car sometime between about 1934 and 1936. Bruce Denman Sr. lent the car so the students at the Unionville School could go for a last-day-of-school picnic and swim.

The children of Herbert and Esther George pose on Red Hill with the family dog. From left to right are Linda, Vincent, and Ruth. Evelyn is hidden behind Linda. The family later moved to Sundown, where they lived for many years. The George homestead in Sundown was sold in 2013.

This photograph of Louis N. Clark was taken by Hillig Studio in Liberty in May 1919. (Clark family collection.)

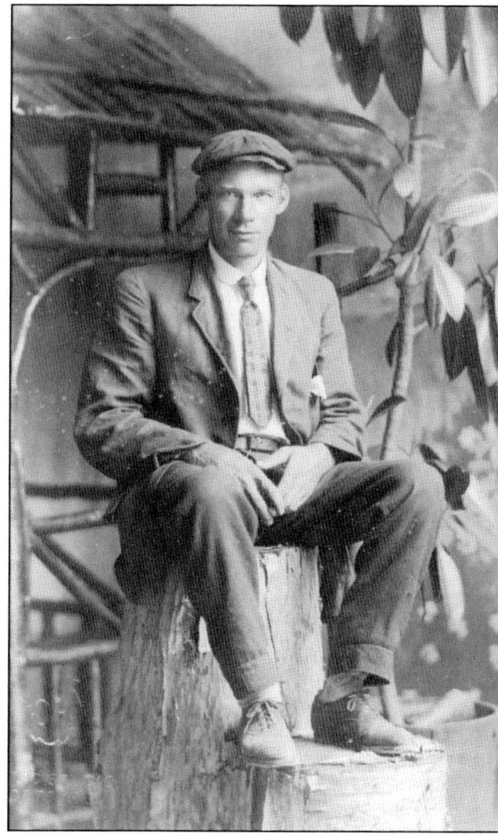

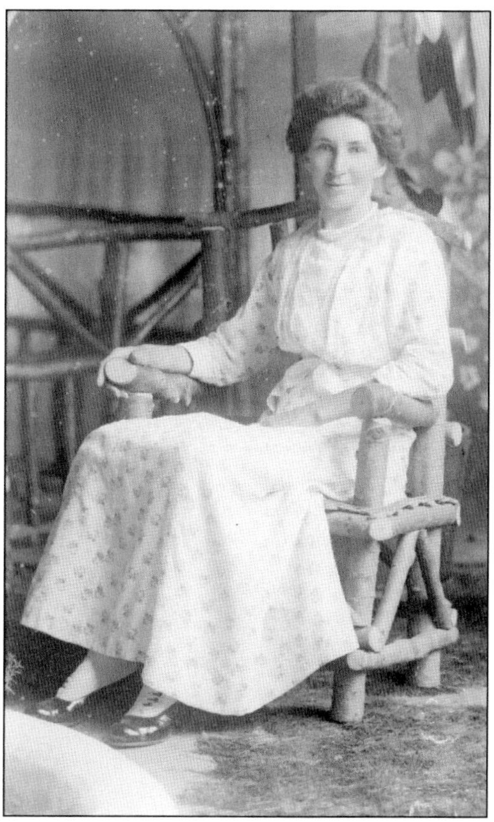

Kate J. Brackman of Denning, New York, was also photographed by Hillig Studio in Liberty in May 1919. (Clark family collection.)

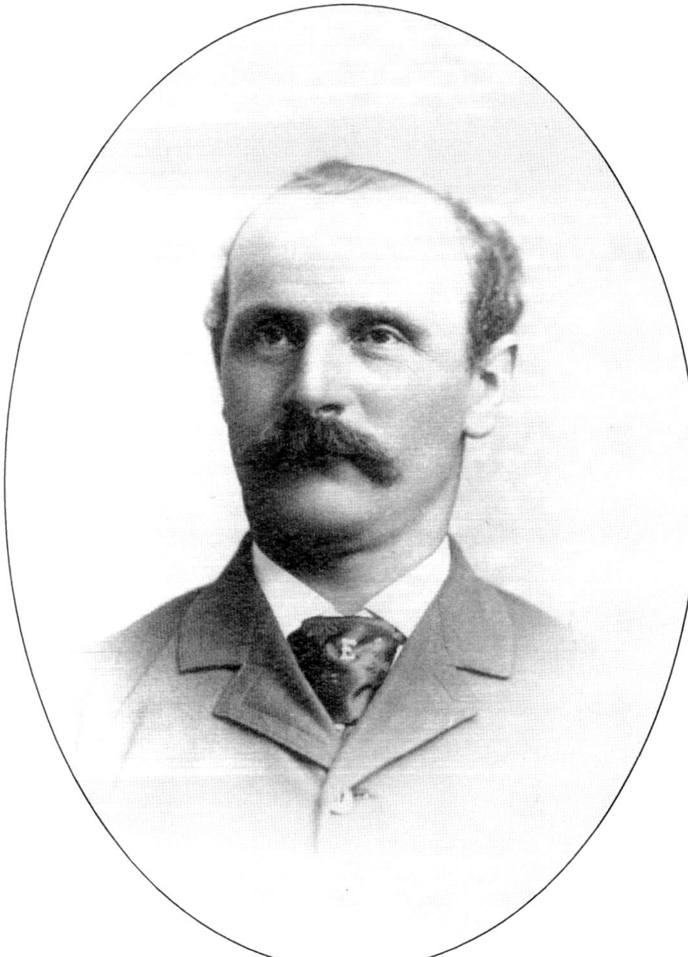

The first George Erts recorded by a family genealogist was born in Prussia around 1813 and died in 1863. It is believed that he is buried in Dutchess County. Pictured here is George W. Erts, who was born in April of either 1856 or 1858, the son of Joseph and Emma Erts. His son was George Walter Erts, who was the unofficial historian for the Town of Denning for many, many years. (Cathy Keator collection.)

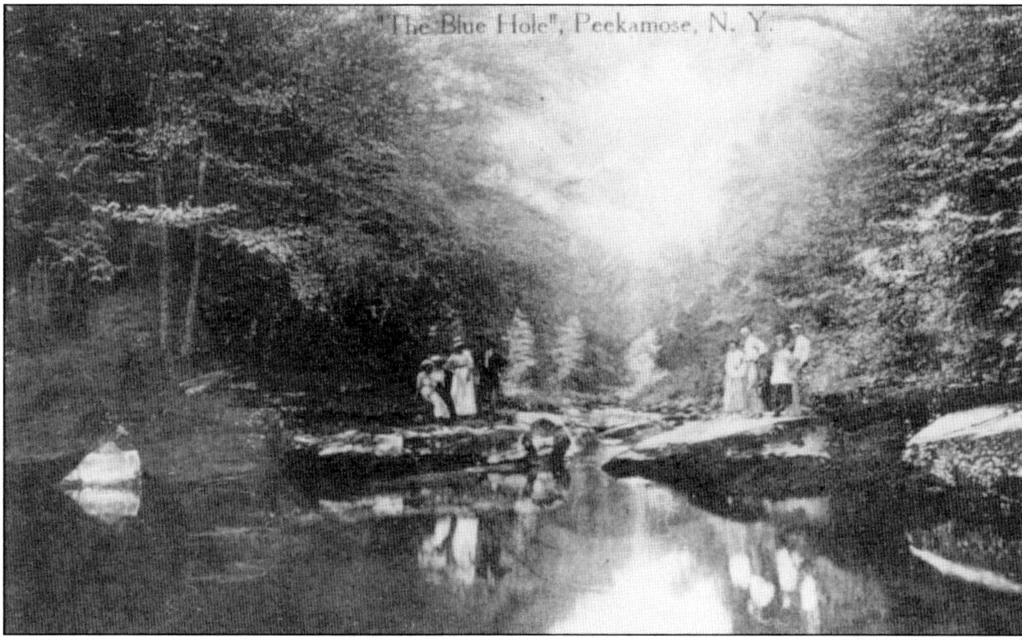

This c. 1910 photograph was printed with a blue tone. It captures young men and women dressed as though for a party, and their reflections can be seen in the water. This is the Blue Hole in Peekamoose. Generation after generation has visited and swum in the deep, chill pool here. The Blue Hole gained some attention when it was chosen by multiple groups nationally as a special swimming hole. (Philip Coombe Collection.)

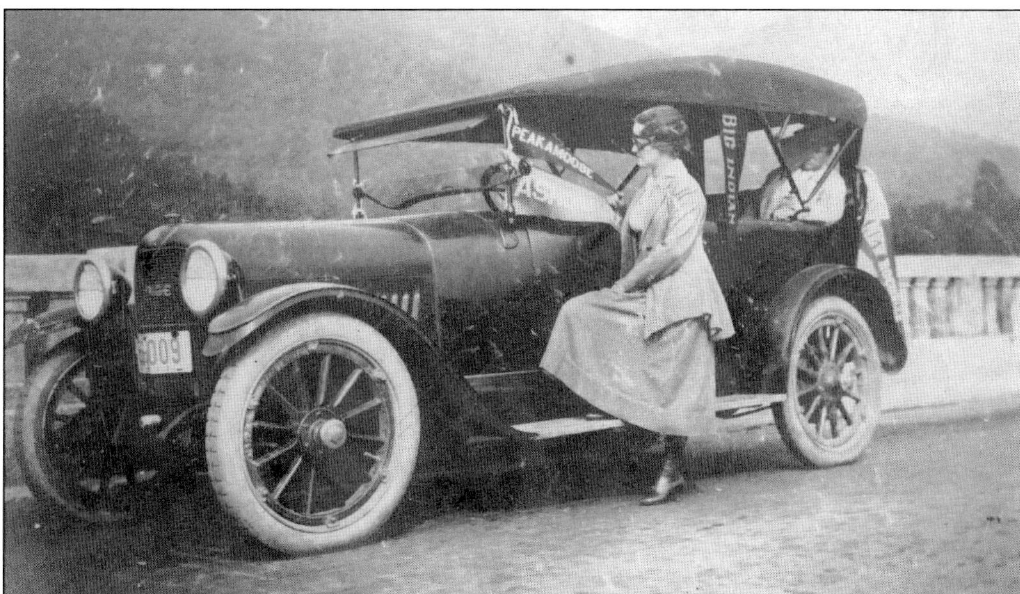

The Ashokan Reservoir had been built by the time of this image, and this car is parked on the road that goes across the dam. The banners hanging from the vehicle say "Peakamoose," "Big Indian," and "New Rochelle" respectively. The year is approximately 1915. If the driver had driven up to Peekamoose, they would no doubt have had to get out and push to get up that very steep incline. (Richard George-Murray Collection.)

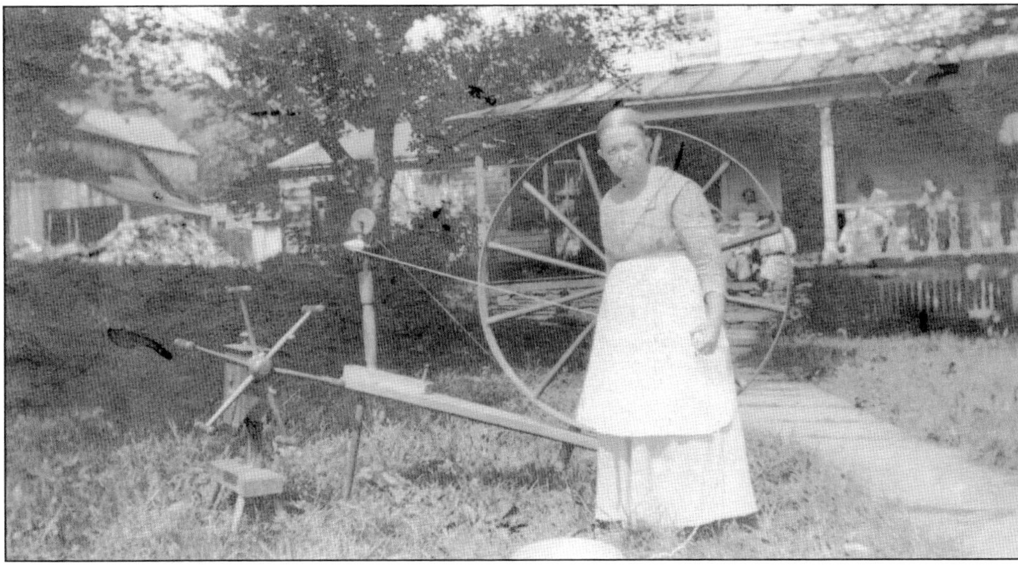

Savina Walter stands with her spinning wheel and yarn winder in the front yard of the home presently owned by Michael and Lisa Garigliano. Michael is a descendant of Savina Walter. Items were often carried outdoors to be photographed because of the lack of light in the house. In the late 1800s, many homes still had spinning wheels.

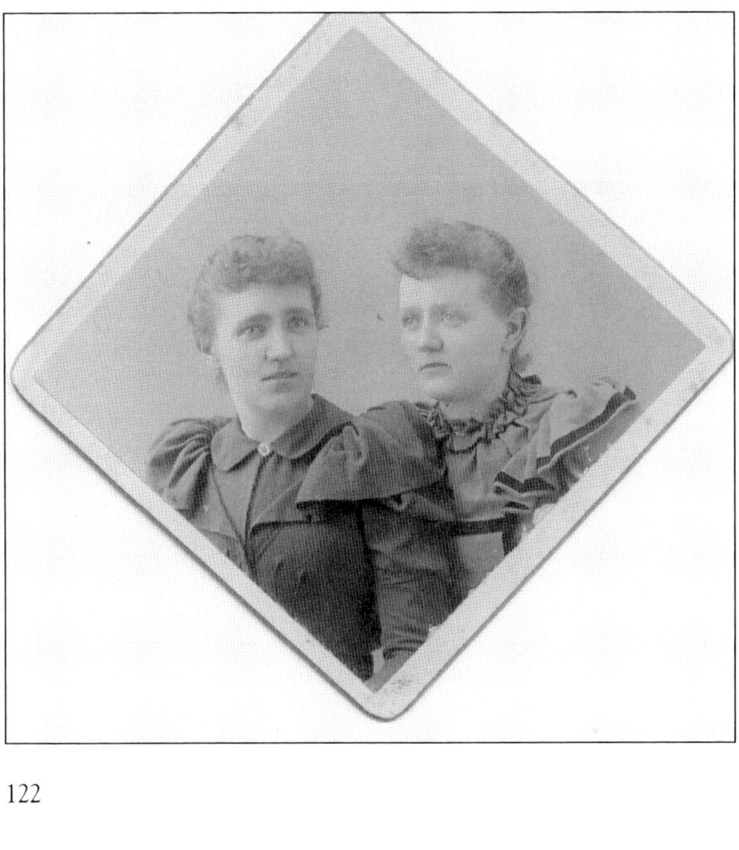

Sisters Alice and Harriet Slater pose for this interesting diamond-shaped photograph. W S. Davis of Ellenville was the photographer. Alice went on to marry Harold Smith of South Hill, and they had one son, T.H. Smith. One of their great-grandsons, Kyle, lives on part of the property to this very day. (Dale Houghtaling Collection.)

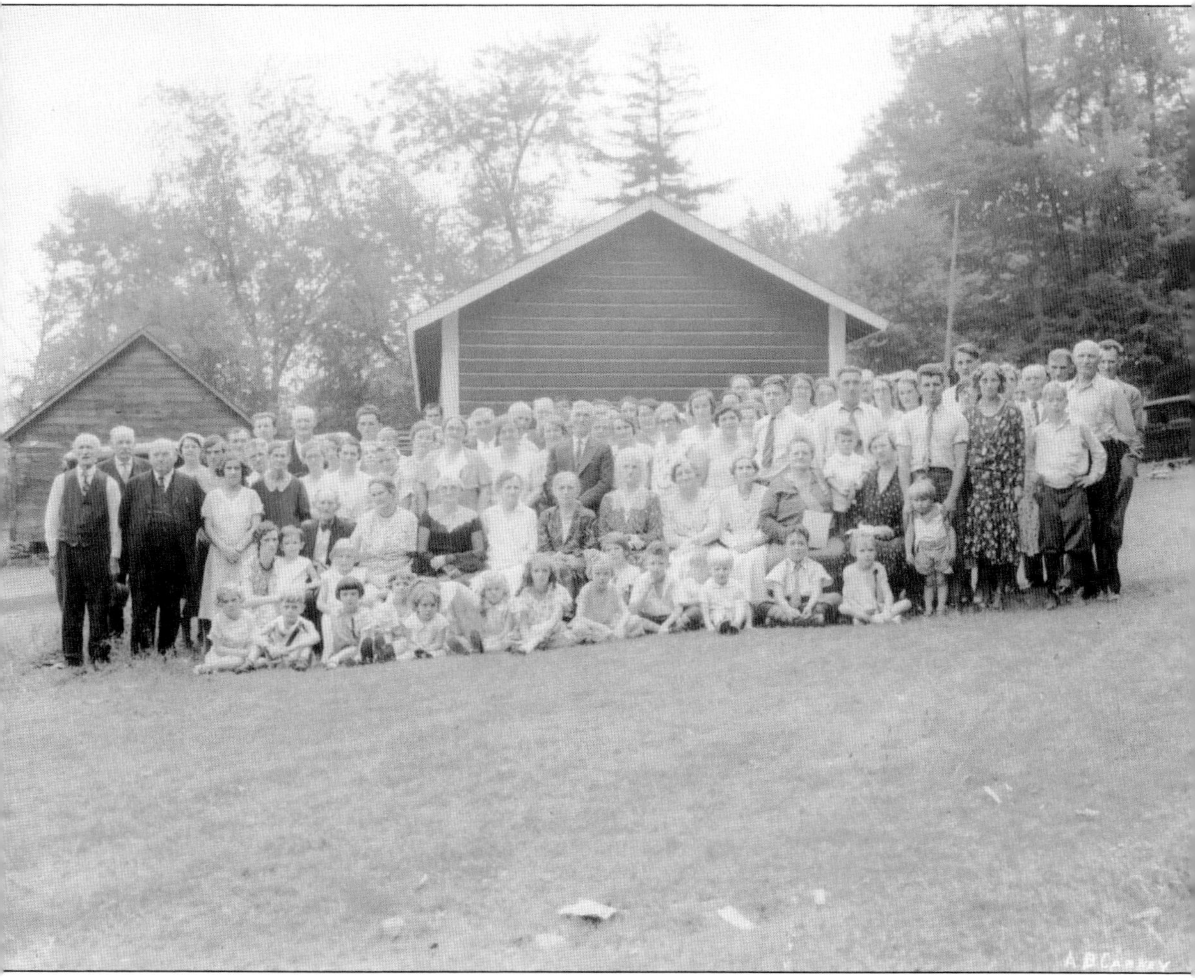

This Curry (sometimes spelled Currey) family reunion photograph was taken at the Grahamsville Fair. It is believed that this was the 11th reunion, held in 1931. In attendance were 84 descendants of Stephen and Anna Vail Curry. The fairgrounds were originally part of the late Andrew Curry's estate. Officers elected for the subsequent year were Vail Curry of Curry, president; Charles Curry of Grahamsville, vice president; D.C. Decker of Nutley, New Jersey, secretary; and Mrs. Burr Moore of Grahamsville, treasurer. Officers would take charge in planning future reunions. The group was treated to a talk by Gabriel Curry of Liberty, the oldest member present. "Uncle Gabe," as he was known, was an 87-year-old Civil War veteran. (Wanda Terwilliger Collection.)

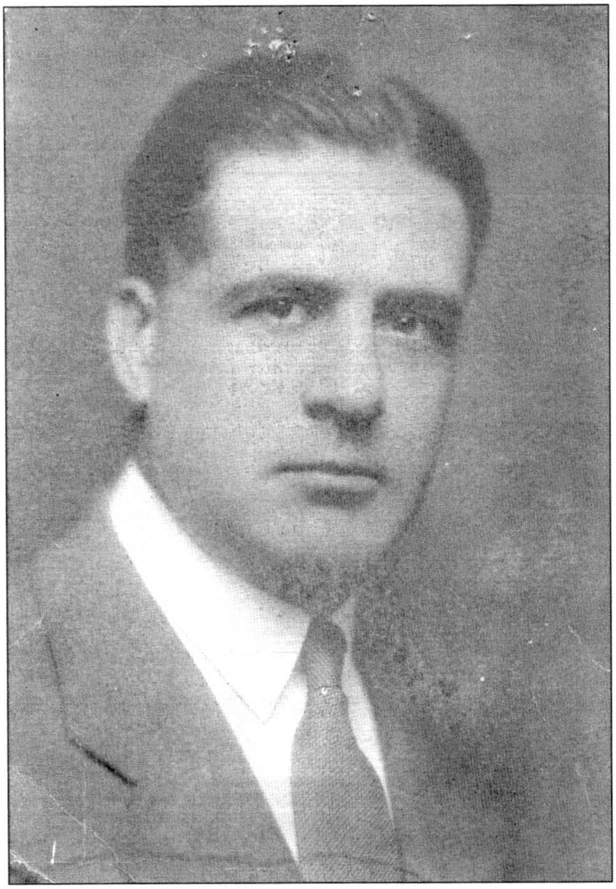

Charlie Cross, then of Neversink, is pictured here. He married the former Ruth Green, and they eventually made their home on Sundown Road at the site of the Lows Corners School. Charlie was a well-known musician who, with his band, made many an event merry with music. (Clark family collection.)

The Clark family house in Denning is pictured here. (Clark family collection.)

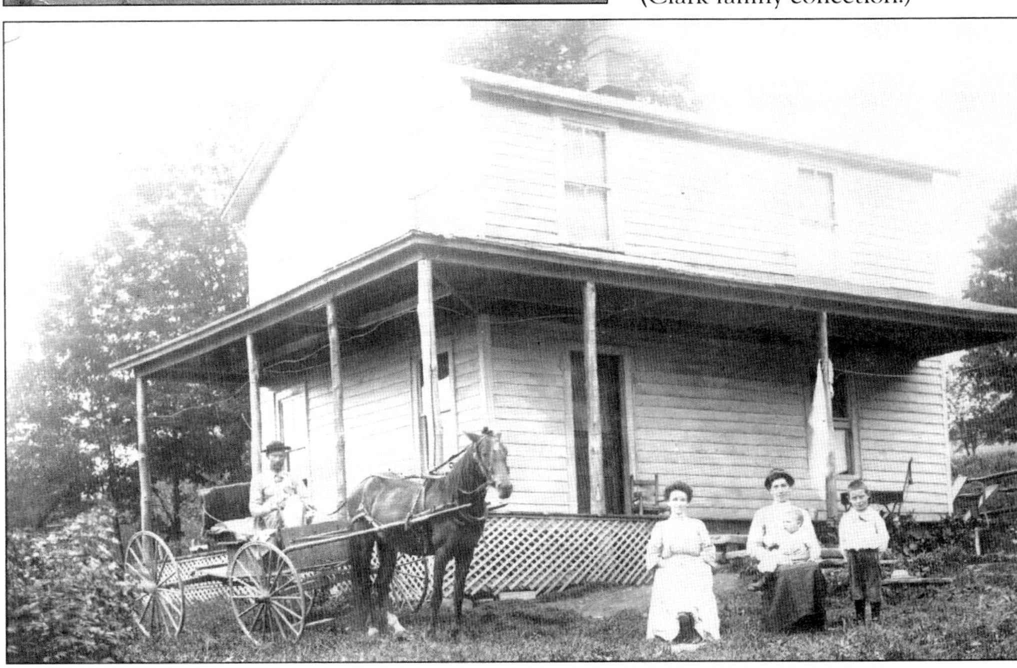

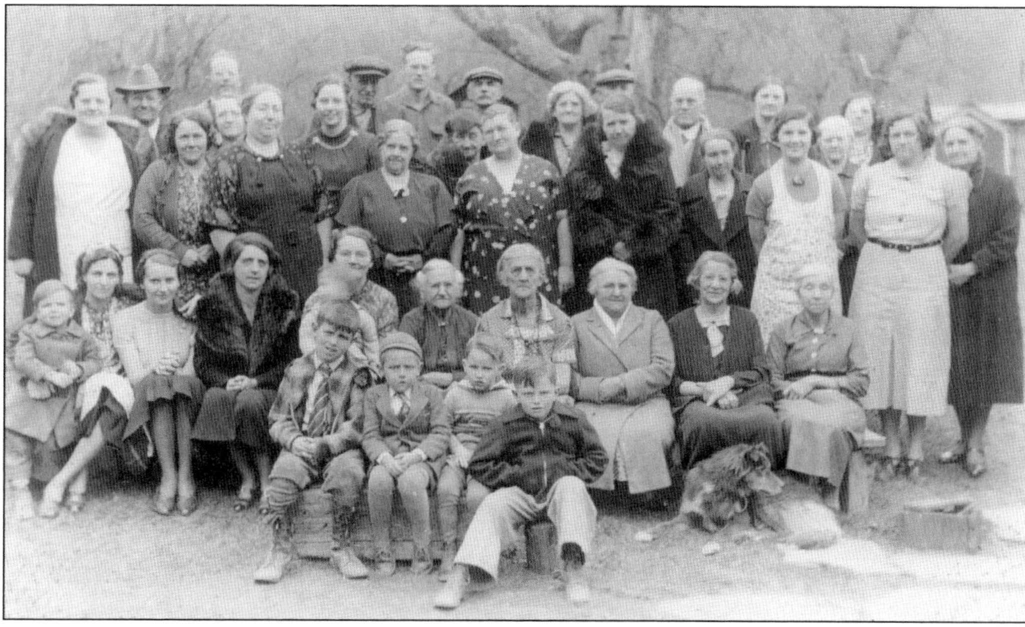

This Sundown-Eureka community picture was taken around the 1930s. An attempt has been made to identify everyone pictured, and they include Herbert Brooks, Clarence Brisack, unidentified, Lorin Quimby, Grant Brooks, Ann George, William Bevier (?), Reverend Haris, Lula Carlile, Beatrice Burch, "Aunt Effie" Sheeley, Emma Brooks and James, Verta Brooks, Dorothy Brooks, Madge Brooks, Minerva TerBush, Susan Hornbeck, Phoebe DePuy (Verta's grandmother), Mrs. John I. Brooks, Janie Brooks, Fanny Brisack, Mrs. Frank Brooks, Carrie Lievre, Hazel Low, Caroline Low, Mrs. Harris, Ada Smith, Maude Eck, Mrs. Oscar Banta, Ethel Bevier (?), Effie Everett, and Mae TerBush. The four boys in front are Delos Brooks, Art TerBush, Randall Brooks, and Richard Brooks. (Wanda Terwilliger Collection.)

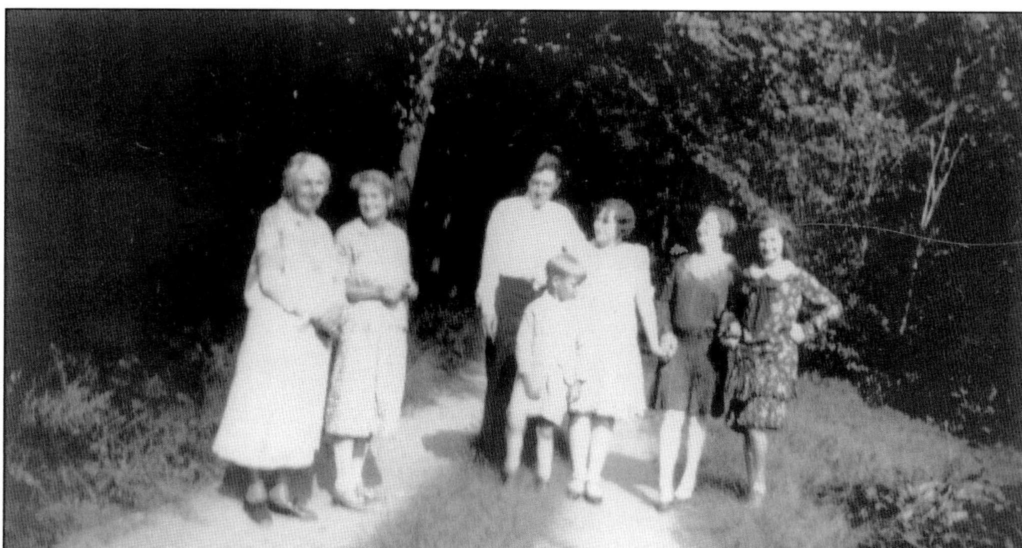

This early-1930s group includes, from left to right, Alice Smith, Juliana George, a Mr. Joslin, John McKenna (in front), a Mrs. Joslin, Linda Smith, and Mabel Joslin. They are standing on the dirt road that went to Sundown and ran along a portion of the Upper Rondout or Sundown Creek.

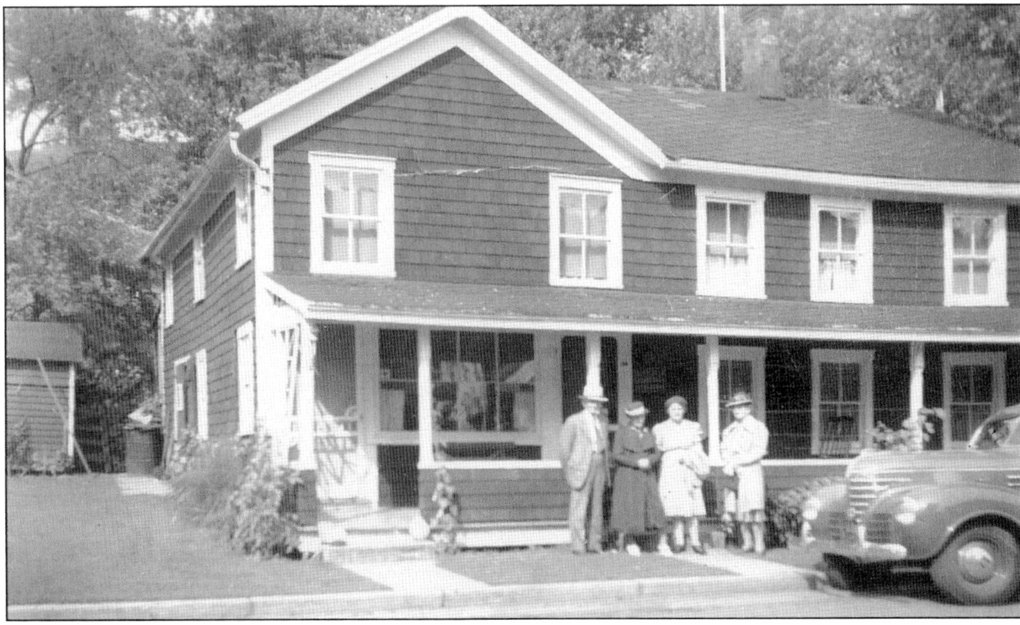

Mark Slater (1872–1956)—undertaker, cabinetmaker, clock repairer, and barber—was an icon of Grahamsville in the 1940s. The two couples pictured here look as though they might have just returned from church. The caption on the back of this photograph identifies this as Mark Slater's house and notes that it is the afternoon of Sunday, July 12, 1942. The house, which doubled as clock-repair space, barbershop, and mortuary, was torn down along with another to make room for Grahamsville's Bicentennial Park. (June Tillson collection.)

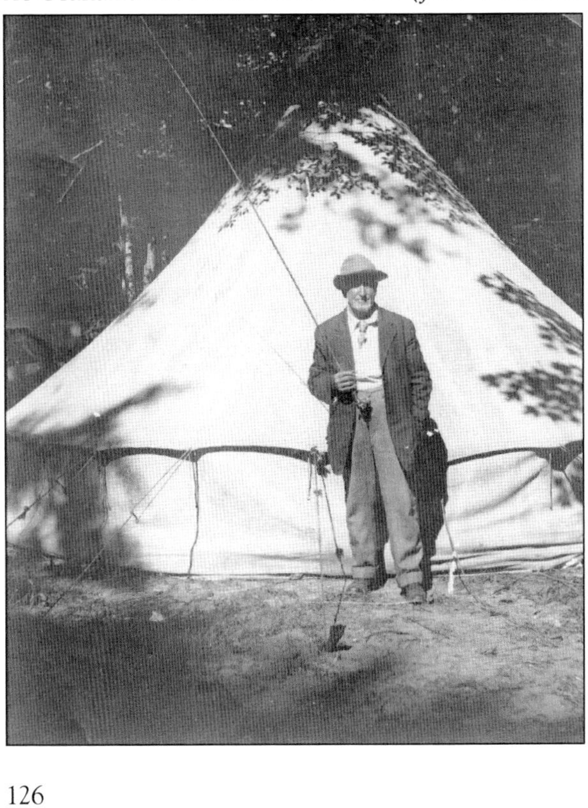

James B. Smith of Eureka stands with his fishing pole in hand. He was married to Angelia Reynolds, and they had 11 children, one of whom passed away as an infant. The others were Harry, Eva, Mary, Nellie, Harriet, George, Arthur, Walter, Nancy, and James.

Ward Eugene Dierfelter was the son of Ollie Donaldson Dierfelter and George Anton Dierfelter. (Virginia Caldwell Bishop Collection.)

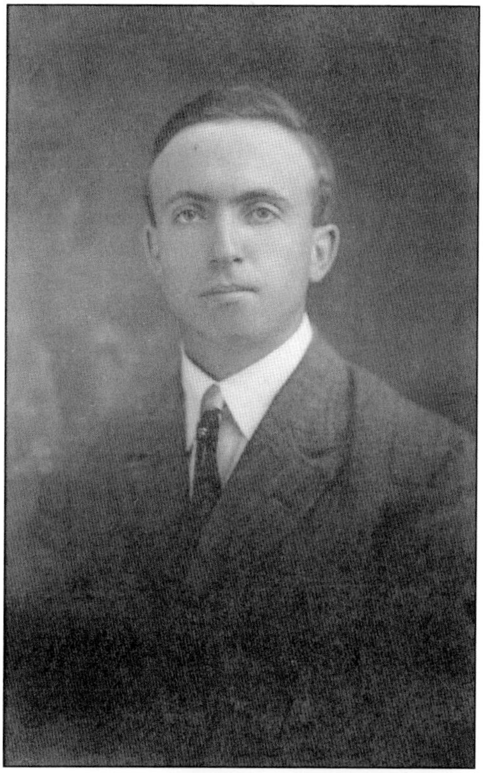

This is the Michael Charter house in Curry. Pictured from left to right are Clarinda, May, Juliette, and Michael Charter. Clarinda became well known for her fringe mittens, which she made to be sold in New York City stores. The house was later known as the Huson house and was torn down to make way for the Town of Neversink's refuse station and the Highway Department. (Shirley Smith collection.)

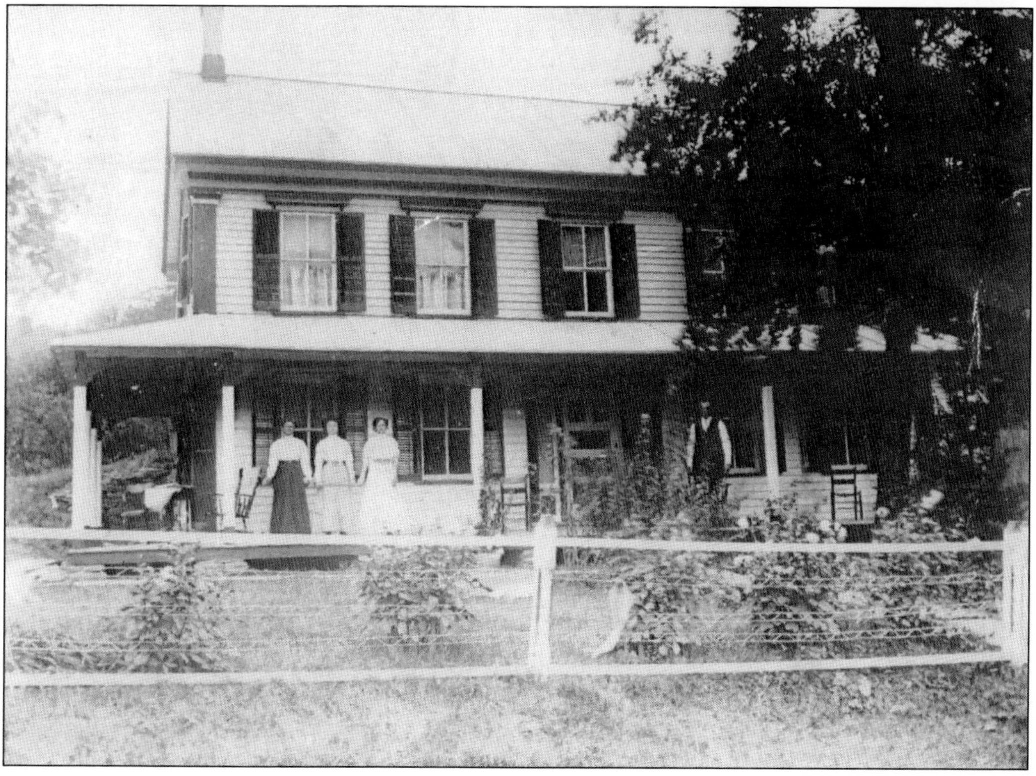